# SWEET MOTHER

■

# SWEET MOTHER

## MODERN AFRICAN MUSIC

■

WOLFGANG BENDER

With a Foreword by John M. Chernoff

Translated by Wolfgang Freis

■

The University of Chicago Press
Chicago and London

Wolfgang Bender teaches at the Institute of Ethnology and African
Studies, University of Mainz.

The University of Chicago Press, Chicago 60637
The University of Chicago Press, Ltd., London
© 1991 by The University of Chicago
All rights reserved. Published 1991
Printed in the United States of America
00 99 98 97 96 95 94 93 92 91   5 4 3 2 1

Originally published in Munich under the title *Sweet Mother:
Moderne afrikanische Musik,* © 1985 Trickster Verlag.

Library of Congress Cataloging-in-Publication Data

Bender, Wolfgang.
    [Sweet mother.   English]
        Sweet mother : modern African music/Wolfgang Bender :
translated
    by Wolfgang Freis.
        p.   cm.—(Chicago studies in ethnomusicology)
    Translation of: Sweet mother.
    Includes bibliographical references.
    Discography: p.
    ISBN 0-226-04253-7 (cloth); 0-226-04254-5 (paper)
    1. Popular music—Africa—History and criticism.   I. Title.
II. Series.
ML3502.5.B4613   1991
780'.96—dc20                                      90-20316
                                                       CIP
                                                       MN

⊗ The paper used in this publication meets
the minimum requirements of the American National
Standard for Information Sciences—Permanence of
Paper for Printed Library Materials, ANSI Z39.48-1984.

Sessa!
Rocafil Jazz presenting you

## SWEET MOTHER

Sweet mother, I no go forget you,
For the suffer wey you suffer for me, yeah,
Sweet mother, I no go forget you,
For the suffer wey you suffer for me, yeah.

When I de cry, my mother go carry me.
She go say, my pikin, wetin you de cry, oh,
Stop, stop, stop, stop,
Make you no go cry again, oh.

When I want to sleep, my mother go bed me,
She go lie me well well for bed, oh.
She cover me cloth, say make you sleep,
sleep, sleep, my pickin, oh.

When I de cry hungry, my mother go run up and down,
She de find me something that I go chop, oh.
Sweet mother ah, ah sweet mother, oh.
Sweet mother, sweet mother.

When I de sick, my mother go cry, cry, cry.
She go say, instant when I go die, make she die, oh.
She go bed God, God help me,
God help me pikin, oh.

Oh my mother!

If I no sleep, my mother no go sleep.
If I no chop, my mother no go chop.
She no de tire her.

Sweet mother, I no go forget,
For the suffer wey you suffer for me, yeah.

Sweet mother, I will never forget you,
For if you forget your mother,
You have lost your life.
When I de cry, my mother go cry,
She no no wetin to do,

you no well,
No wetin de worry you, my pickin?
You fit get another wife,
You fit get another husband,
But you fit get another mother? Mother, no, so yeah.

My mother is great,
Greater than the world.

(Prince Nico Mbarga and Rocafil Jazz; record without title. Produced
in Nigeria by Roger's All Stars 1976. ASALPS 6, Decca France
278.159.)

This book is dedicated to guitarist, band leader, poet,
and broadcaster Ebenezer Calender of Freetown, Sierra
Leone, West Africa, who died on Good Friday, 1985.

In memoriam Alic Nkhata of Zambia, Njemanze alias
Israel Nwaoba of Nigeria, Aboubacar Demba Camara of
Guinea, Joseph Kabeselé "Grand Kallé" of Zaire, Todd
Matshikiza of South Africa.

# CONTENTS

■

# FOREWORD

by John M. Chernoff

■

At the time when Wolfgang Bender first tried to hear the different
popular musical styles of sub-Saharan Africa, the task was difficult. The kind of exposure that African musicians now enjoy was
just a dream. In the 1960s, here in the United States, I dreamed in
vain. My college buddies and I could get amazing mileage from a
single record: a few tunes from one place could inspire fantasies of
dance halls and nightclubs in many far-flung cities with resonant
names. By the 1970s, like Bender, I was roaming and getting the
experiences I wanted. Meanwhile, in the States, radio coverage of
African popular music, if any, might have been found on a campus
station, hosted by an expatriate African professor. Only a few
stores in the country had African records, mostly folkloric. Ethnomusicologists were still heir to a small body of essays that dis-
missed the whole area of popular music as artificial. Jazz people, as
usual, had been the first to respond positively to the potential inspiration of African music, much in the same way as their previous
generation had responded to Latin American music: a few expatriate African musicians, usually percussionists, found their way
onto records in the 1960s and 1970s. But well into the 1970s, if
you wanted to find out what was actually happening with music in
African countries, you had to go to Africa. If there was an occa-

sional touring band, its mission was generally privately sponsored and celebrated at cabarets by the small African communities that had recently established themselves in a few American cities. The situation was a bit different in Europe, just because there was a more significant African presence. But one cannot compare the situation in the 1970s with what we now see at the beginning of the 1990s.

Twenty years ago, even going to Africa did not ensure that one could get the music. In 1970, when I first went to Ghana, there were only a few 33-rpm highlife records in distribution—African Brothers, All Brothers, Ramblers. The main medium was 45s. A few reproduced 45s from Zaire and Nigeria were also available, along with Rex Lawson's ten-inch LP. But the place was not really set up for sounds, nor was the world for that matter. I used a reel-to-reel tape recorder at the time. Things were easier than they had ever been, but the gear was still heavy. I forget whether there existed a portable cassette recorder with Dolby, but if there was, it was beyond my means. Most drinking bars in Ghana and Togo were fortunate to have a monophonic record player with a tiny external speaker attached. Discos were only a coming thing; with a few exceptions, they were attached to restaurants for the well-to-do, and the music was international. It was not until the mid-1970s that Ghanaian LPs became relatively abundant. Konadu released an astonishing number of them in a single year. And then, when Ghana's economy withered, production was effectively halted by the lack of foreign exchange for raw materials. The record stores converted their business to audio-cassette dubbing, which, over and against the appeals of copyright claimants, was officially sanctioned just because the government recognized that the people needed music and could not afford records, and there were too few records anyway. Abidjan, Lome, and Ouagadougou had more resources and better distribution, at least within the French zone, though it was not until the mid-1970s that the number of different records became impressive. When I traveled to those towns, I bought what I could, and I made friends with a couple of people in record stores who could dub cassette tapes of new releases and send them to me. I do not know how Bender managed. I know that I struggled: getting records and, later, getting cassettes was a major goal of all my traveling outside of Ghana; yet I spent a lot of time collecting with limited results.

In West Africa, those few years from 1970 to 1975 saw many changes in music technology, notably in terms of the availability of cassettes and component stereo systems. I do not know much about the move from 78s to 45s or the introduction of radio, but in 1970 there was not even a lot of Ghanaian pop music on Ghana Broadcasting. I have the feeling I caught the tail end of the situation when almost all pop musicians made money primarily by playing their music live at small venues. During the early 1970s, even the top musicians were easily approachable. They were very aware of the relative limitations of their respective recording markets compared to the rest of the world. They were also open to any expression of interest by an outsider, and in this latter regard they resembled the traditional musicians I also befriended. They were proud of their music, and they believed that it had a rightful place in the world scene. They had the same attitude about their cultural heritages, with which they believed their musical work shared many characteristics. Nonetheless, the local musical contexts were limited. In African societies, many people participate in music-making, but their idioms have appeal mainly for particular groups in particular contexts. Like traditional musicians, the pop bandsmen hoped for recognition, sincerely, but they were not all thinking of themselves in terms of international stardom. They were still focusing on their own countries. Recordings were a way of making their music available and certifying their musical standard. Many of the crucial developments that Bender documents occurred on a very small scale, when it was still not clear that the "popular" music in a country, despite the fact that it could be classified in distinction to "traditional" music, was indeed something "popular" that could represent the country as a whole.

In the early 1970s, if it was premature in Africa to anticipate the potential impact of African popular music on world music, in the United States it was eccentric. After all, African-American music had found its way into the mainstream only a few years before, often more indirectly than directly. In 1975 I was full of eccentric conviction, and I obtained agreements with many musicians in Ghana and Nigeria to represent them in looking for American recording interest. Among them were African Brothers, Sweet Talks, Ramblers, Sonny Okosun, Fela Anikulapo Kuti, Sunny Ade, Victor Uwaifo, Tony Benson, Godwin Omabuwa. I had no particular qualifications, though I did have a few good contacts; I believe

most pop musicians would have dealt with anybody they felt they
could trust. Most were not making a lot of money from their records, and some who had international licensing arrangements had
been disappointed. A couple were just beginning to record on their
own independent labels. At any rate, I could not find anything for
them in the United States, and I wrote them all to continue looking
toward their national markets. At the time, the biggest problem in
the States seemed to be fears of parochialism about songs in other
languages, though some of the harmonies may also have seemed a
bit strange. Maybe some people somewhere heard the tapes I sent
around, and a few isolated ideas were assimilated. Whatever, the
decade was well over before African musicians became major
news.

Bender is not writing the history of the Western impact of African popular music, though he notes a few significant points of
contact. Perhaps he is deliberately avoiding a forum in which so
many know so little about what they write. Perhaps he is reflecting
his efforts in the 1970s, when it was difficult to get a perspective
just in terms of Africa. Information now is easier to get and easier
to get with. The Western media have special words to classify music from beyond Western boundaries. Like many modern words,
these define by indiscrimination, a genre of criticism one might
call "nouvelle vague." World-beat, ethno-pop, techno-hut: these
words enable us to talk about the different styles of music without
knowing the names of countries or cities, without thinking of the
inspiration of the artists, without acknowledging the meanings of
the songs, without wondering about musical roots. To be sure,
conscientious world-beat disk jockeys try to pronounce the names
and titles, and some printed information comes with recordings.
All in all, though, I believe that most people are responding to the
music for new kinds of sound, curious textures, intriguing
rhythms, fresh harmonies. We are looking at African music as a
source of new ideas, as an addition to what we have, as a style to
take parts of, as music to be co-opted under the formulas of the
business. But I do not believe that most people care much about
the actual local uses of the music.

I can understand that position. Both here and there, patronage
is what creates the conditions that make the music possible, and
what a type of music is about in its own environment is often quite
different from anything we can understand. For example, while

the lack of English lyrics was an early stumbling block, more in the United States than in Europe, a greater barrier might be created if we knew what many of the songs are about. How would Western audiences react if they found out that they were dancing to Nigerian juju music whose lyrics praise the bourgeois or corporate sponsors of the gigs? An element of expressive dissonance might be introduced by thoughts like "Shegun and Hawa, best of luck on your marriage" or "Star Beer is the best." What of songs that praise political bureaucracies? I have heard some that say, roughly translated, "Let's hear it for the national airline corporation because they're doing a such fine job," or "Let's all pitch in on the back-yard gardening campaign so that we can become self-reliant in food." Some liberating political stuff is there, as are the philosophical proverbs and the commentaries on modern love, but perhaps it is a good thing we do not know all the lyrics.

Bender, on the other hand, is interested in the relationship between popular music and the new elites during the period after independence. That theme is only one part of his book, but he points to a cultural gap that is a hidden force in the way the music has developed both here and there. We can sympathize with music that mobilizes freedom fighters, but when African musicians praise the rich and powerful, it is difficult for democratic souls to appreciate a musician's pride in being able to contribute praise that elevates one person over another, difficult to understand a musician's modesty in seeing a musical destiny as an opportunity to render a service that not everyone can give. You really have to be there to appreciate how a given type of music fits into the patronage system that must be in place to make the music possible. This situation is what the musicians are singing about. Sometimes they are making it funny, but more often, like their traditional counterparts, they are telling the people who support them what they want to hear. In its own environment, African popular music is more than just musical sounds.

Given the nature of our market, though, musical sound is the essence, and there is no need to understand the way the music works in its own context. As African music penetrates our music market, more people may want to know more about it, but the common ground among devotees, critics, and businessfolk is a simple interest in turning more people on to the music. Nonetheless, the sounds alone are still not enough. Critics and producers do not just approach the music as dance music or modern music and leave it alone. It must be simultaneously refined and rendered exotic to become commercially viable. Stars must be created to facilitate marketing in the European and American scene. Ideally the star should be politically sensitive to the alienation of the masses. Reggae, partially understood, filled that bill for a while, and it makes sense to think of African music as coming from the same place. A lot of things happen to the music itself in its migration, too. We initially receive some predictable compilations, in which songs are shortened for radio slots. First to be edited out are the extended jams, which originally made the music a hit with dancers, as with music from Zaire. Lyric sections are placed first instead of following long instrumental introductions, as with Fela's music. Eventually some players start making shorter songs by themselves, as in the Antilles and in Zaire. Western-style funky passages are excerpted and African-style highlife passages are cut, as with Sunny Ade's early releases. If the songs themselves are not edited, then at least fuzzy and dirty mixes must be cleaned up in mixing or remixing. The bass is moved back, along with rattles and bells.

Thus has African music developed further, taking another step in the process of Westernization. Yet if all the talk nowadays is about the Westernization of African music, Bender knows that that development has not been the only thing happening. Two generations ago, African popular music was viewed as an inauthentic type of syncretism, unworthy of discussion. A generation ago, a few people started to talk about the Africanization of ballroom and dance hall music. When Bender writes about the re-Africanization of such music, he is looking at the penetration of traditional elements into popular forms, at the use of Western instruments to play traditional musical motifs, at the way Africans infused Western social contexts with the motives of the traditional spirit. But more important, he is also looking at the way the music was extended to new uses beyond the musical contexts with which it had been associated. Perhaps the era about which Bender writes may one day be viewed as the flowering of African popular music, as a kind of period in between periods, when assessing African and Western musical fusions and influences may not be the salient issue.

Some African musicians consciously seek a Western market;

others concentrate on indigenous audiences at home and abroad. Everybody would like to strike it rich, of course, but it is worth remembering that there is money in Africa. Some African musicians are getting from the Western market what they can get, which is something but not millions. Most, however, as musicians and creators, are thinking about recognition, respect, and the love of audiences. What makes being a musician sweet is playing the music and being appreciated. African musicians are grounded in their own musical situations. It is rather the promoters and critics who flutter around. Those from outside who go to foreign countries are either lucky to meet local enthusiasts who know the scene or unlucky to meet local hustlers with narrow-beam spotlights. We see only a small part of the modern African musical scene. For every musician we can name, for every recording we can get, there are many we do not know about. In areas with which I am familiar, you can read all the books, and you still will not hear of many of the better players and singers.

What is happening with African popular music is more related to Africa than to our Western markets or to the cross-fertilization of the world music scene. I am not denying the increasing significance of the latter factors, for international success is now a palpable model, but my experience tells me that it is difficult for musicians to reach musical heights with styles and material they get from elsewhere. It takes years playing even an inherited style before one is comfortable inside it. What of an imported style? In a complementary vein, that is why outsiders like Mickey Hart or David Byrne, and many others who begin with musical curiosity and an openness to influence, find that the path into African music has to be approached spiritually and that the music's depth is of a different nature than mere listening can grasp. Musicians in Africa are still working from their musical roots. We overvalue the various histories of musical influence because we require documentation—evidence of such-and-such an instrument and such-and-such a musical presence. But we do not know enough about what was already there, the full range of traditional repertoires and the prototypical forms of evolving popular styles. I believe that creative developments are rooted in local affinities which take the names of imported styles they only resemble.

The Western marketplace is not much concerned with the local African environment, in which music is only a part and which mu-

sic has little to do with shaping. The more significant cultural penetration of African music is not outward but inward. Kwabena
Nketia, our leading African ethnomusicologist, once advised me
not to be so preoccupied with identifying African prototypes that I
neglected the fact that music needs places where it can be played.
What is involved in calling a type of music "popular," he noted, is
that the common people have to be ready to get with the music.
For the music to become something that is part of the culture, the
people need technical means and certain social contexts to be in
place, as a matter of development, before music moves away from
its elite forms. At that point, the society itself has become something else. This development continues. What we think of as African popular music is still penetrating its own cultural environment
and, to an extent, presaging a culture that has not yet emerged. In
Ghana, for example, the beats you hear at a nightclub are not all
that different from what you hear at a funeral, a church service, a
festival, or a wedding. You can hear something like highlife in all
those places. But highlife has not reached the point where there are
highlife bands at state occasions: Ghanaians still use traditional
drumming to welcome foreign dignitaries. In Zaire, however,
dance band music is the order of the day, and a visiting head of
state would find a dance band as the chosen cultural component of
political pomp. Nketia reminded me that when we speak of popular music in Africa, we have to look at the conditions which allow
for the creation of the music, whether the various systems of patronage or the technological and civil environement of the society
or the presence of people who can dance to it.

It is because of Bender's sensitivity to these issues that I find his
point of view refreshing. There is no way for any one person to
know all that is happening with music in contemporary Africa,
and no book can claim to be comprehensive. No mere catalogue of
the cavalcade of current stars will demonstrate how the music both
responds to and depends on politics and economics. Within a ca-
pable introduction to the prominent musicians of major African
genres, Bender highlights the kinds of real problems we cannot
easily imagine, from professionals who do not own their instruments to national shortages of vinyl. What distinguishes Bender's
book from much of the available work by journalists and critics is
Bender's perception of music as a source of documentation about
political, economic, and social life. What distinguishes his work

from much of the academic work is that he is not afraid to voice an
opinion or to comment as an observer. He strikes a balanced tone
that is both droll and political at the same time. He has an eye for
the ironic anecdote and a cosmopolitan interest in what people are
doing. These special qualities provide a foundation of subtle so-
phistication as he moves from region to region: Bender communi-
cates a sense of discovery, while his love of the music keeps the
book within the world where the music has been created.

# PREFACE

■

My first encounters with African music date back to the early 1960s. I was in Lagos during those promising years that followed independence: it was the heyday of Highlife music in Nigeria.

On Saturday nights the bands played outdoors. The closer we came to Kakadu, the famous dancing club, the better we could hear the electrifying music, especially the trumpets and saxophones. Street vendors besieged the entrance and offered various tidbits: peanuts, cigarettes, candy.

Inside, behind the wall and fence, the band could be seen in the semi-darkness. The concrete dance floor was in front of it, and chairs and metal tables were placed around it. Star beer was sold to drink. There was much passionate dancing. On the dance floor, couples nudged each other rhythmically around in circles. After a few faster pieces, the band played slower music, rumba, cha-cha-cha, blues—all Highlife—well into the early morning.

I could never get enough of this music, which, fortunately, one could hear also on the radio. Once in a while I made a few tape recordings. In the years after my return from Nigeria, they accompanied me, along with some singles. I listened to them again and again. When people did not immediately understand this music, I suggested that they just listen to it more often. Even though I did not realize then how crucial this music would become to my later life, I liked it better than any other music.

In the years following I traveled many times to various African countries. My experiences in these travels brought about a steadily growing enthusiasm for the music of other regions of Africa as well and the great variety of styles, musical cultures, dances, and texts.

With this book, I hope not only to give the reader an incentive to listen to African music—especially modern African music—but also to provide a broad general survey. Because of the complexity of the material, however, not all important details—musicians, orchestras, and styles, for instance—could be fully presented. That is, unfortunately, a necessary concession in such a work. I will be grateful, however, for further communications and findings; occupation with the numerous aspects of music in Africa is a life's work. It is to be hoped that the musical histories of individual countries will be subject to more comprehensive study in the years to come.

I am grateful to all who, in the course of years that this book was written, helped make it possible.

W.B.

# 1

# THE GRIOT STYLE

■

## The State as Patron: Guinea

Adieu, de Gaulle, adieu!
Adieu, de Gaulle, adieu!
We have not insulted you.
We have not dealt you a knock-out punch.
Adieu. Return home without provoking a brawl.
Even if you don't want to, adieu!
Those who have chosen you will follow you.
Adieu, de Gaulle, adieu!
Those who have chosen you will rejoin you.[1]

This song was addressed to the departing General de Gaulle. He had come to Conakry on a trip through the French African possessions from Madagascar via Brazzaville in Congo and Abidjan. Guinea was the only country to reject his proposition of independence and continued close alliance with France. De Gaulle's visit in 1958 was also the occasion for the now proverbial remark by Sékou Touré, chairman of the Parti Démocratique de Guinée (PDG) and subsequently president of the state: "Nous préférons la pauvreté dans la liberté à l'opulence dans l'esclavage" (We prefer poverty in freedom to wealth in slavery).[2]

The song was sung by members of Touré's party and was part of the campaign for complete independence. From its founding in 1946, the party had used songs and music to spread its political

1

ideas. It had realized that this was one of the best vehicles by which
to influence the opinion of a largely illiterate population.

After Guinea's categorical "no" to de Gaulle's propositions, the
French left the country. Public installations and facilities were destroyed or rendered useless in order to weaken the new state and to
diminish its chances for survival—so that it might then return re-
pentantly to the French confederation. That, however, did not
happen: Sékou Touré turned to the Soviet Union and asked for its
support. The association with the East continued throughout his
tenure of office until his death in 1984.

## KEITA FODÉBA

On his travels to Paris as a representative to the French national
assembly, Sékou Touré met his countryman, Keita Fodéba, who
has to be considered the founder of national ballet companies in
Africa. Their acquaintance was of the greatest consequence to the
cultural policies of Guinea and the development of music.

Keita Fodéba, born in 1921, attended the École Normale
William Ponty in Dakar. He grew up as the son of a griot and was
familiar with the traditional arts of composition and performance. As a student at William Ponty, the colonial elite school, he
became acquainted with European theater practice. Later he spent
some years as a teacher. During that time he deepened his knowledge of the music and tradition of the Mandingo people, especially
through association with the guitarists Facelli-Kante and Soba Di-
eli. In 1948 he moved to Paris where he studied law at the
Sorbonne. He financed his studies with publications of poetry and
short stories. From 1951, his poems were banned in French West
Africa because of their nationalistic tendencies. In 1947 he founded the Ensemble Fodéba-Facelli-Mounangue, which developed
later into Les Ballets Africains and eventually into the National
Ballet of the Republic of Guinea.[3]

Keita Fodéba had found many talented musicians from all of
West Africa in the Quartier Latin of Paris. Thus, they could perform dances from countries from Senegal to Congo, but the main
emphasis lay on Mandingo traditions. The realization of traditional dances on a stage with European choreography was new
and original. In the beginning, the ballet performed only for Africans in Paris, yet the group soon received the unofficial title

"Ambassador of African Culture" and traveled throughout the world for many years.

Fodéba had recorded numerous songs with guitar, balafon, and kora accompaniment on 78 rpm shellac records, which were a great success in West Africa. Here the French administration again intervened with a ban on those recordings that implicitly attacked aspects of colonial domination. In 1951 Keita Fodéba published a number of his songs and stories under the title *Aube africaine*. Political allusions having been removed, excerpts from these texts were incorporated into the newly "Africanized" school curriculum.

Keita Fodéba was considered the most popular writer and artist in French West Africa during the 1950s. In 1956—the year in which Sékou Touré's friendship with Keita Fodéba began—the Ballets Africain went on a tour to West Africa during which new members joined the company. Among them was the famous tenor Sory Kandia Kouyaté, about whom more will be reported below.

In the course of administrative reforms in the French colonies, Keita Fodéba was elected a representative of his native district of Siguiri to the Territorial Assembly of Guinea and, in 1957, was appointed Secretary of Internal Affairs. He continued to meet his artistic commitments. Fodéba was primarily concerned with cultivating the traditional heritage but, at the same time, with expressing the modern Africa. In order to avoid a radical break, he simultaneously reinforced old values and new goals. His vision of cultural development became the foundation of Guinea's cultural policies.

According to official announcements, "a fight against the aftereffects of the colonial era, against all reactionism" was waged during the first ten years of independence. These aftereffects included "religious mystification, polygamy, ignorance, alcoholism, illiteracy, dissolute lifestyle, lying, laziness, larceny, rural exodus, parasitical behavior, intellectualism, unreasonable power of the griots, etc." At the same time, however, certain aspects of the country's pre-colonial history and of the history of colonial resistance were taken up. Famous epics were rediscovered and pressed on records.

The masters of the old versified chronicles, the living libraries, storytellers of all kinds, all the educated people who jealously guarded their knowledge of authentic African culture, all those were appointed honorary fighters and now contributed to the restitution of Africa's inexhaustible heritage.[4]

The second phase of cultural development was initiated with the proclamation of a socialist cultural revolution in 1968. The task of revolutionizing the culture fell to the party and especially to the youth organization, La Jeunesse de la Révolution Démocratique Africaine (JRDA). All areas of cultural life were taken into consideration: the JRDA was in charge of recreational activities as well as ceremonies; it had to participate actively in arts education and to develop literary, folkloristic, and theater activities. Old people, women, workers, and adolescents were to be given special attention. As one result of JRDA's activities, a poem of Sékou Touré's in praise of women was spoken on record and distributed:

Man of Africa, just as you,
I want to live in freedom and dignity,
Under the just sunrays of rehabilitation,
Sun of Africa, having reached our people
After the long eclipse inscribed with red letters
Into the register of living history.
The night weighs too heavy, without moon and without stars.
Everything was a mystery to me, dear companion, whom I carried on
    the back when you carried the colonialist or his feudal friend in the
    hammock of shame
In the time of forced labor.
Women of Africa, let us rise.
Just as fire, we are energy.
Just as air, we are indispensable.
Just as water, we are the source, the source of everything living.
Let us unite and act together.[5]

It is not at all an exaggeration to describe the period after Guinea's independence as a period of cultural rebirth. It was a time of awakening, of united effort and united action. As the field of experience of the artists grew, the quality of their work improved. The events scheduled at Palais du Peuple in Conakry—constructed by the Chinese—all reflected the vitality and enthusiasm that were inspired by the current cultural policies.[6]

The popularity in West Africa of records and artists from Guinea was the result of hard work and rigorous selection. Music and art were tied closely to the policies of construction of a revolutionary society. The great success in the area of cultural policy was, for the most part, due to Keita Fodéba's creativity. But without the full support of Sékou Touré, it would have had no chance. Keita Fodéba belonged to a group of intellectuals that supported Sékou Touré. In March 1969, however, he was accused of having taken part in a conspiracy against Sékou Touré. Fodéba was sentenced to death and executed.[7] Shortly thereafter, the record *Ballets Africains—de la République de Guinée* appeared with jacket notes signed by President Sékou Touré that do not even mention Keita Fodéba. His name did not appear again.[8] In a UNESCO publication of 1979, drafted by the government, he was again passed over in silence.[9] Sékou Touré, on the other hand, was celebrated directly or indirectly on most records released by the state-owned record company, Syliphone. The name of the company alone payed homage to the *syli,* which means "elephant" and is a metaphor for the president. Since most recordings were made by the national orchestras—by state-funded groups—it is not surprising that the benefactor is praised repeatedly. Besides, songs of praise are common in traditional Africa and are readily adopted by modern musicians.

A short survey of the regional distribution of traditional music follows. A larger subject, the griots, will be considered later.

## TRADITION AND THE BEGINNINGS
## OF MODERN MUSIC[10]

The traditional music of Guinea was handed down and developed from generation to generation. Before colonization, our region was under the influence of several large kingdoms. The music of four regions influenced the development of our traditional music: the first can be ascribed to the Mandingo people, who lived in an area stretching over most of the former French West Africa. This music has a courtly orientation and is interpreted by traditional instruments like the kora.

The second influence was that of the Fouta Djallon, a mountain region whose music has a very religious character and is also very melancholy.

The music of the coastal region, played by farmers and fishermen, was a third influence. It is a spontaneous music that reacts to events and describes their progress. Initiation music constitutes the fourth influence. It plays a part in the education and instruction of every young man. This music originated in the forests of Guinea and is very polyphonic.

European instruments like the saxophone, the guitar, the trumpet, and so on were imported during colonial times, and that developed into the so-called modern African music.

Before independence, musicians slowly began to modernize the traditional forms of music. This was done for the purpose of motivating people to dance with music they knew from their villages, so to speak. The synthe, which could not be danced without traditional instruments, became especially popular.

Musicians then began to introduce the old traditional instruments into their orchestras. On the other hand, elements of traditional style were taken over by European instruments. Traditional music included singing and rhythm. Dancing belonged to it as well. Musicians now were concerned with integrating this rhythm into the modern music, and with supplementing it without interfering with traditional dance steps. The well-known songs and rhythms from the countryside had to be orchestrated in new musical arrangements.

The first Guinean orchestral groups included La Douce Parisette—which already had been founded before independence—the Symphonies, and Harlem Jazz. At first they were imitation orchestras and played imported music like tango, waltz, and so on. In the early 1950s, shortly before independence, they began to discover and take up regional folk music.[11]

The French had pursued a policy of assimilation in their colonies. They disseminated French and other European music in schools, religious associations, dance halls, concerts, and brass bands. At the same time, records, song anthologies, and printed music of European origin were imported. The resulting influence, of course, was more noticeable in the city than in the country. Only a few Africans could afford a phonograph. In the novel *L'enfant noir* by the Guinean author Camara Laye, the uncle of the main character is a senior accountant in a French trade firm, and his position enables him to own a phonograph:

My uncle would leave his gramophone and records for us, and Marie and I would dance. Of course we would dance very circumspectly: it is not customary, in our land, to dance in one another's arms: we dance facing each other, but without touching; at the very most we hold hands, but this is not usual. Need I say that, in our shyness, we desired nothing better? But would we have danced together if it had been customary to dance in one another's arms? I hardly know what we would have done. I think we would have abstained, although, like all Africans, we have dancing in our blood.[12]

Mural in a bar in Conakry.

The scene in the uncle's house takes place in capital, Conakry. At home, in the eastern part of the country, the main character has no phonograph but plays a guitar instead:

"Don't brood over it so," Kouyaté would say. "Play us your guitar." I would go and take down my guitar—Kouyaté had taught me to play.

In the evening, instead of staying in my hut, we would go strolling through the streets of the town, Kouyaté and I, picking on our guitars, while Check played the banjo and we all three sang in harmony. Girls who often were already in bed when we passed their compound would wake up and listen to us. Those who were friends of ours would recognise our voices; they would get up, dress hastily and run to join us. Though only three of us had started out, soon we would be six, and ten, and sometimes even fifteen, all of us rousing the echoes in the sleeping streets.[13]

Especially interesting in this short excerpt is Camara Laye's description of playing the guitar: he says "picking." It suggests that the youths used the "guitar-picking style" practiced in large parts of Africa. This technique, also called "finger-picking style," is especially characteristic of African guitar playing and allows the traditional plucked stringed instruments to be replaced by the guitar (there are, of course, also bowed stringed instruments). One should not make the mistake, however, of assuming this transfer to be a natural one, as it were, for every African musician.

## THE BUREAUCRATIZATION OF CULTURE

During the Sékou Touré era, music festivals were organized every other year on regional and national levels in order to discover and promote talent. Local dance groups, bands, theater groups, and traditional music ensembles were called upon to participate in competitions in the various *arrondissements:* that is the source from which to take water.

The selection began on the local level. The best of the regional groups were integrated into the cultural work, as were, for instance, Bembeya Jazz, the Amazones du Guinée, Kaloum Star, and others.

The government employed them as cultural officials and they received monthly salaries. In the individual regions, half of the salaries for regional music and theater groups were paid by the local administration.[14]

A concrete result of this cultural policy is, for instance, the record entitled *Folklore et ensembles instrumenteaux,*[15] which consists of a compilation of eight pieces by seven groups. The record jacket states that the recording is of folklore and music by traditional instrumental ensembles. One would expect that the titles of the individual pieces would allude to folklore. The themes presented, however, are absolutely political: *Horoya,* meaning "independence"; *Aggression,* surely referring to the attacks on Sékou Touré's regime; *Le complot ne passera pas,* alluding to constantly uncovered conspiracies; *PDG Lannata Dyabi,* dealing with the Parti Démocratique du Guinée; and *Festival*, a song about the festival itself.

What has happened here to tradition, to the traditional cultural property of the people? On the one hand, it certainly experienced a re-evaluation, compared to the disregard it had received during the colonial period. On the other hand, it is secularized and probably deprived of its essential content through its heightened political consciousness. What remains is a residue of form—dance steps, melodies and rhythms; the meaning of the form, however, appears to have been lost. Instead, it was replaced by political content. It is difficult to determine whether the traditional culture was thus dominated; it appears doubtful whether the traditional culture will continue to assert itself. The revolutionary cultural policy was able to accomplish with much greater efficiency what the colonial attack on traditional culture was not able to achieve.

## STATE MOURNING FOR A SINGER

Aboubacar Demba Camara, the vocal soloist of Bembeya Jazz National, died on April 5, 1973, in Dakar, following a "stupid" traffic accident. Here is the story, told by Ibrahima Khalil Diare:

Since April 1 [the day of the accident], the whole city of Conakry has been in turmoil. The radio stations broadcast optimistic bulletins about Camara's condition daily until the evening of April 4. It is no exaggeration to say that all the people of Guinea were shocked and stunned by the news of Demba's death.

In an official communiqué, which was translated into all six national languages, the party and the government called for two days of national mourning. On Thursday and Friday all flags were to be flown at half-staff, and the singer was granted a state funeral.

An important party and government delegation, accompanied by a member of the politburo, flew to Dakar to escort the body of the artist home. On Thursday at 7:00 P.M., the airport of Conakry-Gbessia was crowded with people who gathered spontaneously to meet the remains of Demba Camara. The state funeral began there. It was continued in the Palais du Peuple with a long wake, attended by all members of the central committee of the PDG and the government in turn. All dance halls and bars in Conakry were closed.

Never had the funeral of an artist triggered so many expressions of sympathy and collective compassion: a true tide of processions and funeral marches swept through African countries as far as Zaire, Sierra Leone,

LP cover showing A. Demba Camara, on right. (SLP 44).

Burkina Faso, Senegal, Ivory Coast, Mali, and Liberia. The singer and
composer of Bembeya Jazz had his fans in all these countries and was appreciated as one of the greatest representatives of modern African music.

In Conakry on Friday, April 6, more than ten thousand people, all
dressed in white—including two government delegations from Senegal
and Sierra Leone—escorted the singer Aboubacar Demba Camara to his
last resting place in the cemetery of Camayenne. The Fanfares of Camp
Boiro opened the funeral procession with the great Mandingo hymn for
brave warriors, *Boloba*.

Born in 1944 in Conakry, Demba Camara spent his early school years
there living with his father, who worked for the administration of the
Conakry-Niger Railroad, as it was then called. He caught the attention of
his friends by always picking up current songs here and there. After he
finished school, his father enrolled him in the regional craft school in Kan-
kan, from which he received a diploma as an ebony craftsman. In 1963, he
encountered Bembeya Jazz in Beyla. The group was just beginning its diz-
zying rise to becoming the most famous orchestra of Guinea . . .

He joined the orchestra as a singer, which his family . . . viewed as an
escape from more serious tasks, such as establishing a workshop. His se-
cretiveness came to an end in 1966: Bembeya Jazz was established as the
national orchestra and had returned from a triumphant tour to Cuba.

On this big island of freedom, he moved the old Afro-Cuban *animateur*
Albelardo Barroso to tears when he performed, in Spanish, one of the biggest successes from the rich career of the seventy-year-old man.

In his position as first singer of the national orchestra, Demba quickly
realized that it was necessary to cultivate his voice and expression, to master and discipline his breathing, to train his ear, and to increase his feeling

for rhythm and meter . . . He worked at it with passion and per-
severance, inspired by the expression of the African bards. Demba proved
to be a researcher who loved the music of the people, passionately ob-
sessed with dance and music, attentive to various rhythms that
characterize African music, without showing contempt for other genres.
A tape recorder in hand, he knocked at the doors of all traditional artists
in Conakry. His touching masculine voice with its rugged gentleness
helped and eased his performance in all genres and styles.

Demba was more than a singer; he became a giant of show business, a
master in his field.[16]

## BEMBEYA JAZZ NATIONAL

The city of Beyla in the extreme southeast of Guinea did not have
much of a social life in the early 1960s. Apprentices, masons,
drivers, administrative officers, physicians, etc.—that is, mostly
people who had completed a European education—joined forces
to bring some life into the province. They founded an orchestra
and named it after the river that runs through the area, Bembeya
Jazz. At the next national festival, in 1962, they received second
prize, a silver medal, and then, a gold in 1964. In 1965, Bembeya
Jazz represented Guinea at the Festival Tricontinental in Cuba.
After winning additional prizes, the orchestra was accorded the
status of a national orchestra in 1966. Now the band had to move
to Conakry. In 1969, at the Pan-African Festival in Algiers, it was
again Bembeya Jazz who represented Guinea, at least in the modern division. They placed second, behind the host country.

In the years from 1969 to 1973, Bembeya Jazz became one of
the most famous bands in West Africa, especially through their
singer, Aboubacar Demba Camara. Their records were played in
all the discotheques, and many other groups performed their titles.
Following the death of Aboubacar Demba Camara in 1973, it was
difficult for the group to compensate for the loss, and they did not
play at all for the next two years. Personally and musically it was a
time of search. The Trio Bazouka was taken into the orchestra to
fill the place of Demba Camara. Then, in 1977, Bembeya Jazz performed at the Second World Black and African Festival of Arts and
Culture (FESTAC) in Lagos, after they had just lost their bassist
Mory Kouyate II as well. The solo guitarist Sekou-Diabate-
Bembeya, "Diamond Fingers," was elected the "majeur guitariste
d'Afrique" by the attending international press in Lagos.

Meanwhile, Bembeya Jazz has experienced a continuous renewal of musicians and repertory. In the years since 1980 alone, nine new musicians have joined the band, which now includes players of traditional instruments as well. Besides traditional drums, a xylophone, and a balafon (a xylophone with gourd resonators) are now part of the orchestra. In addition, three female dancers perform sometimes in grass skirts, sometimes in modern Guinean dress. All this appears to reinforce a folkloristic tendency that until now was not noticable.

The song texts of Bembeya Jazz have above all an educational character corresponding to official policies, but love songs are not excluded. Just like the instrumentalists, the singers draw on the rich tradition of the Mandingo for melody and rhythm. Traditional songs are adopted and trimmed for recordings. Thus the traditional Mandingo "hymn," which celebrated brave warriors, becomes a song of praise of the new national army, titled *Armée Guinéenne:*

Guinean army, the defense of the Guinean homeland is a basic demand.

Oh, Guinean militia, the defense of the Guinean homeland is a basic demand.

National Politburo and the government,
All Guineans, men and women, bless you.

The army that nobody brings to contempt.
The war of contempt has not ended
The treacherous war has not ended.

Eliminate the enemies, the traitors.
Eliminate the enemies.
Eliminate the spies.
The destruction of the spies consolidates our honor.
Nobody will ever again betray us our newly-won honor.[17]

## ARMÉE GUINÉENNE: SIGNAL MUSIC OF THE NEW MILITARY GOVERNMENT AFTER THE DICTATORSHIP OF SÉKOU TOURÉ

On April 3, 1985, a group of military men under the command of Colonel Diarra Traoré seized political leadership of the country. After only one or two days, an updated version of the song *Armée Guinéenne* by Bembeya Jazz National was broadcast by the radio station Radiodiffusion et Télévision Guinéenne (RTG). The "Com-

Bembeya Jazz at a concert in Frankfurt during their European tour in 1985.

mitée Militaire du Redressement National" appears inserted in the text at the appropriate place. When the first version of the song had been included on a Bembeya Jazz National record more than ten years earlier, it was dedicated to the military. Now this salute was even more befitting. Other national orchestras followed. The Boiro Band and the Ensemble National Instrumental et Choral, for instance, also sang the praises of the new government. Now the change in government could be perceived acoustically as well.

It appears that the official agencies are not entirely pleased with this seamless continuation of musical homage to the ruling government. The current thinking is that music should stay out of politics completely. This will certainly take its toll on the repertoires of orchestras which, after all, have been almost exclusively concerned with political subjects since 1960.

Radio broadcasting, which is to say the station Radiodiffusion et Télévision Guinéenne, played an especially important part in the transition from the dictatorship to the liberating military regime. One of the most dramatic reports broadcast the voices of just-released political prisoners from Camp Boiro and their relatives.[18] A sigh of relief, which rippled through the whole nation, was heard day after day on the radio. The radio network acted as a driving force of liberation. People were interviewed by telephone. The listeners could voice their opinions about the liberation without censorship. They cried, they began to rave. The radio constantly broadcast announcements of new rules by the government—for instance, that all citizens of Guinea were allowed to open bank accounts and that confidentiality would be kept.[19]

The songs of Bembeya Jazz and other orchestras[20] celebrate martyrs of Guinea's colonial days. Moral principles are propagated just as in traditional song, which also uses proverbs as subjects. Moralistic views and popular music may constitute a contradiction in our Western eyes (popular music here even appears to be appreciated because of its amoral tendencies), but in Guinea and, as far as I can judge, in all of black Africa, that does not occur to anybody. The text is important and the music is incredibly good. What else is needed?

The epic narrative of Samory (a Mandingo ruler who resisted the French and subsequently was deported to an island of Gabon where he died in 1900) lasts an entire LP. It is entitled *Regard sur le passe* and is called "le premier grand concert africaine."[21] It is African in the politico-cultural sense of "Africanization." Consisting of continuous recitation in the traditional style, it is nevertheless comparable to an orchestral composition in scope. It also shows how inept and misleading it would be to apply our distinctions of popular and traditional music to African standards.

Yet, not only historic recitation and current political events were incorporated into songs. Modern achievements of the new state were included as well: one of Bembeya Jazz's songs is dedicated to the new national airline, Air Guinée.[22]

Most pieces appeared first as singles, at least in the 1960s. As a consequence, most individual pieces on LPs were at first approximately the length of a single. Longer tracks, however, are found even in the early 1970s. The composition *Nganakoro* on the Bembeya Jazz record *Authenticité 73*, for instance, lasts almost twelve minutes. It is advertised as a piece "du long-play de Bembeya," and is based on an initiation song from Wassoulou.[23]

Dance styles and rhythms indicated on the records are for the most part rumba, or rumba versions other than simple rumba: "rumba lente" and "rumba guinée." Then there is also the tentemba, a dance type of which a fifteen-minute example (*Super*

*Tentemba*) has been recorded on *Discothèque 73*, SLP 45, by Bembeya Jazz.

Bembeya Jazz is certainly the best known orchestra in and from Guinea, but there are at least forty-four similar ones throughout the country. Eight of these are national orchestras: Horoya Band National, Super Boiro Band, Balla et ses Balladins, Camayenne Sofa, Bembeya Jazz National, Syli Authentic, Kélétigui et ses Tambourinis, and Les Amazones de Guinée.

Balla et ses Balladins grew out of the Orchestre du Jardin de Guinée, the group of the dance hall Jardin de Guinée. Kélétigui et ses Tambourinis used to be the house band of the Paillote.

Both dancing clubs existed for more than twenty years. The quality of music and musicians grew steadily, due to the festivals. In order to solve the central problem of all modern musicians in Africa—procuring useful instruments—the state founded Enterprise National d' Importation et de Vente des Instruments de Musique, Articles de Sports, et de Distribution des Disques et des Cassettes (ENIMAS). Through this state agency, European instruments of good quality could reach even the most remote regions. Thus, in Guinea, musicians are dependent on the state, whereas in other parts of Africa, musicians frequently depend on a band leader or nightclub owner who has the final say because of his financial power or, more often, because he owns the musical instruments.

## LES AMAZONES DE GUINÉE

Les Amazones de Guinée are a group of female police officers. In the beginning, they performed in their unsightly police uniforms under the name L'Orchestre Féminin de la Gendarmerie Nationale. But soon they could be admired in their Guinean wraparound skirts and blouses with "tails." As early as 1979, they had performed at the "Erstes Festival der Weltkulturen. Horizonte '79" in West Berlin. They had come with the famous South African singer Miriam Makeba, who lives in exile in Conakry and maintains her well-known *Club Zambézi* there.

Before their modernization, Les Amazones performed with mandolins, bongos, congas, violins, cellos, double basses, etc. Then, beginning in 1965, electric guitars, saxophones, trumpets, and—not to be overlooked—drums were purchased. The group visited many African capitals on their tours. In 1977, they performed at FESTAC in Lagos. It was their declared goal to create a place for women in Guinean society where they are neither enslaved by men nor subject to general sexism.

In 1983, Les Amazones went on tour to France and made several records among them a recording of a live concert on April 6, 1983 in the Théâtre de la Mutualité. In addition, two other LPs were released. One of them features M'Mah Sylaah, a singer of the group, together with Mamadou Aliou Barry from the Orchestre Kalum Star. The second record, called *Sons de la Savane* (Sounds of the Savannah), presents the guitarist and singer Sona Diabate, who is married to "Diamond Fingers," guitarist of Bembeya Jazz, in collaboration with the guitarist and balafon player Demba Camara of Super Lion.[24]

Every morning the musicians of Les Amazones report for duty at the Palace du Peuple and practice. These beautiful African women are richly garbed with reputation and pride.

One Guinean musician who ought not to remain unmentioned is Sory Kandia Koyaté. Unfortunately, he died at the early age of 44. As a griot, he belonged to the Ballets Africains from the beginning and later directed the Ensemble Instrumental et Choral de la Voix de la Révolution. On his first LP, he is accompanied by the Ensemble National Djoliba (side one) and the Orchestre Kélétigui et ses Tambourinis (side two). A series of three records by Koyaté (entitled *L'Epopée du Mandingue*) that appeared later is in the style of a classic recitation of his traditional trio.[25] Koyaté thus followed the instruction of Sekou Touré, who had called on musicians to maintain the cultural heritage. In the words of Justin Morel Junior, he was "toute sa vie un artiste de combat"—all his life a fighting artist.

## Griot—Griotte

In the whole area of the geographic Sudan—from Senegal to Niger and Chad—there is a type of musician that has entered the literature under the name "griot." The griot, however, does not exist. The assumption that there is one universal type has led to the common mistake that all African musicians are sometimes described as griots.

Les Amazones de Guinée used their sojourn in France in 1983 for the production of records.

In its present form, the word is not part of any African language. Attempts to explain its etymology have given rise to a number of speculations without producing a conclusive result. One theory suggests that the word stems from the Portuguese word *criado* (servant), another that it is a French corruption of the Wolof term *gewel* (*Dictionaire des civilations africaines,* Paris 1968). The word was introduced into French and thus spread over all of French Africa. Spelled "guiriot," it first appeared in the eighteenth century in reports by French travelers to Senegal. Its present-day spelling was adopted in the nineteenth century.[26]

The term "griot" encompasses musicians and singers (male musicians, that is; the female form of the word is "griotte"), who fulfill a variety of important social functions. They are either wandering musicians or part of a courtly establishment and may be compared to our bards, court musicians, or minstrels. In their respective homelands, they are called a variety of names: in Mande (the language of the Mandingo people) they are called *dyeli, yeli,* or *jali;* and in the language of the Fulbe and Toucouleur, *awlube;* the Soninke and Wolof refer to these musicians as *gesers* and *gewel* (*jewel*), respectively.[27]

All have in common an education in their own families from

early childhood on. They learn to memorize texts and recitation, and the men are also taught to play instruments. The genealogy of the ruling houses, the history of their dominions, great battles, conquests, and so on, are among the subjects of this oral transmission. The griots are rightly referred to as the archives and libraries of this part of Africa. Thus the famous proverb, "wherever a griot dies, a library dies,"[28] is increasingly true in our times, since the transmission of their enormous knowledge has not continued to the same degree as in earlier periods.

At the center of the history transmitted by the griots lies the interest of a ruler in legitimizing his right to rule. The griot performs in this functional context: he lauds the ruler and his family, and sings praises of his deeds. Since the griot is supported by the ruler, in most cases he is also dependent on him. Griots could also function as speakers for the ruler. They were interpreters of current politics, transmitting messages and orders from the governing power to the people. As musicians with contacts with musicians outside the court, they were able to learn the opinion of the common people and could convey sentiments of the populace to the ruler. Thus, the griot, as the ear and voice of the people, also may have been feared as a spy. He became potentially dangerous if he publicly and forcefully attacked and defamed someone.

Based on their position at court, griots might enjoy great esteem. In the realm of the Sudan, however, they belonged to the lower end of the social hierarchy, at the same time respected and despised.

In general, the griots were the preservers—the guarantors of tradition, oral transmission, customs, and morals. Their songs denounced aberrant behavior and showed the true way. Christianity and Islam were, and still are, a threat to these musicians. The introduction of a monetary economy, especially, dealt a severe blow to the existence of the griots. Instead of giving the griots natural produce, their lords and patrons now had to pay them with money. But the funds of the traditional rulers, who had been robbed of their sources of wealth (for example, colonial powers had deprived them of their tax monopoly), did not suffice any longer. Griots are still invited to feasts for such occasions as the birth of a child, a wedding, or a funeral, but even in this area they have lost many commissions.

The following song by the kora player Foday Musa Suso dem-

The kora player Abdoulaye Cissoko, in Ziguinchor, Senegal.

onstrates that griots are able to incorporate modern phenomena into their traditions:

> Ah, dindin ka nyin, Apollo
> Ah, the young woman (lit. "child") is beautiful, Apollo
>
> Dinding kunsinyi ka nyin, Apollo
> The woman has beautiful hair, Apollo
>
> Dindin kan fala ka jan, Apollo
> She has a beautiful long neck, Apollo
>
> Dindin nyin kese ka ge, Apollo
> She has lovely white teeth, Apollo[29]

The song praises a young woman; an especially impressive word, "Apollo," is interpolated, leading to the conclusion that the song was composed at the time of the Apollo moon landings, which caused much excitement everywhere in Africa. Interjections of this kind often have an additional, sometimes purely functional significance in the formal structure of poetry: they allow the poet to consider the words to follow, and in this way this kind of padding aids in the continuation of the poem.

The griots, or, in Mande, *jali,* accompany themselves or are assisted by a female singer, most often the griot's wife, who is called *jali muso.* The performance, the activity of the griot is called *jaliya.*[30]

The kora is probably the best known and most impressive instrument of the griots. A twenty-one-string instrument, it is categorized as a harp-lute in ethnomusicological terminology, its name being justified not by its technical construction, but rather by its bell-like tone. The neck, a round wooden staff, is fastened to the resonant body, which is made from a large gourd or a calabash bowl. Today, pick-up microphones for amplification are hooked into the sound hole at the side. Across the bridge or at the end of the neck a snare sheet may be fastened, which the vibrations and other movements of the instrument will cause to rattle and ring. This corresponds to the ideal sound quality desired by the listeners in many parts of Africa—quite the opposite from our ideals of a pure tone. It is exactly the clarity and transparency of the tone that is intentionally avoided, or at least weakened.

According to region and function, the griots do also play a number of other different instruments. The five-stringed spike

Glasspainting by Sylla: a griot playing a khalam.

lute, khalam (xalam), and the one-stringed godji (as it is called in its eastern area of dissemination) are stringed instruments.[31] The balafon, distinguished by its gourd resonators installed under the sound bars, is a type of xylophone. Most often, a bar is also furnished with a snare resonator whose sound hole is covered with a web. In addition, a variety of drums serve griots as accompanying instruments.

## Great Female Singers: Mali

Although the socialist regime of Guinea remained in power until 1984, the government of Modibo Keita in Mali was removed in a coup d'état by the military in 1968. The first president of independent Mali had ideas similar to those of Sékou Touré of Guinea, even in areas of cultural policies. The two states formed a confederation in which they were joined by Ghana under its president, Kwame Nkrumah. The alliance of Ghana-Guinea-Mali was intended as a first step in the direction of a later pan-African union.

The alliance—intended to be a signal to other African states, a model to be emulated—was celebrated in songs composed in all three countries. In Ghana the famous Highlife tune *Ghana-Guinea-Mali,* by E. T. Mensah and His Tempo's Band appeared in English. This was unusual for Mensah, for he sang most of his songs in native languages. Obviously he intended to reach a wider audience beyond the borders of Ghana.

> Singer: Ghana, Guinea, Mali Union
> has laid down a strong foundation
> for redemption of Africa,
> for which we've been strongly fighting.
>
> Chorus: Ghana, Guinea, Mali,
> Singer: the nucl'us of the great union,
> Chorus: Ghana, Guinea, Mali,
> Singer: Africa's strongest foundation,
> Chorus: Ghana, Guinea, Mali,
> Singer: the nucl'us of the great union,
> Chorus: Ghana, Guinea, Mali,
> Singer: has now been laid forever.
>
> Singer: As it was Ghana and Guinea,
> later Ghana, Guinea, Mali,
> soon it will be all Africa
> the achievement of a greatest t'ing.
>
> Chorus: Ghana, Guinea, Mali,
> Singer: the nucl'us of the great union, etc.
>
> (instrumental interlude)
>
> Singer: Africa is now awakened,
> that unity conceived,
> all leaders of mother Africa
> are called to join this great union.
>
> Chorus: Ghana, Guinea, Mali,
> Singer: the nucl'us of the great union, etc.[32]

In Mali, a song entitled *Mali and Guinea Have Joined Hands* was recorded by a modern orchestra and broadcast on the radio.[33] A booklet enclosed with the record names the singer of this piece as Mondan Tape, but unfortunately the band is mentioned only as a "contemporary orchestra." The musical style is classified as "Highlife," and the singing and the music of the orchestra are described as "definitely African" and being under Cuban influence, respectively. In my opinion, however, the orchestra is not really a Highlife group. Such a classification would claim a direct relationship to those groups indigenous to Ghana and Nigeria. This group includes an acoustic guitar, maracas, and a muted trumpet, and, indeed, they perform a Latin American piece—one of the most beautiful pieces of the period—in their manner. As the comment indicates, the style of singing is certainly African, but it is significantly faster and adapted to the rhythm. Here is the text of a song with the same theme:

> Modibo's people are in Mali
> Their likes are in Guinea
> And similar men are in Ghana
> The moment for being alone has arrived . . .
>
> The evil whites who were here
> I say those evil ones have gone . . .
>
> The evil hunger that was here
> I say that hunger has ended
> It is the time of the five-year plan
> Let us unite to work
> It is the time of socialism
> Misery has ended . . .
>
> The evil prisons that were here
> I say these evils are gone.[34]

Like the potentates of imperial Mali, the politically responsible of the modern state consider themselves patrons of art and music. Today as yesterday, they regard musicians as servants to their cause. Famous singers, griots, were interested in broadcasting and reinforced the efforts of the new government to build a socialist Mali.

Before independence, when it was still called Radio Soudan, Radio Mali already broadcast in five native languages in addition to French. The largest portion of the programing was in Bambara. The broadcasting system was expanded significantly with independence in the early 1960s. The people of the country voluntarily raised two hundred million CFA to finance a new medium wave station, which also demonstrates how important the radio was in those days to the people.[35]

The late 1960s was the time of cheap transistor receivers. Powered by batteries and thus independent of a power supply system, they disseminated popular music. To the great astonishment of the rural population, they now could hear those wonderful songs not only at local feasts and festivities, but practically any time: they only had to switch on the radio.

Recordings from the pioneer days of Mali's independence are contained in a two-part collection. One record is devoted entirely to political songs, and the other contains historical and cere-monial songs. With few exceptions, all the pieces are entirely in a traditional style. The political songs celebrate the five-year plan or the withdrawal from the French confederation. Appeals like "Mali must work" were intended to spur the population's creativity and dedication. Songs like *The French Have Gone* commemorate the early days of colonial times. All songs are sung in Bambara or Malinké.[36]

In addition to the radio, the National Ensemble provides an-other means of survival for some griots. The members of the Ensemble National du Mali are employed by the state. All griots are integrated into the Association des Artistes Traditionalistes. During Modibo Keita's administration, this organization was rep-resented by a party official who was a high ranking member of the government at the same time. The competition-like character of this politico-cultural organization corresponds to that found in Guinea.

After the military seized power, a campaign to "re-evaluate the artistic and cultural heritage" was launched in 1969. The "Bien-nales," festivals held every two years since 1970, lend an organiza-tional frame to the campaign. The series *Mali Music*, a production of the Department of Information, documents the first Biennale of 1970, a musical highpoint in the history of Mali.[37]

The pieces performed by Rail Band begin in perfect arrange-ment and immaculate balance of tone. First a solo electric guitar plays sequences of high pitches descending into the low register, with the reverb effect turned on. Then, on the last low pitch, the conga enters and, shortly after, the trumpet follows, slightly dis-placed. After this short intro, the basic rhythm begins and continues throughout the piece. The voice starts to sing in the clas-sical manner of the griots. It is kept distinct against the brass section, who one after another are heard imitating speech pat-terns. In all, the piece is a dense web full of tension which still creates a wide field: it appears to reflect the open spaces of the native geographic area, the Sahel. Dances taken over from Afro-American dance music have become more relaxed and lighter, yet,

The Rail Band of Bamako, Mali, appropriately depicts the Malian railroad on this cover.

at the same time, new arrangements produce an increased density and tension. Only a superficial listener could speak here of plagarism. Ingeniously, Afro-American elements are adopted in a sparkling and creative manner. The listener perceives and catches the fascination and enthusiasm of the early 1970s, even if he is thousands of miles away.

The instrumentation is that of a standard rock band—lead guitar, rhythm guitar, bass guitar, drums—and, in addition, a brass section with trumpets and saxophones, as well as a set of Latin percussion instruments, mostly congas, maracas, and guiro. And, finally, there are voices.

Among the outstanding singers of modern Mali and beyond—today even worldwide—is Salif Keita, who had been present at the foundation of Rail Band in 1970. He was born in 1949. As an expression of highest honor, he received the epithet "Domingo de la Chanson Malienne."

After Rail Band, the Ambassadeurs du Motel followed, and they became Ambassadeurs Internationaux in 1978 in Abidjan. Since 1984, Salif Keita has resided in Paris, and there he released his first French production, *Soro*. *Bingo* (a magazine for the African market published in France) assesses it as "a leg on his way to universalism."[38] The modern, refined and perfect production—and that of Mory Kante as well—is marketed as Mandingo rock. Mory Kante also sang with Rail Band. His song "Yeke yeke," which appears on his LP *Akwaba*, even found its way onto the French hit parades. The compositions in this new style enthusiastically pull out all the stops of modern electronic rock and pop music. Nothing for purists! Salif Keita and Mory Kante and another former Rail Band member, Kante Manfila, follow a new path and thus assure a higher estimation and a larger audience for African music.

The group Las Maravillas du Mali, under Boncana Maiga is the most extreme example of the admiration of Cuban dance music. Having just graduated from the A. Garcia Conservatory in Havana, eight young Malian musicians returned to Africa in late 1969, after they had performed with great success in Cuba. They recorded a very popular record album. One of the pieces was entitled *Radio Mali*. Unfortunately, the group broke up because they lacked adequate instruments. Four of the original members later formed a new group under the same name: in 1973 they performed again in Bamako and had great success in Dakar in 1974. Afro-Cuban music is still, for many Africans, the paragon of all good dancing music. The bonds to the Caribbean are stronger in former French colonies than in former British territories. Apparently even today Paris is an important center of exchange for this music. In addition, many blacks from the French Antilles with French educations were sent as colonial officers to Africa, where they acted as "multipliers" of this kind of music: they brought African-American dances to Africa, from Senegal to Congo.

In 1977, Les Ambassadeurs participated in FESTAC in Lagos. So did the other big band of Mali, the orchestra Le Super Biton National.[39] The trumpeter Amadaou Ba is the leader of this band. As a trumpeter, he of course considers Louis Armstrong to be the god of jazz. Biton was founded through the merger of two well-known groups, Ségou Jazz and Renaissance (both had existed since 1953). In 1968, the new group advanced first to regional, then to national orchestra status under the supervision of the Direction Régionale de Jeunesse, Sport, Art, et Culture (DRJSAC). As a consequence, it was at least supported by the state, though not formally employed by the government as orchestras were in Guinea.

## FANTA DAMBA

Fanta Damba and Mokontafe Sako are two of the most famous female singers in Mali. Today, when they reach their audience through radio and records, they still continue tradition in their style of singing and in the content of their songs. The fact that women accompany male griots as singers may explain why so many became popular *vedettes,* that is, stars. Popular culture in Mali, however, still is a culture for all. Distinctions between classes, generations, and other target groups are developing only slowly. Thus, the *vedettes* are stars with very broad appeal, true darlings of the people, comparable, perhaps, to a star in our culture, who would be admired as an actor and a singer of serious, popular, and folk music, all at the same time.

Fanta Damba was born in 1938 in Segou, the fourth region of Mali. Both of her parents were musicians. In early childhood she was introduced to the art of singing and, at the age of seven, entered a sort of griot school which was supervised by the greatest masters of the region. At sixteen, she had already made a name for herself as a singer and performed at weddings and other festivities. Her great talent quickly became known all over the country thanks to the help of Radio Mali.

It caused quite a sensation when she joined the Ensemble Instrumental National du Mali in 1960. She performed with the best musicians and singers of the country and was soon recognized as number one among female singers by the public. "She owed her triumph to the timbre of her voice, an inimitable mixture of melancholy and gentleness . . . Her songs are the results of her own research. Filled with images, parables, and symbols, they are taken from the traditional song repertory."[40] Concert tours took her to Africa, Europe, America, and Asia. In 1969, the Ensemble Instrumental National du Mali competed at the First Pan-African Cultural Festival in Algiers and won a gold medal.

Fanta Damba was hailed as a "Miriam Makeba." Unfortunately, the success in Algiers was only short-lived, and the ensemble was dissolved a few months later to everybody's dismay. This apparent act of political arbitrariness surely is one of the darker sides of a cultural scene supported and controlled too strongly by the government.

Fanta Damba then founded her own group, which included the well-known kora player Batourou Sékou Kouyaté and the guitarists Mady and Mody Tounkara. The general public was grateful, and their records *Loterie National, Malamine,* and *Hadire* were great successes. *Hadire* was dedicated to El Hadji Omar Tall, a hero of the resistance against colonialism.

In an interview in 1978, Fanta Damba stated, "It is our task to demonstrate the wealth of our cultural heritage to the people of Mali and foreign nations. Some day I would like to earn the title 'Ambassador of Africa's Traditional Music'." "As if you haven't done that already!" answered the interviewer.[41]

### MOKONTAFE SAKO

Mokontafe Sako is also one of Mali's great female singers. She, too, comes from the province of Segou and was born there in 1937. The circumstances of her birth describe a piece of African reality we often disregard because it is so foreign to us.

Her mother had lost one child after another at birth, two boys and two girls. Following an African tradition, Boura Sako and his wife decided to give their future children ridiculous names and no obvious affection. This would avert bad fate and ensure long lives for the newborns. Thus, Boura Sako and his wife named their third daughter "Nobody loves you because you are so ugly." She survived, but by no means did that prediction come true.[42]

Both Mokontafe's father, Boura Sako, and her mother, Fatoumata, were renowned griots: he played the guitar and she sang. In the city of Mopti there was never a lack of events such as baptisms, weddings, and official ceremonies to which they were summoned. The children of griots customarily accompany their parents to these festivities. On one occasion, the little Mokontafe made her debut, singing with her mother; from then on her little voice captivated her audience. She lost her father at the age of ten. Moving from Mopti to Bamako, her mother continued her education. Soon little Mokontafe was discovered by audiences. During the

1950s, when she still was a growing griotte, a French record company pressed her first record, entitled *Kala*.

Mokontafe Sako became one of the best *animateurs*, that is, radio announcer, of the new national radio. She married and followed her husband to the provincial city of Kayes. Yet soon she was called back to Bamako and was asked to join the Ensemble Instrumental National du Mali. Concert tours with the National Ensemble made Mokontafe Sako an international celebrity. After the dissolution of the Ensemble in 1969, she founded her own group.[43] One of her records, *Farafina Moussow,* was dedicated to African women.[44] It pays homage to famous African women such as Bell Bellow, singer of Dahomey (today called Benin), M'Balia Camara, the queen of Kokou, and others who are examples and symbols of bravery to their sisters.

On another record, she sang in honor of Malian soccer.[45] *Aigles du Mali* refers to Mali's national team, the Eagles of Mali, and another song praises the famous soccer team Le Djoliba de Bamako.

Mokontafe Sako on the problems of African artists:

> African artists deserve a better lot. They should be aided by national authorities or other public or private corporations.
>
> The well-being of singers and musicians is a source of foreign currency to our country. No artist in Africa can hold his own without support, and without support there are no concert tours, no recordings, in short, no promotion. That is the end of a career. Nothing is more detrimental to an artist than want of international contacts, of openness to other currents, or of confrontation with different styles. On our continent, there is an abundance of songs and art in general. But young talents often are afraid to express themselves and to pursue an artistic career when they realize the poor conditions under which older artists live. A further danger to Africa's artistic heritage is the tendency of many of our colleagues to make it too easy for themselves. There is a lack of serious research and respectability in music. Art is an inexhaustible treasure, good for those who produce, and good for those who consume.[46]

### FANTA SACKO

Fanta Sacko is younger than both singers presented above. Like Mokontafe Sako, she transforms traditional tunes into new songs. She reflects a concern to cultivate the traditional heritage without letting it decline into a purely historical document.

On a record produced by Bärenreiter for the Malian Department of Information, Fanta Sacko is accompanied by two guitarists, Foussenou Diabaté and Mamadou Tounkara. Their acoustic guitars are tuned throughout with a capodaster at the fifth fret. Fanta Sacko sings a song composed at the city of Kita in honor of the griots of that town:

> God has created the world,
> God has created mankind,
> But he has overwhelmed more than any other
> Him whom he has gifted
> With a certain personality, with dignity,
> And above all with a sense of honor.
> Do never forget,
> O griots of Kita!
> That treason
> Is the most fatal thing
> To honor and dignity.
> I salute you, I, Fanta Diali,
> O griots of Kita!
> And tell you:
> That God has created nothing
> That is beyond the reach of fortune,
> And has created nothing worse
> Than treason and hypocrisy.
> Now, some, in our time,
> Say their prayers without conviction
> While others, who do not pray,
> Yet believe in God.
> Avoid, therefore, treason and hypocrisy
> And be always honest,
> O griots of Kita!
> For nothing escapes God,
> And God forgives nothing to the perjurer.[47]

## BAZOUMANA SISSOKO

Bazoumana Sissoko, the "Old Lion," is among the famous griots. He accompanies himself on a four-stringed nkoni, referred to as a spike lute in the ethnomusicological literature. The notes enclosed with the Bärenreiter record read:

He is modest, and his modesty is a sign of his gift. I, who was born when his fame already sparkled, must introduce him.

The National Ensemble of Mali, in Berlin (1979). Photo by Walter Kranl.

Bazoumana, the "Old Lion," has made history since independence . . .

He is popular and feared. He is venerated so much that his nkoni is
credited with magical powers: it would continue to play by itself if the
sore fingers of Father Zoumana were unable to pluck it.

This legend may cause Western people, who are rationalists, only to
smile. But I believe in it somewhat, since I know him. Indeed, when Bazoumana Sissoko's nkoni whines like a child torn out of sleep, and he
comforts it in his voice full of wisdom, then his noble figure fades to make
room for the great men of old times: Malinké warriors following the call
of the emperor; Bambara horsemen on the way to Segou, crowned with
honor and carrying trophies; El Hadji Omar . . . El Hadji Omar on the
way from Tekrour to Ségou country. Sometimes, a smile appears to relax
our mind, the smile of a beautiful copper-brown Fulbe woman, the bright
smile of a clear spring that we approach to drink.[48]

Bazoumana Sissoko is a cousin of Diely Baba Sissoko, who was
among the first griots whose music was transmitted by Radio
Mali. In 1960, when a staff member of the station suggested that
he make a program, he had his doubts: "No, really, radio is nothing for me, a griot." Nowadays, some thirty years later, and even
now, after his death, millions listen to him every week in Mali, Senegal, Ivory Coast, Zaire, Congo, and Sierra Leone.[49]

## Wrestling and Music: Senegal

In the mid 1970s, a *musique Sénégalais* began to emerge in Senegal; this music can immediately be discerned in style from the music of neighboring countries. An exception, of course, is Gambian music, which belongs to the same Senegambian cultural region.

Until 1980, the capitol of the Republic of Senegal, Dakar, was strongly influenced by the official cultural policies of President Léopold Sédar Senghor and his concept of *nègritude*, though trends imported from Paris have always made their presence felt. Senghor, a poet, was the most famous representative of nègritude, a notion intended to give Africans humiliated by colonialism a sense of self-esteem through a revival of their own culture. Until independence, it was an important, though controversial, ideological force in intellectual circles, especially in Paris. It had, however, no significance whatsoever for the "normal" African population, which could not afford the luxury of a quest for identity à la Senghor in its social stratum.

Senghor often composed his poems in view of their being recited to the accompaniment of certain, instruments, mostly traditional ones such as the kora, the four- or five-stringed khalam, or the small double-headed hourglass-shaped tama drum. In his instructions on the performance of his poems, he called for the combination of traditional and modern instruments—for instance, clarinet and balafon—or he simply indicated a "jazz orchestra."[50] Lamine Konté and two other musicians recorded some of Senghor's poems to balafon and kora in Paris on a record entitled *Chant du nègre . . . chant du monde.*[51] The interested audience was, however, mostly European.

For twenty years, the ideology of nègritude set the tone for cultural policies in Senegal. With a strong hand, the president determined which cultural achievements concurred with it and which were to be supported along these lines.[52] The national ballet, founded in 1961, organized its presentation of traditional dances on the basis of nègritude. The program for its third world tour in 1968 reports on the preparations: "To put the program together, every detail that appeared valuable in respect to music, poetry, and historical aspects of costume was researched in even the smallest village and incorporated. Often, the picturesque was consciously avoided in order to reproduce exactly the life-style of contemporary Africa."[53] It goes without saying that it was impossible to reach this precise goal in this manner.

The traditional music culture of Senegal[54] reflects the many different cultures native to the country: Serer, Dioulla, Wolof, Toucouleur, etc. Late in the evening on weekends, most often on Saturdays, small drum groups play in the country and in popular districts of the cities—"on the block," as it were. People go to the tom-tom and dance, while spectators in the circle around them admire the performance of individual dancers and enthusiastically toss them coins.

Diallo describes such occasions in Dakar:

On moonlit nights all the young people of the district gathered round a huge fire to sing circumcision songs, known as *kasaks*. Our musical instruments were rather rudimentary: we simply inverted calabashes in enormous basins filled with water, and used them as drums. We completed the ensemble by clapping our hands and chanting. The leader held a burning branch in each hand and sang the choruses, which we already knew and which we repeated after him. Sometimes obscene songs were improvised for the occasion. These sing-songs went on until all the young men were healed.[55]

Besides music played on transistor radios and tape recorders, such nightly drum meetings are familiar experiences for most people in Senegal. Radio stations broadcast mainly music in the styles in vogue internationally. During the 1950s, Latin American dances were popular, followed by rock music in the 1960s. Through Senegal's close ties to France, Johnny Hallyday was a special favorite. Soul, reggae, and disco rose to popularity thereafter. In Senegal, however, Afro-Cuban orchestras remained popular all the time and were emulated by local bands.

At the time of its formation on August 3, 1960—the year of independence—the Star Band was inspired by Afro-Cuban and Latin American music traditions. Amara Touré played congas during the early days of Star Band. In an interview with *Bingo*, he discussed the justification of using Latin American compositions.

I came to music at a time when it was difficult to introduce typical African music. Before independence, many musicians still played banjo and accordion, instruments of Western culture. Rhythms like waltz, jazz, and rumba were fashionable. I am part of that generation.

I wasn't able to veer out of that movement. After all, Latin American music—is that foreign music to us Africans? I really don't think so. Just listen to Brazilian samba, the percussion, the rhythm of the drums: all that seems to be very close to our own. We sense it as part of our own culture . . . Music has no boundaries, no language; rather, it is a mode of expression shared by all.[56]

Afro-Cuban titles still predominated on records of the mid-1970s, but there were also other pieces from outside Senegal, such as rock'n'roll and Highlife. Even today Latin American music is still popular, though it is not recorded anymore by the major bands. The Orquesta Aragón de Cuba, for example, was the big attraction during the Christmas season 1984 in Dakar. Complaints had been heard that the group had frequently come to Conakry over the course of the years, but never to Dakar.

In 1975, Le Sahel released its first LP—"le premier 33 tours"—an important occasion for every African band. The record and its first piece are both entitled Bamba!. They commemorate Sheik Ahmadou Bamba, the founder of the Brotherhood of the Murids, who was born about 1850 and dedicated his life to the dissemination of Islam. As an opponent to French colonial expansion, he became part of the history of anti-colonial struggle. In the piece mentioned above, the singers, imitating black American soul music (such as that of James Brown), literally scream the names of Bamba and other illustrious figures. James Brown toured Africa in 1975 and visited, among other places, Dakar. He performed for twenty thousand enthusiastic listeners in the Demba Diop stadium.

About a year after founding Le Sahel, the manager of the group named two things that were foremost on his mind: first, Senegal's music, and second, an opening-up to foreign genres in order to expand the repertoire. This statement prompted a question by one of Senegal's music critics: "N'est pas vouloir concilier l'inconciliable?" (Isn't this an attempt to reconcile the irreconcilable?) That, after all, is one of the basic questions regarding the development of modern African music. Le Sahel perceived audiences' great enthusiasm for African-American pop music and set out to prove that musicians from Senegal could make this kind of music, too. In addition, the group surely enjoyed playing this music, feeling like James Brown themselves.

At that time, the Star Band, by contrast, had accumulated fifteen years of experience. Titles like El Vagabonde, for instance,

had been number one on the hit parades for a long time. But that
did not deter the band from recording Senegalese pieces again and
again.

A number of equally famous orchestras emerged from the Star
Band: first among them was Star Number One, which later be-
came Orchestre Number One and, finally, Number One du
Sénégal.[57]

Attempts to create a new Senegalese music were characterized
primarily by the use of certain traditional instruments, such as the
tama (a small, double-headed, hour-glass-shaped drum) and the
sabar (a mid-size closed drum), and, by singing in the style and
tradition of the griots.

Certain pieces had already been based on Senegalese melodies
and rhythms even before traditional instruments were introduced
more frequently. After all, Latin American instruments were used
for the percussion elements. Today the music is given a more
"native" sound—electrically amplified, of course, and thus considerably more effective. The sound of the tama (the bang, or even
the pitch manipulation achieved by stretching the ropes connect-
ing the two drumheads during a lingering sound) can be imitated
quite well by a guitar or synthesizer, allowing for dialogues between two such instruments played alternately. High-pitched
singing amplified by short and sharp-sounding words so abundant in Wolof (the language contains many one-syllable words) is
characteristic of the new style as well.

The content of the song texts are determined by traditional values, mostly those of the predominate Wolof people. Connections
to and influences of the Islamic Brotherhood of the Murids, which
controls practically all of the economy, are frequent as well. Because it controls the cultivation and export of peanuts, the
Brotherhood is so powerful that the government cannot take action against it without difficulties. Ousmane ("Ouza") Diallo,
singer and bandleader of Ouza et Teranga International Band, illustrates his connection with muridism on the cover of his record
Wethe. The record then extols the critical values of the Wolof tradition, such as respect, bravery, and patriotism.

## YOUSSOU N'DOUR

Youssou N'dour's orchestra, Super Etoile, has been the most
successful popular group so far. It was formed when the original
Star Band, then called Etoile de Dakar, broke up. The remaining

members of that group formed a new band with the singer El
Hadji Faye, Etoile 2000.

Today Youssou N'dour is regarded as the undisputed king of
Mbalax music (also M'balah). Günter Gretz, the organizer of
Youssou N'dour's first West German tour, spoke with him:

[Q] How did you come to music?

[A] I started very early making music and singing. My mother's ancestors were *gaulo*, courtly singers of the former feudal rulers. They
passed on to me the gift of singing. My father never had anything to do
with music.

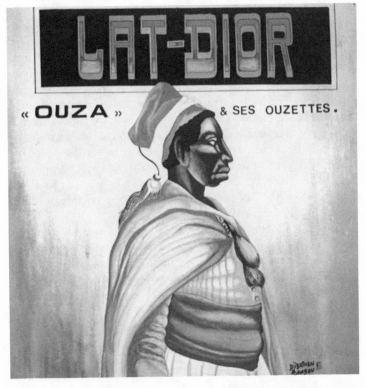

The influence of traditional Senegalese music during the second half of the 1970s became apparent in cover designs. The graphic artist Djibathen Sambou of Dakar
designed an entire series of record covers: the records of Production Jambaar, numbers 5000–5004, are signed works of art. Number 5004, for example, bears the title
Lat-Dior, after a king who offered resistance to French colonial soldiers. He has been
portrayed in the style of popular glasspainting.

Youssou N'dour at Frankfurt during a tour of Germany (1984).

I sang publicly for the first time at a circumcision ceremony. At these ceremonies, an entire family and all of its friends meet. Anybody may sing or play the sabar or tama. I went with friends to such a ceremony, and because there was such a great atmosphere, I sang. The people present liked it so much that they clapped, asked to hear more, and tossed me money. We bought a whole lot of stuff with the money. The next night we took off again and were successful once more. So we continued every day during school vacation, and I didn't tell my parents. But one day a friend of the family talked to my father and praised my singing. He immediately exploded, yelled at me, and forbade me to sing publicly again. I stopped and kept going to school. From time to time, I went to concerts or cultural events with other musicians. My interest in music grew steadily.

When I was about twelve years old, some members of a theater group in our part of town asked me to join them. Secretly I went to rehearsals. I told my father about it one day and he seemed to have nothing against it. During National Youth Week we performed our piece, in which I sang a beautiful, sentimental song with a woman. At the end of the presentation, the musicians of the Jamano Band came over and asked me to sing in their group. I didn't tell anybody for three months, and they urged me more and more. Finally I went to rehearsals. I had absolutely no idea of notes, tempi, harmonies . . . We practiced and practiced. Soon we had a piece together which was to be recorded by a radio station. First, however, we had to talk to my father. The band suggested that I make use of my talent and enroll in music school. He thought that was all right; it even sounded like school. But he didn't want to see me performing publicly with a band. Nevertheless, we recorded the piece, and one day it was played on the radio. From then on I had many problems with my father again. He even threw me out of the house, and I had to live with my grandmother for a while. During summer vacation I secretly disappeared to Gambia to perform with the band. Immediately my father contacted the Department of the Interior and I was taken back home by force.

Again we had big discussions, and finally my father allowed me to keep making music, under the condition that I remained in Dakar. Soon after that, Kassé, from the Star Band, contacted me. He talked to my father and guaranteed a monthly salary. So, during the day I went to music school, and I rehearsed and performed with Star Band at night. We had so much success that I had less and less time for my studies. Since 1975 [Youssou was born in 1959] I have been a professional musician, as it were.

[Q] Listening to Star Band's first records, it becomes apparent that up to three quarters of the titles are of Cuban origin, and only one quarter is based on Wolof rhythms. The proportion is already reversed on the first record you recorded with the band. And today, there is no Cuban music at all on your records.

[A] We continued to develop and have taken responsibility to dedicate our music directly to Senegalese folklore. This concept immediately had great success. People liked the music from the beginning. Our music is based on traditional drum rhythms of the Wolof, Peul, and Serere; it transcends all tribes. We travel throughout Senegal all year, especially on weekends. If there is no electricity, we set up a generator. Everywhere, when people hear that Super Etoile will perform at 9:00 P.M., they turn out at 7:00 P.M. and wait for us.

[Q] How about these concerts? Where do they take place, how is admission paid? . . .

[A] Dakar has a theater seating 1,200. In the country, there are stadiums [for soccer and, above all, the traditional wrestling, *M'balah*, which are very popular in Senegal] with 2,000 to 3,000 seats. In smaller cities, there are youth centers, and in villages, the main square will be fenced in. In Dakar, we perform in our own night club, Thiosanne. Admission is charged everywhere, but people also give us money when they enjoy the music.

[Q] What importance and function do the dancers and the mime have?

[A] The mime tells a story, makes jokes, and has a way of dancing all his own. He is the second most important person in the band. He captivates the audience and makes them laugh.

Male and female dancers are primarily soloists. They dance exclusively to the [fast] beat of the tama. The dances originate in old traditions, especially in the tradition of wrestling [M'balah].

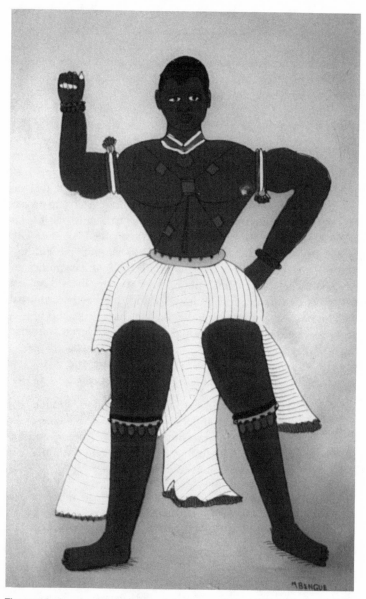

The wrestler is a popular motif of Senegalese glasspainters. This picture was painted by Mbengue, one of the best-known artists of this genre.

Youssou N'dour primarily releases cassette tapes. He sells approximately 150,000 copies per recording. Every other household in Senegal owns at least one of his cassettes.

What is behind this success? Youssou N'dour is looked upon as an attractive, nice young man. He could be practically the boy next door. His success makes him an example to the nation. He does not drink or smoke, and he does not take drugs. Because of his commitment to the orchestra, he cannot afford to be married. He respects his parents, honors tradition, and, in addition, is open to novelty and change. He suits all age groups as a person with whom to identify, especially since he has become somewhat an anti-star.

He picks up folk tunes and then turns them into songs; this has contributed considerably to his popularity. In Senegal, and probably everywhere in Africa, fans remain true to a musician for his entire life. They will continue to follow and assess Youssou with great interest. Which woman will he marry? Senegal's most important newspaper, *Le Soleil,* reports on his tours and examines his personality in long articles. Since taking part in the live aid concert and other charitable gigs, Youssou N'dour has become an artist who addresses a worldwide audience. This has affected his music; he has become more international and open, yet has maintained his tradition.

## LE XALAM AND TOURÉ KUNDA

Le Xalam and Touré Kunda are two other famous groups that move, however, in totally different directions. The music of Le Xalam is a combination of jazz-rock, pop music, and traditional rhythms and melodies. Abdoulayé Prosper Niang, drummer and leader of the group, says about traditional music:

Traditional music is most important to me: it is the basis. In Senegal, we have many different types, and all of them are sung. Every language carries its own history, a philosophy, and behind it, in each case, we find a music. Every dialect implies melodies and rhythms. For that reason we have indicated the origins of the rhythms on our records.[58]

Le Xalam is probably a more intellectual group that speaks— at least as far as the music is concerned—to an intellectual and more critical audience. Their pieces are created rather "in the head." The group is sponsored by a Lebanese citizen. That enabled the group for two years just to play and to follow their ideas, to do "research," and to develop their style.

For years, Touré Kunda was Senegal's most recognized group internationally, especially in Paris. At the same time, it was the most commercially-oriented group, the one most likely to exploit the vogue for African things. The success of the Touré Family (*kunda* means "family" in Soninke) is probably best explained by its diverse repertory. The musicians of Touré Kunda sing in Soninke, Mandinke, Peul, Diolla, Wolof, and Portuguese Creole. Besides different Senegalese music styles, they play Afro-rock, reggae, and Afro-disco. Thus they appeal to a broad audience that is normally not drawn to African music.

The Tourés come from Casamance, a southern province of Senegal. Its different people and diverse musical cultures present an almost inexhaustible source for compositions and improvisations. In the beginning, the trio consisted of the brothers Amadou, Ismailia, and Sixu. Amadou, the oldest, taught his brothers to play guitar and a number of traditional instruments, among others, the Diolla-"bougguer," (a set of four drums played by one musician) and the Mandingo drum saourouba (played by three musicians).

In 1977 the brothers Ismailia and Sixu made their first record. All three brothers have been in Paris since 1979, and the group developed its own musical style in the early 1980s. Amadou died in 1983, and his place was taken by Ousmane. Today the band consists, in addition, of a saxophonist from Cameroun, a north African drummer, a bassist from the Antilles, and three French musicians.

# 2

# FRANCOPHONE CONNECTIONS

■

## African Jazz: Congo and Zaire

Congo (People's Republic of the Congo) and Zaire (Democratic Republic of the Congo) are at the center of a region creating a music that has found the broadest dissemination in Africa within the last fifty years. From Senegal to South Africa, the music of Zaire is highly esteemed. It has given many names in the course of the years: African jazz, Congo jazz, Congo music, musique zairoise, rumba, Zaire rumba, and soucous. Soucous was actually one of the many dance styles that succeeded each other within this musical style.

The great musicians, mostly singer/guitarists, have already become legend; Wendo, Leon Bukasa, Kabasele Tshamala ("Le Grand Kallé"), Luambo Makiadi ("Franco de mi Amour"), Dr. Nico, and Tabu Ley ("Seigneur Rochereau") are among them. These musicians enjoyed success in Zaire's capital, Kinshasa, and in the neighboring capital of today's People's Republic of Congo, Brazzaville, located at the opposite side of the Zaire (Congo) river. Both cities are considered centers of modern African music. In 1977, at least 360 orchestras were active in Kinshasa alone.[1]

Congo jazz became known in the 1950s when it was disseminated on the first labels of Congo-based record companies—all of them in Greek hands—and by Radio Brazzaville. Founded by Jéronimides in 1948, the recording house Ngoma was among the

pioneer companies. It was followed by the brothers Moussa
Benatar with Opika in 1950, and by A. and B. Papadimitriou with
Loningisa. They were joined by Antonopoulos with Esengo in
1957.[2]

At the same time that these recordings appeared in the north of
Congo, the South African label Gallotone released recordings of
songs with guitar accompaniment in the southern province of Katanga, today's Shaba. At that time, this province was more a part
of southern African mine workers' culture. The miners came from
the former British East Africa, Northern and Southern Rhodesia,
Nyassaland, and South Africa. They brought along their own musical ideas and traditions. Dance music echoed European musical
fashions on the radio. Thus, it was strongly influenced by Latin
American styles, especially since this kind of music was well received by the African population; and, after all, it was dominated
by rhythms that had been brought by African slaves to the New
World.

In 1952, the songs of Mwenda Jean Bosco, Losta Abelo, Patrice
Ilunga, and Edouard Masengo were released on 78 RPM shellac
records by Gallotone. The selection of these guitarists was rather
accidental. The recording company Gallo had sponsored a field
and research trip taken by the South African musicologist Hugh
Tracey in 1949. Under the condition that any commercial exploi-
tation was left to the company, Tracey was able to record what and
as much as he wanted. It was thus mere chance that Tracey found
Bosco's playing interesting and recorded him. Bosco's fortuitous
discovery does not at all detract from the quality of his music, but
it indicates that there must have been many more guitarists playing
similar music at the time.[3] Through their recordings these guitarists gained access to a new kind of audience and became better-
known than any others before. Thus they emerged as exponents of
a musical tradition that was carried on by many still unknown
musicians.

In 1952 Bosco's *Masanga* was released as an instrumental piece
on Gallotone GB 1586. It immediately received the Osborne
Award, a prize awarded to the best African record of the year. The
sung version of the composition was released the same year on GB
1700.[4] On the cover of an even later release of *Masanga*, Tracey
wrote that he recorded the instrumental version only to demonstrate better Bosco's skill on the guitar.[5]

Mwenda wa Bayeke (Jean Bosco) during a visit to the Iwalewa House, Bayreuth (1982).

It is surprising that Tracey, one of the greatest authorities on African music, did not scrutinize the solo version (which he himself occasioned) more carefully. He may have thought that Bosco's compositional masterpiece would be more appealing to an European audience without words. From an ethnomusicological point of view, however, that is nonsense. It would be a possibility, of course, if African music were structured like Western compositions: here, for purposes of demonstration or teaching, instruments may be isolated, and others continue to play undisturbed, though even in our music, it is problematic if a piece is played without an intended instrument. In African music, however, all participating parts are inseparable: they depend on each other; they need each other; and without them, the piece simply does not work. This was once described impressively by Gerhard Kubik. For analytical reasons, musicians were asked to play their parts without the others. It turned out to be impossible. The manner of composing and playing makes the simultaneous participation of at least one other musician a condition for the performance of each. It is perhaps best described as the interlocking of musical patterns, and that cannot occur without the simultaneous participation of more than one player.

In the case of *Masanga,* it is "only" Bosco's voice and guitar, but they are interrelated as well. Even if the compositional process, as described by John Low, results first in the guitar piece and then the vocal part, both are still dependent on each other. It is no surprise, then, that the two versions differ from each other.[6] It was an unusual undertaking and, according to Low, Bosco never again recorded an instrumental piece on his own initiative. Yet, when he actually performed solo guitar pieces on his tour through central Europe in 1982, we may suppose that he intended to accommodate European tastes. Since Europeans did not understand the words, they were not very important for them in the first place.

For an African audience, however, it would have been inconceivable for Bosco not to sing. Text and instrumental playing simply belong together. To my knowledge, there is only a handful of pieces on recordings of traditional African music that are purely instrumental. Surely the success of Bosco's songs depended above all on the quality of his lyrics. They touched upon the whole spectrum of social phenomena in the copper belt and dealt predominantly with problems facing those who came as itinerant workers: the issue, for instance, of a large number of unmarried men. Or he told the story of a man returning to his native village, bringing along his family from the city, but then marrying a second wife in the village.[7]

John Low, himself a skilled guitarist, describes what attracted him to Mwenda Jean Bosco's performance of *Masanga:*

First, the incredible grace and control of Mwenda's right-hand playing, a feature always remarkable, but nowhere more than here. The thumb movements were balanced and measured, while to relieve his rather august tempo (at the start of the piece) the index finger performed a quite light, perfectly choreographed dance. Of course, later in the song the interest moves at times to the thumb part, and the index merely fills in; but at all times, watching Mwenda play "Masanga," it makes perfect sense that only thumb and index are used. The piece can be seen, or even better is felt while you yourself try it, as a conversation or competition, between thumb and index-finger. Try to play it with thumb and two or three fingers, and the feeling of pure duality is largely lost; I'd even suggest that if Mwenda played with two or three fingers, the composition would have been quite different. This opposition of thumb–index, low–high, big voice–small voice, is one of the keys to understanding Mwenda's playing and African finger-styles in general. The interplay of opposites becomes particularly interesting in numbers such as "Masanga," "Namlia-e" (Gallo GB 1588) and "Mama Kilio-e" (GB 1728) which are not tied down to "alternating bass" thumb movements, so that both index finger and thumb are free to shake loose and depart, in turn, on phrases or ornamentations of their own, before coming together again in an established theme.

The second noticeable feature of Mwenda's playing was that the phrases of variations that he played were neither completely similar to those recorded in 1952, nor were they played exactly in the same order as those on the records. In fact, each time he played "Masanga" new differences in detail and order were noticeable. Similar differences are noticeable between the recordings of "Masanga" solo and the sung version. This suggests that when Mwenda plays "Masanga" he has certain well-established themes firmly in mind, but that he plays these in any order he likes and in addition sometimes provides new ornamentations or even variations to these themes, in a spontaneous way.

In this connection, another important realization, in seeing Bosco practise "Masanga," is that the variations he produces, and indeed the famous sixteen-pulse opening theme, are tied both to chord positions in the left hand, and to particular finger-styles in the right hand. As far as the left hand (which never leaves first position) is concerned, although at times the fingers are free to fret individual notes (for example to produce a descending line of notes), nevertheless, in each new pattern that Bosco introduces, there is an unerring schedule of basic chord positions that the fingers must return to at the right point in each cycle. As for the right hand, there are five or six distinct picking patterns that emerge, re-emerge, and interweave in the course of the song; these patterns also correspond to the variations identifiable in both versions of "Masanga." It is also worth noting that the left hand and right hand operations described, in combining to produce the themes and variations as described, always follow the sixteen-pulse ground metre established at the beginning.[8]

This detailed description of Bosco's playing delineates a number of the most important characteristics of Katanga guitar style. Low addresses the repetition of rhythmic and melodic patterns, a common and favorite device. A successful repetition, played with slight, hardly noticeable variations, is among the fascinating aspects of African guitar playing. The repetitive element returns again and again in cyclic motions, just as in the exchange of opposing pairs mentioned above. Low describes the movement of the index finger as a "perfectly choreographed dance" and submits that "the piece can be seen."

Kubik has repeatedly pointed out that the aural impression differs from the visual.[9] "In Western music, the motions of musicians as they play are suggestive in view of the sounding results. In African music, however, patterns of movement themselves are perceived as meaningful. They are a source of enjoyment within themselves, whether or not a sound is produced."[10] In the same context, Kubik mentions that a member of a certain African culture may have assimilated motion repertory—"body language," as it were—to such a degree that he will be able to translate "correctly" an audio image into movement. He asked the guitarist Donald Kachamba of Malawi to play a Bosco composition after listening to it on record. Not only did Kachamba reproduce the tuning correctly, but he imitated the associated motions accurately as well. Kubik reached the following conclusion:

The example shows that a member of a given African culture may not only grasp the tuning of an instrument, but may also be able successfully to extract motion patterns from musical products of this culture (records, tapes). From experience, a member of the culture knows how audio manifestations are realized. He recognizes motion patterns through the phenotype "music" and is able to duplicate them. He is also able to recast them at will, into a dance movement, for instance, or a syllabic memorization formula.[11]

For an European guitarist, it is hardly possible to reconstruct movements by listening alone. Transcriptions made on the basis of recordings—such as those of the Englishman David Rycroft—have their limits. Aspects of motion do not appear in standard notation. This is one of the main reasons why Kubik was prompted to use silent film recordings to transcribe African music. Picture by picture (eighteen frames per second) all movements were noted and transcribed in a graphic notation.[12]

The custom of interjecting narrative or witty comments between stanzas is also important and at the same time characteristic of southern African guitarists. Such statements may include spontaneous remarks, or the musician may refer to the current circumstances or introduce himself. Such interjections are received gratefully and with enjoyment by the audience.[13] Other important characteristics include the use of capodasters, which may consist simply of a pencil held in place by rubber bands. Furthermore, the tuning of the guitar does not always correspond to our standard system. Certain chords are especially popular: John Low mentions the use of $D^6$ chords (FAD or FFAD), frequently employed by Bosco and the so-called "dry" guitarists of east and central Africa.[14]

The transcriptions by David Rycroft mentioned above are called "guitar improvisations." Our observations on Bosco's performing style have made it clear that this is a gross misunderstanding: there is nothing improvised in this music. We tend too easily to assume such an attitude about African musicians—partly because of our perception of jazz improvisation. To call such music a "composition" would not identify it as "African," that is, "original." Unfortunately, many Africans contribute to this kind of bias toward their own music by disguising their musical practices as an art of improvisation.

Assuming that there is a direct and immediate dependence on traditional music also leads easily to a mystification of African music. The finger-picking guitar style, in particular, is often attributed to traditional techniques such as those of the regional hand-piano, the likembe: "Certainly, hand-piano playing often has that counterpoint of high notes against low notes that is so characteristic of Katangan guitar finger styles."[15] Even John Low maintains that this cannot be a direct influence, but he does not exclude the possibility of a more or less unconscious adoption by guitarists observing local instrumentalists.[16]

There is no doubt that certain elements of the traditional found their way into Katangan guitar styles. "Bottle rhythm"—rhythmic patterns beaten on a bottle corresponding to a variety of rhythms used with traditional instruments such as gongs and wooden percussion instruments—makes this clear. John Low indicates two beating patterns, of sixteen and twelve pulses, that are also found in traditional Shaba music:

16   XX.X.X.X   X.X.X.X.
12   XX.X.X.X   X.X.X.[17]

He elaborates:

Taking into account that Mwenda refers to the bass notes as strong beats, it is worth paying a little more attention to the triplets that Mwenda plays, in other words to the finger pattern as the guitarist feels it. If we express the thumb stroke as a cross and the finger stroke as a dot, the played pattern can be expressed as 12‖: X..X.. ׀ X.. X.. :‖ To look at the pattern this way acts as a reminder that the guitar here, as much as anything else, is a rhythm instrument; the guitarist, although playing all the pulses, makes definite and unvarying subdivisions of the twelve-pulse cycle. Even the relation of the pitches to one another (bass—high treble—low treble) does not vary. So, despite the tricks that inherent rhythms may play with the listener's ear, it is justifiable to describe the pattern, from the player's point of view, as a rhythmic interplay of thumb and index, "big voice" and "small voice." Styles such as this one where the thumb maintains a regular beat, and the index fills in, I refer to as "regular bass and fill-in" styles.[18]

## MWENDA JEAN BOSCO

An authenticity campaign by the Mobutu government, which introduced a new rule on names, changed Jean Bosco's name to Mwenda wa Bayeke. Bayeke is the name of his ethnic group. Bosco was born in 1930 in the village of Bunkuya, near Jadotville (Likasi today). His father, an organist in the Roman Catholic church of Bunkuya, stirred his interest in music early on. Kinsago is his mother tongue, but since early childhood he also spoke the Congolese variant of Kiswahili, the language he was taught first in school. Later, French was introduced as a foreign language and gradually became the language of instruction. Bosco graduated from primary school, but he had to leave secondary school prematurely because he could not afford to continue after his father's death in 1946. Eventually, he found employment at a bank.

In his village, Bosco had made music with other young people and shown exceptional talent, which lead to his first performances on a local level. He performed publicly with his guitar, however, only after his father's death—as a sideline, so to say, to his bank job.

In 1959, Bosco spent half a year in Kenya with Edouard Masengo, a relative as well as a guitarist, advertising Aspro, a pain reliever. He sang, "Aspro ni dawa ya kweli!" (Aspro is true medicine). Masengo worked for some time for Coca-Cola and sang, "Drink Coca-Cola with Edward Masengo!" The emerging guitarists from Kenya, who oriented their style toward Katanga musicians, were likewise interested in these jobs: Jim Lasco worked for Tusker Beer, and John Mwale advertised cigarettes, even though he was a non-smoker. It was good money for the guitarists and, as John Low reports, they became better known at the same time and sold more records.[19]

Hugh Tracey released Bosco's first record in 1952. During the following ten years, eighty more were released. Thereafter, no more records seem to have been produced on Gallotone. The time for 78 RPM shellac records had passed. In addition, the market in Zaire for a record company from South Africa was no longer as attractive and accessible as under colonial conditions.

In 1961, Mwenda Jean Bosco flew to the United States where he had been invited to the Newport Folk Festival. Pete Seeger was among those who received him. Upon his return, President Mobutu granted him an official appreciation. Bosco and Losta Abelo, along with such illustrious stars as Miriam Makeba, were part of the musical program at the championship fight between Muhammed Ali and George Foreman in Kinshasa in 1974. Five years later, the Belgian ambassador invited Bosco to perform in Lusaka, which comes as no surprise: according to Bosco's own statement, he had been on good terms with the Belgians during colonial rule.[20]

A husband and father of nine, Bosco is an important man to-day—a *grand patron*, even driving a Mercedes. He is supervisor of the housing authority of Gécamines, the national mining company, and oversees repairs and maintenance of company-owned housing projects. Moreover, he runs his own businesses, among them a hotel, and a local dance band with ten musicians, Super Shaba. Mwenda Jean Bosco makes no secret of his affluence. In one of his songs, entitled *Advice on How to Procure Wealth*, he reveals a recipe for prosperity:

In order to become wealthy, you should start with small savings. These can lead to the first steps in an independent business, for instance, selling tea in a cafe. One day, you will notice with amazement how your own wealth multiplies.[21]

Wealth brings prestige. Bosco captured this experience of life in his songs as well; *Public Appreciation* is an example:

In the big cities you have to be rich to be appreciated and to have prestige in the public eye. If you cannot obtain wealth, you will not be noticed and, often enough, you will be treated with contempt. In our villages, on the other hand, you have to till the fields to satisfy your basic needs: otherwise you would be condemned to a slow death.[22]

In 1982 Jean Bosco toured Europe, which confirmed his eminent position as one of the originators of Zaire's modern music.[23]

The music of the so-called "dry guitarists" of the Katanga province (Shaba) had a strong influence in eastern Africa, especially on guitarists in Kenya and Tanzania. With the introduction of electric guitars in the 1950s, as well as the rise and increasing success of large orchestras in the major cities, this kind of music has receded into the background. It does exist, however, even today. Now a rather rural phenomenon, the guitar style is kept alive by many young (tin can) banjo players.

After Zaire's independence, the musicians from Shaba—singing for the most part in Kiswahili—no longer had a chance on the national level: Lingala, which had developed in the nineteenth century as a communication idiom based on various native languages for black colonial troops, became the national language. In Kinshasa, the center of the new music scene, songs were sung almost exclusively in Lingala, with the exception of a few songs in Spanish or French.[24]

Naturally, it was not only the language aspect that led to the decline in popularity of the Shaba guitarists and their songs. Their music simply faded in comparison to fashionable, brilliant, and modern electric orchestras playing breathtaking dance music. Nobody could escape their dynamic force: the performance of such a band was a big show! After a short but not very exciting introduction, off it went:

. . . the pace began to quicken. Whereas previously the band had played at half or two-thirds of its strength, now all the hitherto absent members came to the bandstand and threw themselves with great energy into some irresistible Swahili and Lingala numbers, with the others, or rather *against* the others, since when a Zairean band is really in full swing it's quite difficult to discover any two instruments that are playing the same rhythm. There's something different going on in each of the three guitar parts, in the singing, and in the sax-playing; more rhythmic layers still are added by drums and congas. It's this welter of cross-rhythms which makes dancing to a Zairean band so exciting. Listening to and dancing to this music it was not difficult to understand how the old dry guitarists were replaced by electric bands: no guitarist, with an extra singer and bottle player, could ever approach the complexity and drive of this music.[25]

Another reason for the great popularity of these bands is the fact that modern electric guitar music can be heard constantly on radio and television. In addition, it often appears in conjunction with political coverage. Broadcasts of solo guitarists, on the other hand, are rather the exception.[26] Even so, it is amazing how popular they still are, even today.

### TABU LEY, FOR INSTANCE

A detailed account of the complicated and interwoven history of Congolese bands has already been written elsewhere.[27] The Congolese music scene does not differ from the rock and pop scene elsewhere in the world: bandleaders exchange musicians, or change bands themselves. The history of Tabu Ley—formerly called "Seigneur Rochereau"—may serve as an example.

Tabu Pascal ("Rochereau") was born on November 13, 1940, in Banningville (Bandundu). His father worked on the boats of OTRACO[28] on the Congo river. When Tabu Ley was six months old, his parents moved to Kinshasa. He was raised in a Catholic home: "When I went to school, my parents wanted me to become a priest. Since I had no other choice, my family already called me 'Brother.' "[29] He belonged to a new social class created by colonial circumstances. Consequently, he did not experience much of the traditional life of his people, the Bayanzi, during his youth. He did not remain, however, without any knowledge of traditional music and culture. Accompanying his father on shipping trips, he heard songs praising the hosts of overnight stays and other traditional songs. He also participated in hunting trips where spotters sitting in tree-tops sang to indicate the movement of game to the hunters.[30] Tabu Ley attended a Catholic school. At the age of twelve, he sang at festivities in the parish church, and two years later he participated as a singer in scholastic competitions. He received his nickname, "Rochereau," because he was the only student of his class who could name, when once asked, the nineteenth-century defender of the French city Belfort, Colonel Denfert Rochereau.

His success in singing inspired him to compose his own songs. Soon he had collected a repertory of more than one hundred songs and melodies, which serve him as a source of inspiration even today. At the time he also participated in a competition, singing for more than one hundred thousand people, and won first prize in a field of forty-five singers. The title of his first composition, *Besame muchacha,* testifies to the predilections of the time. It was written in 1956, at a time when the people of the Congo raved about Afro-Cuban music. Groups such as Machito, Prado, or the very popular Johnny Pacheco had an enormous influence on local dance music.

At the mission school, Tabu Pascal had been trained as an office clerk, a profession he pursued even long after he had become a famous singer. After receiving his diploma, he first worked for the Domestic Welfare Fund, and later, in 1963, he became assistant to the principal of a well-known high school in Kinshasa.[31] Just having finished his professional training, Tabu Pascal married a young Congolese woman, Georgette Mowana, who is often referred to by the nickname "Tété." She was born in Katanga, but her parents came from Bandudu.

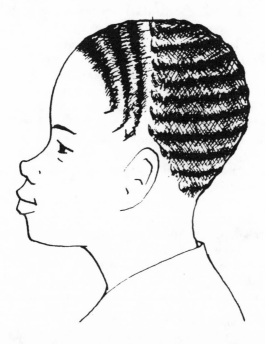

Hairstyle from Zaire. Each style has its own name. This one, in Lingala, is called *Tolanda nzela moko* (Let us walk the same way), after an election campaign song of 1970: "Let us walk the same way / Let us prove our love for Mobutu / Let us again vote one-hundred percent/as we did on the 31st and 1st."
"The hair is separated into two parts and braided in one direction; the hairstyle thus represents men and women pursuing the same path together."

Rochereau had received some European musical training while attending school. He was so interested in music that soon he could not be considered an amateur anymore. Yet he did not consider a professional career in music at the time. In the early 1950s, Tabu Rochereau was an enthusiastic fan of Kallé. In his enthusiasm he composed songs for Kallé's African Jazz orchestra and anonymously passed them on to the orchestra—through the back door, as it were. This lasted for about half a year. One day, he accidentally met Master Kallé at the Cassien, a cafe in Kinshasa. The young fan informed his idol that actually he was the author of many songs brought out by African Jazz. Kallé was surprised and extended an invitation to Rochereau. It started a friendship that opened a musical career to Tabu.

The years from 1953 to 1956 were marked by great success for African Jazz, and Esengo recorded many of their songs. Rochereau mastered the repertory of African Jazz well. Once, when the second singer failed to appear at a recording session, he was able to fill in easily. His time had come. Shortly thereafter, Master Kallé was in need of help again. African Jazz was performing in Vis-a-vis, a bar, and again a singer was missing. Kallé was alone at the microphone which the bar owner saw as a breach of contract. Tabu Rochereau saved the night and sang with the band.[32] Rochereau began to collaborate regularly with African Jazz. He became the artistic director, as it were, and the band recorded his song *Kelia*. At the same time, Tabu Ley developed a personal friendship with Patrice Lumumba.[33]

In 1963, a new band emerged from African Jazz under the leadership of Rochereau, African Fiesta, and in 1965, Rochereau founded the orchestra African Fiesta Flash. During these years, Rochereau—who was generally referred to as "Seigneur Rochereau"—celebrated several great successes with titles such as *Afrika Mokili Mobimba*,[34] *Mokolo Nakokufa*, and *Madina*. Tabu Ley, himself, had this to say about the time following 1963:

At the beginning of 1963, I joined Dr. Nico and African Fiesta. It was a difficult period since competition was fierce. We were two leaders: Franco Luambo Makiadi's almighty OK Jazz, and African Fiesta. In order to beat the opposition, I used the weapons of my opponent against him. I built my success by modeling our songs on Franco's, arranging them in our own style and in such a manner that the author did not recognize them. Science is the organization of people's everyday lives. I have put many hardships

Record label of an Ngoma ET (extended play) single from Zaire.

on me and my collaborators since I foresaw that the road to success would be long and we had to plan according to the circumstances.[35]

In the late 1960s, Tabu Ley was praised beyond measure: "Tabu Ley is not just a singer; he is also an incredibly inventive song writer. Among all Congolese singers, it is Rochereau who has mastered best the art of fascinating the audience." His full name and title was "Pascal Tabou, dit Emmanuel Rochereau le Maréchal." His voice was called the "magic voice of the Congo's Yéyé." "Often he screams or sings alone against the instruments."[36]

The song *Mass Media* was one of the best-known titles recorded by Tabu Ley:

> What you want to keep secret, keep it in your heart, don't tell it to anybody.
> What you want to keep in your heart, don't tell it to anybody.

What you want to keep secret in your heart, don't tell it even to your
    brother.
An insignificant matter: you talk with your wife about it.
An insignificant matter: you talk with your brother about it.
An insignificant matter: you boast about it to your in-laws.
The secret matter: you share it with the prostitutes.
If you want to keep it in your heart, don't share it with anybody.
If you want to keep it at the bottom of your heart, don't get drunk.
What you tell the musician, he will turn into a song.
What you tell the journalist, he will put it in his newspaper.
What you confide to the prostitute, she will spread all over the village.
What is broadcast on the radio, the whole world will hear.
What you tell your father-in-law, he will boast about.
What you tell vampires, they will shout from the rooftops.[37]
What you broadcast on television, everybody will see.[38]

Early in the 1970s, when the sale of his records went past a
million, Tabu Ley was appointed an honorary knight of Senegal by
Léopold S. Senghor. Shortly thereafter, the Republic of Chad con-
ferred on him the title "Officer of the National Order."

At the height of his career at that time, he performed in 1970 at
the Olympia in Paris, only to retire from the music scene shortly
thereafter.[39] After six years, however, he returned to the international and African music stage. The music of Zaire had reached a
low point in his eyes, and he endeavored to raise it again to its former importance. His comeback was a success. Since then, he has
recorded many new records, including some very exciting ones
featuring joint performances with other famous musicians of
Zaire.

From an interview conducted by Celestin Monga in 1983 it appears that the role of the "grand old musician"—which certainly
appeals to Tabu Ley—is at times controversial in Zaire today. We
may suppose that the artistic and political attitudes of Tabu Ley
(and his contemporaries) have provoked particular criticism.
Tabu Ley replied cautiously to a question on that subject:

[A] When an artist touches politics, he will get burned; even he who
believes that a musician should account for political events in his country.

[Q] It is noticeable, however, that few African singers become famous
without having contact with politics. For instance, Fela and Miriam
Makeba, Manu Dibango . . .

[A] I don't involve myself in politics. Fela is no politician, either. His

actions are that of a commercial enterprise. He will never become a pre-
fect or mayor of Lagos! Manu Dibango is an intellectual . . . who has
accepted responsibilities from the Department for Cultural Affairs to further music in his country. The case of Miriam Makeba, who chose to live
in Guinea, is a special case since her homeland, South Africa, is not
independent.

[Q] You are accused of collaborating with the powers in Zaire.

[A] I am not a politician. But my opinion is clear. You have to respect
the existing powers, regardless of who they are. Each one has his role.
Power lies in the barrels of guns, it is said. A musician doesn't have fire-
arms. He carries only a flower, a present to all.[40]

## "JE VEUX ÊTRE LA TINA TURNER AFRICAINE": ZAIRE'S WOMEN STARS

Whatever brings movement and a new breeze into Zaire's music
happens on the part of women. For a long time, female singers remained in the background, or women danced in front of the band
in a way similar to go-go girls. That, however, changed during the
last ten years. Female dancers turned into singers, recording their
own LPs. Famous male bands call on female vocal stars, or female
singers, having become famous, assemble the best studio musicians they can get hold of.

*Abeti Masikini.* Abeti Masikini, called Abeti for short, retired
from her career as a secretary in 1970 in order to pursue her talent
and to distinguish herself as a singer. She is said to have a warm-
toned voice that is distinguished by her capability "to maintain
an almost continuous vocal line by stretching overrunning
syllables."[41]

Her performances in Paris and New York (1974 at Carnegie
Hall) secured her an international presence. While her early style
was oriented toward Miriam Makeba and folkloristic themes, she
has recently participated in the development of rumba in Zaire's
music.

Her Orchestre Les Redoubtables includes an electronic drum-
olator, an almost indispensable necessity in Zaire's music of the
late 1980s. The development and availability of musical instruments have always been followed with great interest in Africa. To
be up to date is a must for many bands. Tabu Ley expressed his
opinion this way: "Now, my style is always changing in step with
technical changes, new recording developments, and the public's

taste as well as current musical developments. It is important to
play African music but to use the best sound techniques available
in order to convince the public."[42]

*Mbilia Bel*. Mbilia Bel first worked as a dancer and chorus singer for Abeti Masekini. Tabu Ley—Seigneur Rochereau—enticed
her away to join his Rocherettes. After a few years she developed
into a solo singer alternating with Tabu Ley, or performing alone
with Afrisa International. "Before Mbilia Bel it was usual for men
to attack women," Tabu Ley says. "Now the women are attacking
back. The men are curious, the women, proud."[43]

Mbilia introduced a fresh breeze into Tabu Ley's Orchestre Afrisa International and a new counterpoise to the constant rival
Franco (Luambo Makiadi). When Franco attacks women, they are
defended by Mbilia Bel and Tabu Ley. The song *Eswi Yo Wapi,
Amina,* for instance, is intended to support divorced women;
other songs address the misfortunes of older women in polyg-
amous relationships.[44] It remains to be investigated to what
extent Mbilia Bel incorporates her own experiences into her
songs. Although she is not married to Tabu Ley, she bore him a
girl, named, appropriately, Melody, on March 24, 1985. In the
meantime, Tabu Ley's wife is the mother of nine children.[45]

Mbilia Bel once said about her own voice: "I have a voice that is
half male, half female. Because of that I cannot be pigeonholed simply as a 'female star.' I sing naturally; that, perhaps, is the difference
between singers such as Abeti or Tshala Muana and me."[46]

Mbilia Bel has since separated herself from her mentor and has
established herself as a completely independent performer.

*Tshala Muana*. The triad of being born in Zaire, adopted by all
of Africa, and living in Paris—that seems to be the typical path of
female African musicians today. The detour to Paris via Abidjan
appears to have become the fixed route. After having made a name
for herself as a singer and dancer in Zaire, Tshala Muana successfully tried her luck in Abidjan.

She was born in Lumbashi in southern Zaire, the province of
Shaba. She became known when the mutuashi, a dance from the
western province Kasai, became popular. Asked about the erotic
components of the dance, she answered: "What is not erotic?"[47]
The people in Kasai danced the mutuashi on all occasions. About
her relocation in Paris, she explained that "she wants to become

more international and unite styles, as in the past . . . The advantage of Paris is that one is at the centre of decisions, one can see many people, bathe in show-business, and it is easier to revive oneself."[48]

*M'Pongo Love.* M'Pongo Love (her real name is M'Pongo Landu), born in 1956 in Kinhsasa, is another celebrated female singer of modern Zaire. She began her musical life in 1976. Before that, she was a secretary at an automobile company. She left that position to pursue singing outright. Now she makes a living by her present profession, and she had at least ten LPs on the market in 1986. Being handicapped herself (she had polio at age four), she toured Scandinavia during the International Year of The Handicapped. "La chanson, c'est ma vie," she says, and in her songs, again and again, she advocates especially women's rights. She died on January 15, 1990, following a long illness.

### CONGOLESE RUMBA

Rumba, the most-performed music of Zaire, underwent a number of changes in the course of the years.[49] One rumba dance style superseded another: rumba (1955–59), kara-kara (1960–62), boucher (1964–65), soucous (1966–68), kiri-kiri, mombette, and Apollo (1969–70), and ngwabin (1970). The first variant of rumba was the kara-kara, which means "indifferent." Both partners danced separately at a distance, moving about on the dance floor; when they came together again they acted indifferent toward each other. Coming from Brazzaville, the boucher was a relatively harmonious dance in which the dancers moved their hips up and down. Later it developed into the soucous, a shake. The similarity of the soucous with some traditional dances resulted in an increased release of suitable traditional music. Records by James Brown and Aretha Franklin introduced soul music to Zaire in late 1966, and it was soon to be emulated by local orchestras. From this music emerged the kiri-kiri, meaning "excitement" or "anger." After the successful landing on the moon by the Americans, the Apollo became a popular dance for a short time. Here the dancers imitated the moon-walk of the astronauts.

After that period, the rumba experienced an increasing integration of Afro-American rhythms, or simply an increase of rhythmic elements into improvised sections. This aspect of rumba initiated a

A Mama Wata painted by Cheri Samba, a "dessinateur" from Zaire. The Mama Wata motif can be found all over black Africa from Senegal to Zambia. It combines traditional images of water spirits and river and sea deities with representations of mermaids, which first came to African shores as ship figureheads, and figures from Indian movies. A mermaid is an ambivalent figure: it may bring good or bad luck. In any case, its sighting brings about fear and insecurity, suggesting a parallel to the experiences of many Africans following the appearance of white men: these, too, brought things pleasant as well as frightful.
The Mama Wata—also called Mami Wata or White Mama—is praised by many African musicians in songs addressed to her or composed especially in her honor.

gradual "re-Africanization," which gradually developed into Zaire-music. During a *montuno*, the musicians could realize their own musical ideas. In addition, Spanish texts of the original Cuban pieces were slowly replaced with Lingala texts. This, in turn, also lead to modifications of the melodies. Many more crazes and fashions came up and will come up, season by season—too many to give them adequate recognition here.

## THE ADVENTURE OF SAM MANGWANA

Leaving Zaire to turn to all of Africa, the singer Sam Mangwana became a star. Here he explains how:

[A] I came to music in 1963 under the direction of Tabu Ley. After spending five years with him, I participated in founding the orchestra Maquisards. It consisted of eleven young men under thirty. Our success began with the release of our first record, entitled *Zella Ngai Nassalla.* We made sufficient money that each one of us could afford to buy his own car. Unfortunately, the success was short-lived: it was more than some of us could handle. Being just 24 years old, it was difficult for me to stop this disorganization. Finally, in 1969, the group broke up. I still own recordings that never were produced. Slowly I gained recognition. Each of Zaire's two great orchestras (OK Jazz and Afrisa International) offered me contracts. I alternated between the two orchestras, depending on the length of the contract. This procedure has proven to be fruitful: up to that point no opportunity had existed for a musician to come and go. My fluctuations,

Record cover of an LP by Sam Mangwana, *Sam Mangwana et l'African All Stars* (Celluloid CEL 6638), with a popular painting, signed G.P. d'Art—V.N.—1978.

therefore, were the first step in a process of standardization and convergence advancing the music of Zaire. So much about my beginnings. In 1976 I left Zaire to dare the adventure . . .

[Q] Listening to you, one might almost conclude that you could not gain recognition in your country.

[A] On the contrary. I left Zaire at the high point in my career. Through the system of contracts, I had become the best-paid singer in the country, which also created some difficulties for me. Certain persons did not tolerate the fact that I had left the clan of African Jazz (headed by Kabasele). The African Jazz orchestra was one of the first modern groups from Zaire. These persons were also opposed when I joined other groups to further my own development. They threatened me in anonymous letters, to the point that I was forced to live in a state hotel under government protection.

[Q] Why, then, did you leave Zaire?

[A] I wanted to broaden my field of action, to search for different music. I had proven myself on the national level. It remained to conquer the international audience. Thus I left Zaire and ventured on a real 'safari,' to Bangui, Yaoundé, Douala, Enugu, Onitsha, Lagos, Cotonou, Lomé, Accra, and finally, in 1977, to Abidjan.

[Q] What did you gain?

[A] What I was interested in: I performed in concerts with all the modern orchestras in these cities. At my arrival in Abidjan, I tried to synthesize all that I had absorbed. It became clear to me that black African music is largely uniform, with the exception of some local variants. From there on, I tried to proceed accordingly. I think I was successful. My first record, *Georgette*—a big hit—seems to prove it. It is almost my calling card for modern music.

[Q] Could you tell us what changes in style your Africa tour brought about?

[A] Certainly. This tour made me an African star.

[Q] Is there a Sam Mangwana style?

[A] Some believe so. For me, it is the reaction of an artist who wants to express himself and communicate in his very own way. I sing in Lingala and Spanish, which I didn't learn in school. During my time with Tabu Ley, he insisted that I memorize the complete repertory of Orquesta Aragon.[50]

[Q] Why do you sing in Spanish?

[A] Modernism obliges us to do so. It is a way to free our music from constriction.

[Q] You are part of a movement of young musicians that is gaining more and more ground in Africa. What is the difference between this new generation and the older musicians?

[A] The older musicians did not have sufficient opportunity to meet each other—I mean, to meet with musicians from different regions. With us, that is not the case anymore. Unfortunately, there is the phenomenon of a star cult that was forced upon us by the profiteers. Their goal is to enrich themselves behind the musicians' backs. Only the exchange of ideas and cooperation among artists can help to create the African music of tomorrow.

[Q] You speak of profiteers. How do you judge your present agent?

[A] He is one of the few people inspired by good will to help artists without deceiving them. He is from Cameroun, thirty years old, and does a tremendous job at my side.

[Q] In your opinion, how is African music doing?

[A] It is doing well and makes great progress despite difficulties. It is a music that has many great names: Tabu Ley, Manu Dibango, Luambo Makiadi [Franco], Miriam Makeba, Ernesto Djédjé . . . The list of names is long.

[Q] How many records originated with you?

[A] I can give no exact number of songs I have already composed. Certain production companies have forced me to compose and record . . . As I remember, however, I have made eleven 33 RPM and seventeen 45 RPM records.

[Q] What does it mean to you to be a star?

[A] To be a star with moral values for those who help me live. The fact that fans take a great interest in me does not mean that I take it easy. I prefer, therefore, to show earnestness and modesty. If all artists would be the same, our products would sell very well. For my part, I sell forty to sixty thousand records per title.

[Q] Are you married?

[A] No. I have one year of marriage experience. And, therefore, I am afraid to start anew because I don't like to be unjust. In my opinion, love should not be governed by material interests. In my songs [*Georgette, Matinda, Suzanna Coulibaly*] I address fictitious persons.

[Q] What does a song or singing mean to you?

[A] My whole life! If I hadn't taken up singing, I would have gone into painting. I would have become a landscape painter.

[Q] What are your future plans?

[A] I will start a music distribution business and release two LPs, *Maria Tebo* and *Zimbabwe*.[51]

Finally, a song from Sam Mangwana's repertory:

*Life*

This world is a world of problems;
Days pass by quickly, my friends.
And I have become old, oh mother.

Our departed ancestors, long ago,
Could not imagine
That an object such as a car exists,
That an object such as a plane could fly.
Where does this world lead us?
We don't know, mother.
Man has made a rocket to go to the moon.
But he has also made cannons that destroy the world.
What are we looking for in this world?
We don't know.
Oh, my God, here again are problems;
A man and a woman get married,
The man wants to have a second wife,
The woman, too, wants to have a lover.
What is the reason for this marriage?
We don't know.
Is that love?
The world into which we were born is the world of people.
Days pass by quickly, my friends.
And I have become old, oh mother.
Man has made a rocket to go to the moon.
He has also invented bombs that destroy the world.

What are we looking for on this world?
We don't know.
Sin, perhaps?
A man and a woman get married,
The man wants to have a second wife,
The woman, too, wants to have a lover.
What is the reason for this marriage?
We don't know.
Sin, perhaps, my friends?[52]

## Capital, Religion, Hypocrisy, and, Above All, Ziglibithy: Ivory Coast

The capital of Ivory Coast, Abidjan, the Paris of West Africa, slowly became the center of modern music for all of francophone Africa between 1975 and 1980. The reason is probably the stability of the Western-oriented government of Houphouet-Boigny as well as the tolerable economic conditions of the country.[53]

At the time, a number of small studios and record companies emerged in Abidjan. Soon they were joined by promotion firms such as Sako Productions, owned by Mohamed Sako, a citizen of Mali. The young *vedette* Tshala Muana of Lumbashih (Zaire) chose Abidjan for her comeback. And for Moni Bilé, a singer from Cameroun, this city proved to be the gateway to Paris. In 1982, the establishment of the eight-channel recording studio JBZ by Jacques Bizolon finally linked Abidjan with international standards of music production. Many of the companies recording and producing records and cassette tapes are associated with French partners. Such contacts present the possibility of opening the domestic market and a chance to enter the international music scene. Paris is the emporium for black music, from the Antilles to Africa and Europe, and Abidjan participates as the "first branch," as it were. Aboudou Lassissi, a record producer of Sacodis, entered the business as early as 1968/69 and recorded traditional music on seven-inch 45 RPM records. In the late 1970s, he even began to record in New York. Now he owns a warehouse there and stores in Paris and Abidjan.

Many singers recording their first singles and later their first LPs orient themselves above all toward U.S.-American and European tastes in popular music, with an African touch, of course. The situation is similar for musicians and orchestras. Even if only a few make the big breakthrough, Abidjan now correctly has a reputation as an Eldorado of African music, especially in recent years, when the city witnessed the rise of such greats as Sam Mangwana, Salif Keita and, before them, Manu Dibango, who had conducted the radio orchestra of Ivory Coast.

The numerous musical currents that meet in Abidjan exert an influence on the modern music of Ivory Coast as well. Amadou Balaké's record *Taximen* (which also gave rise to a new style by the same name) is a good example. The title song about Abidjan's taxi drivers is composed in Afro-disco style, with the rhythms of Congolese guitar music. The band is completed with brass and chorus, singing in French. The next piece is in the by-now-almost-classical form of Afro-reggae. It follows a song that borrows music of Portuguese-speaking Africa, possibly Cabo Verde, Guinea-Bissão, or Angola. The flip side starts out with Amadou Balaké singing in the manner of the Sahel griots; this is followed by another piece in Afro-disco style. The record concludes with an Afro-beat song à la Fela Anikulapo-Kuti from Nigeria, whom Amadou Balaké attempts to imitate both musically and idiomatically.

### ADIEU ERNESTO

On June 25, 1983, the musicians' association of Ivory Coast staged a concert commemorating the recently deceased Ernesto Djédjé. An audience of two thousand attended, and the performers included, among others: Luckson Padaud (who is considered the heir of the Ziglibithy style), Amédée Pierre (the spiritual father of Ernesto Djédjé and regarded by many as the father of modern music in Ivory Coast), Cissoko et son Kora, and Perpétué Kassi et son groupe traditionel.

Shortly thereafter, a commemorative pressing of Djédjé's last song, *Amaguhewou,* was released. Ernesto Djédjé had been called "le roi du Ziglibithy." He was the founder of that dance and music style, which was known beyond the borders of Ivory Coast and

Record cover of Amadou Balake's *Taximen*, Ivory Coast.

had become somewhat of a trademark for the music of that country. For years he had been at the top of the music world in Abidjan, and many local music groups copied his style. Ziglibithy may be described as a web of drums and African percussion with guitars and organ, interspersed brass sets, and continuous bass drum beats. Its sound is a synthesis of Afro-beat and Congo rumba: an extract of the musical mix of francophone Africa.

### RELIGION: AICHA KONÉ AND KATY LOBO

Aicha Koné is a star who in recent years gave rise to much comment and has found many admirers in many parts of Africa. She was born in 1955 in the north of the country. She sings primarily in Bambara and Malinké. Thus, she is understood by much of the population in the neighboring countries. In her own words, Aicha says:

I sing about the things I see every day: poverty, suffering, death, love. In a word, life is the subject of the poor, and I sing for the poor. We live in a country in which we don't know the humiliations that certain brothers are subjected to elsewhere . . .

I am inconsistent, . . . it is God who has bestowed this gift on me. I fear him. I pray every day. One day I hope to be rich enough to stop singing without regrets.[54]

That was her synopsis in 1984 after ten years in the music business. On the occasion of the tenth anniversary of her musical career, she received at a free concert, transmitted live on television—a gift of ten million francs CFA (about forty-four thousand dollars)—from the president.

The frequently close ties between the pop music business and religion may come as a surprise to us. Aicha Koné openly declares her devotion to Islam. Asked where she would like to travel to, she mentioned a pilgrimage to Mecca. There is no reason for her to fear losing her followers for mentioning this.

Almost inconceivably to us, the young singer Katy Lobo, born in 1954, is even more outspoken. She had a vision of Jesus Christ and apparently possesses the "inner word," as it is called in Christian mystic tradition, which is nowadays received by many believers in Africa. Here are extracts from an interview by the women's magazine *Akoua* from late 1984:

[Q] How did you come to singing?

[A] I always dreamed of becoming a singer. I went to all the festivities in the village and participated actively, without forgetting religious hymns.

[Q] You see yourself as a singer who believes strongly in Jesus Christ. God says in the Bible, in "Ecclesiasticus," chapter 9, verse 4: "Do not keep with a singer, or you may be caught by her tricks." What is your opinion?

[A] The Bible is right because it speaks of certain circumstances: a singer whose goal it is to beguile people for her own selfish interests. It is only natural that the Bible seeks to protect the children of God from such a singer. That, however, has nothing to do with my case. As you know, my songs are true messages of evangelism and praise of God, because I have been redeemed by Christ; I am a Christian.

[Q] Should a singer seek inspiration from the Bible in order to compose? What themes are you addressing in your songs?

[A] A Christian singer is not obliged to look for inspiration in the Bible. God respects the free will he has given to each of us. Nevertheless, a truly Christian singer cannot avoid being inspired by this source of mercy, the Bible. (Compare Joshua 1:8: "This book of law must ever be on your lips; you must keep it in mind day and night so that you may diligently observe all that is written in it. Then you will prosper and be successful in all that you do.") Joy, sadness, the assembly, used to be my themes. Now it is the true glorification of God.

## APARTHEID IS NAZISM: HITLER HAS RETURNED, THIS TIME TO SOUTH AFRICA (ALPHA BLONDY)

Alpha Blondy, "the rasta of Cocody," comes from Ivory Coast and has become the greatest reggae star of Africa. Hits such as *Bintou Were-Were* and *Brigadier Sabari* may be heard in all the discotheques of West Africa and are played by many bands. Alpha Blondy, who became famous with a rasta hairdo, then shaved his head bald, supposedly in memory of his deceased grandmother, who had raised him. His relationship to reggae and Jamaica began with a stay in the United States and a visit to Jamaica itself. It is said that he taped a record at Bob Marley's studio. That happened even before he released the successful record *Brigadier Sabari* in Abidjan.

Alpha Blondy's band is named Solar System, and it consists of musicians from Ivory Coast, Togo, Cameroun, Jamaica, France, and England. His Afro-reggae sold well and generated high proceeds. Alpha Blondy is generous with his money. For instance, he donated about forty-three thousand dollars to each country in the Sahel zone on his last Africa tour in 1985.

In Conakry, the capital of Guinea, a serious incident happened on this tour. On June 20, the beginning of the Islamic Ramadan, a concert was scheduled to begin at 4 P.M. Thirty thousand people had gathered in the stadium ("September 28"), and had been waiting since 11 A.M. During the dictatorship of Sékou Touré, hardly any of the great bands from other parts of Africa had performed in Guinea, so the anticipation of the audience must have been tremendous. Since the rainy season had started, it is not surprising that it began to rain heavily. Naturally, Alpha Blondy refused to perform at the stadium. Instead, a compromise was negotiated, and Blondy played at the Palais du Peuple, which could seat only two thousand people. The masses at the stadium were left out, and they did not put up with it. Protest turned into violence, and the police lost control of the situation. The army was called in and armored cars were brought up. The official report: seven dead and dozens wounded. Under these circumstances, Guinean officials delayed Alpha Blondy's departure and committed him to wait until an open-air concert was possible. Five days later, the sun was shining and he finally performed for forty thousand people.

The rastafarian image that Alpha Blondy assumed accounts to a large extent for his popularity. A disclosure in *Ivoire Dimanche* of July 21, 1985, seems to cloud this immaculate picture, and Alpha Blondy is charged with having invented a false biography.[55] The public now wants to know what is the matter with him. Why did he feign a life that did not exist? "Has he become a mythomaniac?" asks the author of the report in *Bingo,* M. Biron. He also says, "Le roi du reggae fait figure du zombie" (The king of reggae has the appearance of a zombie). He suggests that Alpha Blondy should take a look into the Bible he is always carrying about.

## Soul Makossa and African Chanson: Cameroun

Geographically and culturally, Cameroun is a link between West and Central Africa. The musicians Manu Dibango and Francis Bebey come from Cameroun. Both have often had to answer accusations that they are not making "real" African music. In response, Francis Bebey once said the following:

> I see myself as an authentic African, but as an African of the twentieth century. And I have no intention at all of changing my behavior in order to do a favor to some Germans, Russians, Americans, Englishmen, or Frenchmen. I don't want to be an African according to their opinion. I want to be the African I am: somebody who can think and turn out intellectual and artistic products suitable to the African of the present, and to what his ancestors once might have been. To expect me, an African musician of the twentieth century, to produce ancestral music is an insult to me, to my art, and to my audience, which I would have to deceive. I mistrust organizations that, perhaps, believe that African musicians should play tom-toms on stage. Nothing against tom-toms, I use it myself if it corresponds to something in my present life. But I never use it to do a favor to my audience.[56]

Manu Dibango, too, picked up this criticism in his manner:

> Most people of Western thinking want to maintain Africa as a museum. I mean, they want Africa to continue to play tom-toms because Africa *is* tom-toms; that's it.
> They don't think we can play electronics. I think it is most important that people understand that the electric Africa does exist.[57]

Both resist classification of what African music is or what it should be from the outside. Besides that they are two rather different musicians.

Francis Bebey is primarily a solo guitarist, playing acoustic guitar, and a singer, even a bard, a songwriter, a *chansonnier*. He is also a well-known poet who has published a number of novels. Born in 1929, he studied English at the Sorbonne and continued his studies in Paris at the Studio-École de la Radiodiffusion Outre-Mer. In New York he received a diploma as a radio and television journalist and worked finally in Paris for UNESCO in the department for information. He composed a brochure on broadcasting in Africa and wrote one of the few books on traditional African music.[58] Today, his life is devoted completely to music.

Next to Miriam Makeba of South Africa and Fela Anikulapo-Kuti of Nigeria, Manu Dibango is probably the best-known African musician. He is a saxophonist, composer, promoter, and producer. Within francophone Africa, some musical relationships can be followed like tracks. With the example of Manu Dibango, these connections can easily be documented. Born in 1934 in Douala, one of Cameroun's seaports, he grew up with rumba music, according to his own statement. At the age of fifteen he was sent to attend school in France. He neglected his studies in favor of music. Besides saxophone, he learned to play organ and piano. He met the Congolese musician Kabaselé after moving to Brussels. Before both of them went to Kinshasa, they recorded the famous *Independence Cha-Cha* in the early 1960s. Manu Dibango says about this time: "In the early 1960s, I played with countless musicians. You can't imagine how difficult that was since I am from Cameroun: it was simply not my music."[59]

He had his greatest success with *Soul Makossa* in 1973. "Makossa" is the name of a modern dance music style in Cameroun. In *Soul Makossa,* Manu Dibango had arranged a mixture of disco and soul styles that had great success, not only in the United States, but in Africa, too. Dibango was liked especially because of the soul character of his pieces. Soul was very popular, and an African musician who could hold his own in this style was ranked correspondingly high.

Two million copies of *Soul Makossa* were sold by 1977, not including copies released on at least twelve pirate labels.[60] During the period that followed, Manu Dibango commuted between Abidjan, Paris, and Cameroun. He performed with the Radio Télévision Ivrienne orchestra (RTI) and the Orchestre de la Police de Yaoundé. Through Paris he had contact with the modern African film scene and composed and recorded the music for at least three major films: Sembène Ousmane's *Ceddo* (1977), Dikongue Pipa's *Le prix de la liberté* (1978), and *L'Herbe sauvage* (1977). At the same time Manu Dibango founded the music magazine *Afro Music* and successfully published it for more than three years. It offers unique insights into music current in Africa and Paris in the years 1976–1978.

In order to gain a stronger foothold in anglophone areas and to pick up the reggae vogue, Manu Dibango also recorded reggae music. For his LP *Gone Clear,* he selected the best and most experienced studio musicians from Jamaica.

The tremendous success of *Soul Makossa* was naturally a great incentive for many local musicians of Cameroun to develop further their Makossa. The guitarist Toto Guillaume is among the best Makossa musicians. Dina Bell, one of the vocal stars, derives

Manu Dibango at an orchestra rehearsal for his concert at the First Festival of World Cultures, *Horizonte '79*, in Berlin.

his singing style from the smokey sound of Manu Dibango's voice. The blind guitarist and singer Tala André-Marie was discovered and promoted by Manu Dibango. He recorded *Hot Cookie*, which supposedly was adapted and re-composed into *Hustle Baby Do the Double Bump* by James Brown after he had heard it in Cameroun.[61]

# 3

# WEST AFRICAN HIGHLIFE

■

## EARLY CONTACTS WITH EUROPEAN
## MUSICAL INSTRUMENTS

It is impossible to exclude history and politics from a study of musical developments. That holds true as well for West African Highlife, which began its development under colonial conditions. Roughly speaking, West Africa was partitioned in strips of countries running north to south. Areas controlled by the French and British alternated. The regions with similar or related cultures were forced into new political units. Colonial rule established new relationships: countries as far apart as Sierra Leone an Nigeria were part of British West Africa and now often have more in common with each other than with their neighboring countries that were formerly under French control.

The establishment of trade and military bases along the West African coast reaches back to the fifteenth century when the Portuguese built the stronghold of Elmina on the Gold Coast, today's Ghana. No fortress was without necessary musical instruments, and no ship sailed without sailors who played their customary instruments. Thus, European instruments were known on the coast quite early, and were seen and heard. The bugle and all other military brass instruments, the guitar and, later, the harmonica and accordion were part of a new musical culture with which the inhabitants of the coastal region became acquainted.

Slavery spread African music to America, and there it developed into the synthesis that is Afro-American music. The expeditions of the British West Indian Regiments in West Africa led to the first contacts of Afro-American music with contemporary African music in the nineteenth century.

## THE ARRIVAL OF MISSIONARIES

In the mid-nineteenth century, European and American missionaries commenced their activities along the coast and proceeded further inland later. They introduced the harmonium and the entire tradition of Western hymnody to West Africa. In addition, Western common practice harmony became the basis of music education for churches and choirs.

Converts usually were forbidden to play traditional musical instruments since such instruments were considered heathen. Aiming thus to detach the baptized from their traditional culture, the missionaries acted logically. Traditional music was connected in more ways than one with everyday culture, which did not distinguish—as did modern Christianity—between religion and the rest of life. The missionaries worked diligently to stir contempt for the traditional culture in the minds of the believers. That certainly included music.

## THE NEW COLONIAL ELITE

Black Christians became the nucleus of new, native elites, willing, on the one hand, to conform servilely to their Western mentors' way of life, while on the other hand, considering themselves the chosen ones, surpassing their own people, who persisted in "the darkness of ignorance." They wore Western clothing and tried to imitate Western ways of living. Thus, they organized concerts, social dances, and similar festivities. Following British models, drama clubs performed plays, often on Biblical subjects. These plays were frequently intended to parody and ridicule traditional culture. Finally, choral societies practiced English melodies. All that suited the bearings of the early *evolués*, who wholeheartedly took sides with their colonial masters.

A special situation evolved in Yoruba country (Nigeria). Liberated slaves, who had been trained as missionaries in Freetown (Sierra Leone) returned as "educated" Yoruba to bring "enlightenment" to their own people. They had the advantage of

The Hope Wedell School at Calabar, in the far southeast of Nigeria, was among the first schools constructed by the British during colonial times.

speaking the native language and being themselves part of the people to be missionized. The following example illustrates the activities of the Yoruba missionaries:

> European and Yoruba culture met in a particularly evident manner at a concert in 1898, given by the Abeokuta Choral Society under the direction of Reverend Olubi of the Church Missionary Society (*Lagos Standard*, February 2, 1898).
>
> The first part of the concert consisted of Handel's "But thou didst not leave my soul in hell," translated into Yoruba by the Reverend E. M. Lijadu. Mr. Lufadeji sang his own composition *Oye ka fope f'Olorun*, and a piece by E. Sowande of Ebute Metta was performed on the harmonium. The greatest success of this part of the concert was a Yoruba translation of *Evangeline*, sung by Flora Wickliffe. The second part of the program was presented in English. It consisted of the third act of *Julius Caesar*, played by J. Akinanmi. The highpoint of the evening, however, was a Yoruba version of *The Merchant of Venice*, performed by D. O. Lijadu, J. Peters, J. Adegun, J. Ephraim, and others.[1]

## THE DEVELOPMENT OF LOCAL EUROPEANIZED MUSIC STYLES

At the turn of the century, the colonial administration gained more and more control over West African territories. The increasing number of European and African civil servants—not least necessitated by extensive railroad construction and changes in living and working habits in general—required new forms of entertainment. New music and dance styles developed in the coastal regions, growing out of traditional music and, at first, mostly using traditional instruments like drums or bells, gongs, and various kinds of the so-called hand piano (lamellophone). These were combined with the instruments of the sailors, especially the guitar spread by Kru and Krio sailors. The Kru, from Liberia, and the Krio, from Sierra Leone, sailed along the coast and introduced the new musical idiom everywhere they went: thus developed an almost universal West African coastal style distinguished by local variants. The general practice of trading companies and governments was to send workers to work in other than their native territory; this contributed to the dissemination of new styles.

One musical style of this type was the gombe of the Gã people of today's Ghana. The Gã were sent to work in Cameroun. Gombe, like the osibisaba—a Fanti style—is one of the roots of Highlife music and may be called a proto-Highlife.[2] West African gong rhythms, two-finger guitar playing, and European hymns are, according to R. Sprigge, the determining components of Highlife.[3] Western instruments and African rhythms, percussion, and singing are the formulas of modern African music.

## GHANA HIGHLIFE

Highlife developed in the 1920s in the area of the former Gold Coast. John Collins, an English musician, theorist, and producer living in Ghana, characterized the three main categories of bands in those years:

(1) Brass bands—at first exclusively military bands affiliated with coastal fortresses—spread farther inland. Traditional melodies and rhythms supplemented the original military music, thereby creating a very popular form of Highlife.

(2) The second type of band consisted of acoustic guitar bands common among the Akan people, which included singing, guitars, drums, claves, and sometimes the apremprensemma, a large type of hand piano. It is important to understand that the guitar was a successor to traditional stringed instruments like the seprewa or Akan lute.

(3) Large urban dance bands formed the third group, performing the contemporary Western repertory of dance music—fox trot, waltz, quickstep, etc.—alongside Highlife. Since these bands performed for the colonial upper class, the "high ups," they supplied the background for the

The Cape Coast Light Orchestra of Ghana (then the Gold Coast). Its instrumentation of violins, guitars, mandolins, banjo, and others was typical for the large dance bands on the west coast until World War II.

term "Highlife." They also performed in vaudeville shows of Afro-American and African comedians. The names of the bands were correspondingly pompous: The Cape Coast Light Orchestra, The City Orchestra, The Koforidua Royal Orchestra, The Cape Coast Sugar Babies.[4]

The teacher Joe Lamptey holds a pivotal position in the history of modern dance music in Ghana. He accumulated enough money to buy a large number of piccolo flutes (fifes) and formed with his pupils a large "Drum and Fife Band" with up to sixty or eighty members. The older pupils were supplied with brass and wind instruments, which Lamptey supplemented later with stringed instruments and numerous percussion instruments. This school orchestra performed at church and charitable functions, and at social dances. Thus, dance bands emerged numbering up to twenty musicians. During World War II, these were succeeded by smaller professional bands.

In contrast to dance orchestras, acoustic guitar bands performed for the lower-class people in the cities and countryside. "Concert Parties," Ghana's variant of comic opera, were associated with the guitar bands in the 1950s. According to John Collins, it happened at a time when the guitar bands were already well established. The band either supplied the music to a play performed by an independent troupe, or the members of the band were musicians and actors at the same time. Such slapstick comedies took up everyday problems of the post-war period. Next to conventional themes, such as tales of love and jealousy, the political issues of the last years of colonial rule were among the most popular subjects. The guitar bands in those days slowly became electric as well.[5] Brass bands are still in existence today, though mostly in rural areas.

Another interesting development took place: traditional music came into contact with Highlife, and groups performing on traditional instruments created new musical styles.

## E. T. MENSAH AND HIS TEMPO'S BAND: A PIECE OF HIGHLIFE HISTORY

E. T. Mensah, later called "The King of Highlife," came out of Lamptey's school, where he had been a piper. During his secondary education, he studied concert music, playing organ and saxophone. He was born in 1919 and left school in 1939. The following year he joined the Gold Coast Hospital as a pharmaceutical assistant and earned some extra money in his leisure time by playing in a number of bands.

In 1940, a Scottish sergeant called "Leopard" founded a band, which he named Leopard and His Black and White Spots. The name referred to the mixed membership of black and white musicians. The group performed mainly in army barracks and European clubs. (During World War II, many British and American soldiers were stationed on the west coast.) Mostly they played jazz, swing, and the dance music in vogue at the time, but little Highlife. E. T. Mensah was a member of this group and played alto saxophone. Later he switched to trumpet, and it soon became his favorite instrument. In 1947, he joined the Tempo's Band in Accra, which had also started as a dance band for British and American soldiers.

E. T. Mensah was able to devote more of his time to music after he opened his own drugstore. Now, since the war was over and the troops stationed there had left, Highlife music became much more important: the audience was now primarily Ghanaian. The drummer Guy Warren brought along calypso records from London and, much more significantly, Afro-Cuban percussion instruments: maracas, congas and bongos. Both the records and instruments were to determine the music of the Tempo's Band.[6] As incredible as it may seem to Africans today, the gradual re-

The band of St. Mary's Catholic Girls' School, one of the many school orchestras in Accra, the capital of Ghana.

Africanization proceeded in a roundabout way via Afro-American percussion instruments. How easy it would have been for the Tempo's Band to utilize traditional native instruments in the first place!

During the 1950s, when the Tempo's Band regularly toured Nigeria, Mensah was able to organize a second group, which also performed in Ghana. The tours to Nigeria finally ended, however, when Nigerian musicians protested Mensah's coming, since it was ruining their business. In 1955 Mensah visited England for three months and performed with Chris Barber's Jazz Band, among others.[7]

Another highpoint in Mensah's career was Louis Armstrong's visit to Ghana in 1956. Mensah had the opportunity to jam with the All Stars. Later the Tempo's Band toured West Africa, visiting Sierra Leone, Guinea, and Liberia, besides Nigeria. The song *Fire, Fire,* which turned into a famous hit for the Tempo's Band, became known to Mensah in Sierra Leone. There it had been performed by Ebenezer Calender and His Maringar Band:

> Fire, fire, fire, fire de kam
> fire, fire, fire, fire de kam ai
> wan to sie my loveli girl o i love so well
> fire, fire, fire bebi o fire de kam.[8]

It was a very popular song sung to Gombe music before newlywed couples set out on their honeymoon.[9]

In the course of time, many musicians left the Tempo's Band. Most separations proved to be fruitful, and many new bands were formed.[10]

Besides the descendents of the Tempo's Band, there existed— and there still exist—many other dance bands, for instance, Uhuru (named after the Kiswahili word for "freedom"), and the Ramblers Dance Band. Guitar bands should also be taken into consideration. C. K. Mann and His Carousel 7 and P. S. K. Ampadu's African Brothers Dance Band (International) were two of the first guitar bands of the country and also became known outside of Ghana.

## SONG TEXTS OF GHANA'S HIGHLIFE

Highlife music always has been full of life and, before independence, reflected expectations of a better life by self-government. When Kwame Nkrumah was arrested by the British in 1950 (he fought for independence of the Gold Coast colony), songs were composed praising him as a hero and, later, congratulating him on his release. Popular music assumed the role of a social commen-

Two veterans of Highlife performing together: E. T. Mensah (second from right) and V. Olaiya (right, with trumpet). Photo by Robert von Lucius.

tator. At the time of the overthrow of Nkrumah's government in
1966 (he had been president of the new state of Ghana since independence), the African Brothers released a song with the following
refrain: "Even if the driver is different, the truck is still the same."
The song was an attack on the new government, and it was immediately banned. For that reason, political attacks are normally
better hidden![11]

Songs may also include messages to the rulers. Such customs
reach back into the past. For instance, court drummers could warn
a king by drumming slight variations of a song of praise, thus in-
forming him of imminent unrest among the people. A song by the
famous E. K. Nyame's Band, *Nsuo beto a, mframa di kan* ("Before
it starts raining, the wind will blow"), was understood as a warning to Nkrumah about the coming overthrow:

Cover of an 10″ 33 RPM record by E. T. Mensah of Ghana. The "King of Highlife" is
depicted in the photograph (left).

Before it starts raining
the wind will blow.
I warned you but you did not listen.
Before trouble starts,
there will be a flag (to warn you).
I warned you but you did not listen.[12]

Besides political themes of this kind, everyday subjects are the most common. This includes the relationships between the sexes. Male chauvinism becomes especially evident in the following song:

I was traveling with my lover to Accra.
Ampofowa, your character
prevented you from seeing the sea
Darling, get down at Ejisu . . .

The journey had hardly started
when you started misbehaving.
So, get down at Ejisu.
If you marry an educated woman,
you become her interpreter.
Ampofowa your character prevented
you from seeing the sea.
Get down at Ejisu . . .

I won't stay with you anymore
Go away with your mortar
I take my pestle . . .[13]

Geest and Asante-Darko state that this song by Konadu confirms in every authoritarian manner that women ought to be obedient to men and that inequality between the sexes is necessary.[14]

Other songs may deal with philosophical subjects. Death is a common theme in the repertory of Ghanaian Highlife. In the following song, Konadu sings about the death of a man who had supported him:

*The World is Finished (Asaase asa)*
We do not cry because of death itself,
    but because of what happens after it.
Maybe the deceased was your supporter,
    maybe he was the one feeding you.
Now he has left you in sorrow.[15]

The following song text indicates that car accidents are a common cause of death in today's Ghana. Again, Konadu sings:

> *Something Serious Has Happened (Assem bi adi bone)*
> I prepared breakfast,
>     thinking my lover will come and eat it.
> I expected her; she did not come.
> My lover has gone away,
>     and died somewhere on the road.[16]

An important event in the musical history of Ghana was the Soul to Soul Festival held at Independence Square in Accra in 1971. Roberta Flack, Wilson Pickett, Ike and Tina Turner, The Staple Singers, The Voices of Harlem, and others came from the United States and performed for one hundred thousand enthusiastic listeners at this soul marathon. Soul music, however, had long before gained a foothold in Africa. The songs of James Brown, especially, were performed by many bands.[17]

Reggae exerted a strong influence on African music as well. Most bands in Ghana had at least one reggae piece in their repertory. A new variant of reggae emerged that may be best called Afro-reggae.

Highlife dancers in a nightclub at Lagos (1960).

This postage stamp from Ghana, depicting a traditional dance scene, was released on the occasion of FESTAC, the Second World Black and African Festival of Arts and Culture (1977). Numerous dance groups performed at this gigantic festival (with which Nigeria celebrated itself), allowed only two minute each for their performances. Traditional and modern music and dance ensembles met from all over Africa and the black diaspora.

An increasing appreciation of guitar bands led, at least in part, to an abandonment of strict separation of dance orchestras and guitar bands, and so guitar bands nowadays may include brass sections.

Two groups played an important part in Ghana's Highlife scene of the 1970s. On the one hand, there was the group of guitarist Atakora Manu, with his Afro-disco style, who introduced a new sound to the music. Being a sound technician himself, Manu was equipped with the necessary knowledge. On the other hand, there were musicians who were all in one way or another associated with the house band of the club Talk of the Town, Sweet Talks, later re-named Super Sweet Talks. Among others, A. B. Crentsil and Eric Agyeman were members of this band, and McGod and the People's Band also played with Sweet Talks. Their contribution to the renewal of Highlife was to incorporate the tempo of Igbo Highlife from east Nigeria (especially that of Prince Nico Mbarga) and to re-introduce the brass sections of dance-band Highlife. New impulses also came from musicians like George Darko of Berlin, whose so-called "Burgher Highlife" was very successful in Ghana. Not least, the reason was that his music was recorded under studio conditions better than those in Ghana.

Today the life of a musician in Ghana is difficult. Tape piracy is the rule, and records are hard to come by. Musicians receive hardly any royalties. Years of continuous curfew also had severe consequences for night clubs and live concerts.[18] Only a few records are produced in Ghana today though it was once the leading country of Highlife. For the most part, records are recorded and manufactured in neighboring countries like Ivory Coast, Liberia, or Nigeria, if not in the United States or Great Britain.

## Taxidriver: Highlife in Nigeria

Since the colonial situation in Nigeria was similar to that in Ghana, the history of music also proceeded along similar lines. In the 1930s, brass bands existed there as well. The New Bethel School Band of Onitsha, in the east of the country, is considered

This LP by The Supersonics clearly represents the new values: pounds and dollars! Expensive is good! This highlife music, however, is indeed good. Among the musicians are Gasnar Lawol, Ade Bashorun, Peter King.

one of the sources of Nigerian Highlife. It was not, however, the only school band in the country. Presumably, there were brass bands and drum-and-fife bands all over, at least in the southern half of Nigeria. Yet, Bala Miller (one of the few Hausa Highlife musicians), telling about his early musical education in the early 1930s, reports that even in the Islamic north, schools purchased musical instruments (flutes, horns, various drums) from the military supplies of the Niger Company[19] when the company returned its privileges to the government.[20] Later, at the C. M. S. Grammar School, Miller received musical training from a number of music teachers trained by missionaries. The bands used to perform on the road between Lagos and Yaba and were called "Calabar Brass Bands." The name also demonstrates historical references of this music: Calabar was one of the earliest British footholds on the West African coast.

There also were dance bands in Nigeria performing mainly European music. African-Americans from the West Indies were among the first musicians in these orchestras. When E. T. Mensah came to Lagos and made his Highlife popular in the late 1940s, it took less than a year before Nigerian musicians had founded a considerable number of Highlife bands, playing music in the new style and developing their own variants.[21]

Bobby Benson, since his funeral in 1983 called the "Father of Nigerian Music," was a cardinal figure in the development of Highlife in Nigeria, and a catalyst of modern Nigerian music. His personal life reflects much of Nigeria's history and music history. His song texts are vivid documents of almost forty years of cultural and social changes in West Africa.

Robert Benson was a sailor in the British merchant navy during World War II and returned to Nigeria in 1947. He never received any formal musical training. Using his time well, however, he played with musicians everywhere on his travels and, thus, developed his talent.[22] He became a good dancer and singer, and a singular comedian. He played guitar, drums, string bass, saxophone, and "some" piano. Besides bringing calypso to West Africa, he also introduced—rather by accident—the electric guitar. Without sheet music, he played jazz and danced the boogie-woogie and the jitterbug.

Bobby Benson entered show business outright as a professional. Imitating black American "bobs"—the comedians of slapstick comedies—he dressed up in drainpipe trousers and tails, painted his eyes white, and started the "Bobby and Cassandra Show" with his wife Cassandra. In his book *Jazz in Nigeria*, the journalist Chief Bassey Ita of Calabar, Nigeria, described the shock that Bobby gave to the then rather "stalky" jazz musicians and fans among the educated Africans. To them, jazz and social dancing was cultivated entertainment for respectable "tamed negroes." Now Bobby Benson introduced popular jazz that was rather "savage," even vulgar! The reaction of jazz fans was negative, Ita writes, and they simply stopped playing jazz records. Jazz became Bobby's business. He had thumbed his nose at Christian respectability.[23] This reaction surely led Bobby Benson to record the song *Gentleman Bobby,* which was later famous.[24]

In 1948 he formed his Jam Session Orchestra, which toured Nigeria for the next two years. In 1952/53 Nigeria Jazz Club followed, then Agil Jazz Club, and others. In the 1950s, Bobby Benson performed at the Empire Hotel and the Lido Bar in Lagos—until he built his own Hotel Bobby, the Caban Bamboo Nightclub.

His hit *Taxi Driver* made him the embodiment of Nigerian Highlife:[25]

> If you marry taxi driver,
> I don't care,
> If you marry moto driver,
> I don't care,
> If you marry lorry driver,
> I don't care . . .

In his song, Bobby Benson addressed the susceptibility of young Nigerian women of the time to rich men. Professional drivers were still relatively well off among the lower classes in the 1950s and early 1960s. At least they had cash money and could openly and ostentatiously spend it. Drivers were symbols of the new society and of the freedom and laxity of urban living. A driver comes and goes, nothing remains the same, everything fluctuates: all that is an expression of the exhilaration and philosophy of Highlife culture! Modern life and its prestige objects were celebrated. Highlife sang of nylon dresses, lipstick, and, not to forget, the "fast" girls—the "sisis," "titis," or "walka-walka babies." These girls naturally were among the regular patrons of Highlife dance clubs.

Most of these localities were open-air clubs: the bandstand and outer ring with brass tables and chairs was perhaps roofed over, but the concrete dance floor in the middle remained open. Most patrons ordered beer.

The melody of *Taxi Driver* was intoned by the assembled musicians at the funeral march commemorating Bobby Benson. Something of that atmosphere is reflected on the LP *Nigeria* by fuji musician Alhaji Ayinde Barrister.[26]

Victor Olaiya's Cool Cats, later renamed Olaiya's All Stars, is among the famous Highlife bands. Two of their greatest hits were *Trumpet Highlife* and *Omele 'Dele*. In the 1960s, Roy Chicago became a popular Highlife musician, and among the many well-known Highlife bands, those of E. C. Arinze and Rex Lawson, Charles Iwegbue and His Archibogs, Steven Amechi and His Empire Rhythm Skies, as well as Julius Araba and His Afro-Skiffel Group are especially noteworthy.

When calypso became the great rage in London in the 1950s, Nigeria also started its own calypso tradition featuring singers like Benge and Njemanze. Njemanze, also known as Israel Nwaoba, sang with a very high falsetto voice in Igbo and English, accompanied by guitar and kazoo. His vocal style was derived from calypso, but the rhythm and musical style remained in the Igbo tradition.

Highlife bands in the sixties consisted primarily of the following: "eight to twenty musicians, among them two trumpets, one or two saxophones, an upright bass, an electric guitar, and a set of percussion. Sometimes a trombone is added, and currently most popular recordings are supplemented by two muted trombones playing in unison."[27] This orchestration is, of course, completed by drums. (African drums were introduced only later.)

A Highlife piece was structured in such a way that a fast, racy beginning—usually including the full set of brass simultaneously—was followed by singing to the respective rhythm. The text could be sung either in English or in one of the numerous Nigerian languages. The second third of the piece possibly introduced the rhythm section alone, improvising along traditional rhythmic patterns. An immense tension was slowly built up, which was

# Clubs and Restaurants

**Abalabi:** 75 Agege Motor Road, Mushin; Manager: Latunde Vincent; Open: 9 a.m. to 3 a.m.; Admission 2/- to 10/-. Ten rooms; £2 2/- single; £3 2/- double; Dancing 10 p.m. to 3 a.m. (following day). Music: Abalabi Rhythm Dandies led by Roy Chicago; J. O. Araba and His Afro-Skiffle band; four other bands on contract. Ballroom, Highlife and Juju, Cabaret. Meals: 4/-, 7/- and 8/6 (African/European diet.)

**Ambassador Hotel:** 109C King George Avenue, Yaba. Manager: Anthony Rossek. Tel. 44848, 44030, 44038, 44039. Open: 7 a.m. Admission. 10/- to 30/-. 10 Rooms: single £3, double £5 boarding & lodging. Dancing from 10 p.m. Music: Ambassador Down-Beats led by Chief Bill Friday. Highlife and other classical music. Meals. European — 4/6d breakfast; 9/- lunch 10/6 dinner. Beer 3/6; Champagne 60/- Spirit 2/6d to 3/- the glass; Wine, assorted 19/- to 22/-.

**Antoine's Bar & Restaurant:** (Air-conditioned). 61 Broad Street, Lagos. Manager: Tony S. Basmadjian. Open: 12 noon to 3.30 p.m. 8 p.m. to midnight. Admission: Cover charge 3/- and 6/- on Saturdays. Meals from 12/6. Beer: 2/6d. small; Champagne: £2 10s. Spirit 3/-

**Bagatelle:** 208/212 Broad Street, Lagos. Manager: M. Mansour, Tel. 21855; Open: 8.30 p.m. Daily (except Sundays). Admission: 3/6d; Saturdays 10/6d (Ladies free). Music: English, French and Italian. Meals: (European) 15/- to 30/-

Beer: 4/- small; Large 6/-; Champagne £3 10/-; Spirits by the glass 3/6d; Wine from 21/- to 30/-.

**Black and White Caterers Limited:** (Corner House Cafe) 42 King George Avenue, Yaba. Manager: A. M. Osseiran. Tel. 45298. Open: 7 a.m. — midnight. Music: African and European. Cabaret. Meals.

**Caban Bamboo:** 103 Ikorodu Road. Mushin, Lagos. Manager: Bobby Benson. Admission: 5/-. Beer 3/6; Champagne 70/-; Spirits 3/- by the glass. Food: 10/- lunch; 12/6d — 17/6d dinner or a la Carte; Chinese food 7/-; Nigerian food 7/-. Music Bobby Benson and his Orchestra. Special midnight cabaret.

**Caroline Hotel:** 93 Ipodo Road. Ikeja. Manager: Johnson Tenuro Kodesoh, Tel. 33100. Open: 9 a.m. Rates: £2 10/- per day — 6 Rooms £2: 10/- each Dancing twice weekly 8 p.m., — 4 a.m. (following day) Music: Calabar Orchestra. All types of Music. Food: (African) 1/-; 1/6d and 2/6d; (European) 5/- to 7/6d. Beer 3/-.

**Central Cinema:** 20 Lagos Street, Ebute-Metta. Manager: H. Mattar. Tel. 23099/44255. Open: 8 — 11.30 p.m. Admission: 3/6d., 1/9d., and 1/2d.

**Cool Cats Inn:** 40, Abule Nla Road, Apapa Road, Ebute-Metta. Manager: George Weikezi. Tel. 44154. Open: 8 a.m. Admission 5/- flat Saturday night; 3/6 Wednesday Saturday night; 3/6 Wdneesday Music: The Famous Cool Cats Or-

A page from the *Nigeria Yearbook* of 1961. Many famous highlife orchestras performed in the clubs listed.

resolved only shortly before the end when all instruments entered again full volume for a last "swing."

When played relatively slowly, Highlife pieces could also be called "blues," but they actually had nothing to do with blues. In slow pieces, pairs clasped each other and danced in close embrace. An excerpt from Chinua Achebe's novel *No Longer at Ease* illustrates how differently Highlife could be danced:

The next dance was again a high-life. In fact most of the dances were high-lifes. Occasionally a waltz or a blues was played so that the dancers could relax and drink their beer, or smoke. Christopher and Clara danced next while Obi and Bisi kept an eye on their chairs. But soon it was only Obi; someone had asked Bisi to dance.

There were so many ways of dancing the high-life as there were people on the floor. But, broadly speaking, three main patterns could be discerned. There were four or five Europeans whose dancing reminded one of the early motion pictures. They moved like triangles in an alien dance that was ordained for circles. There were others who made very little real movement. They held their women close, breast to breast and groin to groin, so that the dance could flow uninterrupted from one to the other and back again. The last group were the ecstatic ones. They danced apart, spinning, swaying or doing intricate syncopations with their feet and waist. They were the good servants who had found perfect freedom. The vocalist drew the microphone up to his lips to sing "Gentleman Bobby."

> I was playing moi guitar *jeje*,
> A lady gave me a kiss.
> Her husband didn't like it,
> He had to drag him wife away.
> Gentlemen, please hold your wife.
> Father and mum, please hold your girls.
> The calypso is so nice,
> If they follow, don't blame Bobby.

The applause and the cries of "Anchor! Anchor!" that followed this number seemed to suggest that no one blamed Gentleman Bobby. And why should they? He was playing his guitar *jeje*—quietly, soberly, unobtrusively, altogether in a law-abiding fashion, when a woman took it upon herself to plant a kiss on him. No matter how one looked at it, no blame could possibly attach to the innocent musician.[28]

### JUJU MUSIC FROM YORUBA COUNTRY

The purely percussive sections of Highlife described above were called *juju*—not because it referred to magical practices, as the name implies,[29] but because traditional rhythms could indeed assert themselves and dominate a piece. The dance style connected with the music immediately became completely distinct and represented the most variant traditional dance styles, corresponding to the origin of the dancer. On the other hand, juju is also a musical style by itself. Fundamentally, it is based on Yoruba guitar band style.

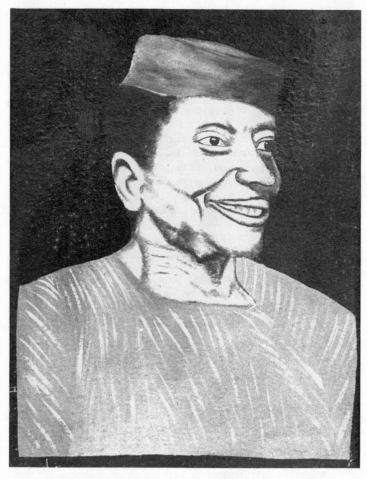

During the 1950s and '60s, Njemanze, also known as Israel Nwaoba, was an Igbo musician who delighted his audience with his songs and high voice. His band was called Three Night Wizards. This portrait is by the signpainter Osuori of Owerri.

Drummers at the entrance of the Alafin of Oyo's palace, Nigeria (1963).

Besides guitars, the talking drums of the Yoruba are the main instruments in juju music.[30] During the 1950s and 60s, larger varieties of dundun drums were used in Highlife and juju bands, whereas today only smaller drums are employed, which are held by applying pressure with the upper arm. The larger drums are suspended with broad leather straps over the shoulders and are carried waist high at the side. They are beaten with a curved drumstick. The talking drums themselves consist of an hourglass-shaped wooden body that is covered at both ends with goatskin. The two drum heads are connected with hide strips to allow a tightening or loosening of the drumming surface. Thus the pitch may be lowered or raised, and extended sliding tones can even be produced. All of this allows the drummer to imitate the speech melody of Yoruba. Yoruba is a tone language and comes lose to singing when only spoken. Essentially three pitch levels—low, middle, high—are distinguished, but in practice many intermediate pitches may be discerned as well.

Each city king of the Yoruba, called *oba*, had his own drummers. Today that is no longer the case. Only few *oba* have the means or the will to support their own group of drummers, since they no longer have the privilege of collecting taxes. The traditional drummer, for instance, announced approaching visitors. Thus the *oba* could hear, even in the most distant chambers, who was standing at the gate.

Traditional drummers also had the ability and knowledge to recite many *oriki*, which are songs of praise. Every important personality has an *oriki* that needs to be transmitted and memorized. Of course, they also have to be brought up-to-date frequently, or actualized, as it were. There are also *oriki* for gods, cities, plants, and animals. The talking drum introduced the tradition of songs of praise even into juju music. Today it is for the most part only the rich who are sung about in live concerts, at parties they finance, or even on records, where these praises can be heard by millions.

Before juju became socially acceptable after independence in the 1960s, it was rated inferior to Highlife. Juju was guitar band music of poorer people who met in palm wine taverns. Since it was strongly influenced by traditional music, it was not "modern" enough for the elite. When traditional music in general was revalued after independence, the time for juju had finally arrived. The breakthrough of juju was largely the achievement of I. K. Dairo. He even tried to dodge the cultural barriers within Nigeria by incorporating rhythms from different parts of the country into juju music. I. K. Dairo was decorated a Member of the British Empire for his musical achievements.

Dairo's songs treat a wide range of subjects, from love and everyday problems, to politics. One of his most famous songs was recorded shortly after the arrest of the former opposition leader

Label of the single *Chief Awolowo* by I. K. Dairo, one of the first singles that was not only produced but also manufactured in Nigeria.

Chief Obafemi Awolowo in 1963.[31] The song was intended to raise the hope among his people that Awo—as he was called— soon would be free again. The prediction came true: Awo was freed a few years later after a military coup. Here is the translation of the song text from Yoruba:

> Who dares to say that we don't have a father
> Who dares to say that we don't have a father
> Who dares to say that we are without a father—pardon me!
> How about our father from the city of Ikenne—Awolowo
> Who dares to say that we don't have a father
> Who dares to say that we don't have a father
> Who dares to say that we are without a father—pardon me!
> How about our father from the city of Ikenne—Awolowo
>
> We are rain, and we are nobody's enemy;
> We are at home, and pray to God
> Obafemi Awolowo, father of Tola

He has only left to become smarter
He has only left to obtain more wisdom
Awolowo, the father, he has only left to become smarter

You don't pull an elephant's tail
Friends at home, pray for Awolowo
We are rain, and we are nobody's enemy;
Rain drenches whom it sees;
Who leaves his home to earn his living, he will not encounter evil;
You will walk the earth for a long time
Who leaves his home to earn his living, he will not encounter evil;
You will walk the earth for a long time
You will go, you will return—father of Olayinka
You will go, you will return—father of Tokumbo
You will go, you will return—father of Oluwole

Who leaves his home to earn his living, he will not encounter evil;
You will walk the earth for a long time
You will go, you will return—father of Olayinka
You will go, you will return—father of Olayinka[32]

I. K. Dairo is also credited with having introduced the accordion into juju music. Whatever happened, it is certain that he integrated it uniquely with guitars and percussion in his Blue Spots Band. *Adupe Baba Oseum* on his LP *Ashiko Music* (volume 2) may serve as an excellent example. By the way, the piece also features the Yoruba talking drum in a purely percussive section. In addition, it is not introduced simply in the background, as in most modern juju bands, but as a central instrument.[33]

I. K. Dairo is still recording today. His emphasis now lies, however, on religious themes. He has founded his own church, in which he performs with his own band.[34]

Chief Commander Ebenezer Obey followed in the footsteps of I. K. Dairo and took the lead among juju musicians with his International Brothers Band. After a few years, however, King Sunny Ade and His African Beats competed with him for the number-one spot.

New record releases are awaited with anticipation. High sales figures—one hundred thousand to two hundred thousand and more—demonstrate their great popularity. Pirated releases of records and cassette tapes are not even included in these figures. The popularity of the musicians is best compared to that of our top athletes. The most important aspect of each new record is

Barbershop signs represent a distinct genre of popular painting in Africa. Hairstyles are sometimes named after musical styles. These three hairstyles from the 1970s represent Synchro System—the distinctive style of Sunny Ade and His African Beats; Miliki line—referring to the music of Chief Commander Ebenezer Obey; and Fella Sounds—relating to the Afro-beat of Fela Anikulapo Kuti.

what the musician and singer (who most often is also the composer, poet, lead guitarist, owner of the instruments, and chief manager of the enterprise) has to say: what he says and how he says it; what expressions he uses; which old proverbs he has dug up; or, perhaps, which well-known saying he disseminates slightly modified. The songs may comment on actual political events, changes in the social structure of the country, or they may simply extol important personalities, who, correspondingly, most often finance the band. The presentation of monetary gifts is done through so-called "spraying." Jeremy Marre has shown such a situation in his film *Konkombe—Nigerian Music:* Sunny Ade plays at a party given by the *oba* of Lagos, and the *oba* passes bill after bill in front of Sunny's face into the open hand of a band member. Others join the *oba,* aspiring to match or surpass his generosity or ostentation. This is quite different from earlier practices, where the audience pasted coins to the dripping-wet forehead of the musician in order to acknowledge or encourage outstanding performances. Today, the exchange of literally thousands of dollars (sometimes reaching five-digit figures) serves almost exclusively the self-aggrandizement of the donor. It is evidence of a smug upperclass corrupted by oil money.

The great juju groups mentioned above are not, of course, the only ones in existence. There is a significant number of other groups and musicians—less well-known to us, but by no means less qualified—that each have their own specific style. For a certain time, his Miliki sound was characteristic of Ebenezer Obey. Sunny Ade's distinctive mark was primarily the use of the steel

guitar, even though he was by no means the first or the only musician to employ it within Nigerian Highlife tradition. It just did not
assume the same characteristic significance with any other
musician.[35]

The final breakthrough of juju music in the Nigerian music
market was brought about by political factors. During the Biafra
war, most Igbo musicians returned home, and thus Igbo Highlife
and Highlife of ethnically mixed groups disappeared for a number
of years. Yoruba juju quickly filled the gap.[36]

### THE FUJI STYLE

The music that developed from traditions of the Islamic Yoruba is
hardly known outside the boundaries of Nigeria, even though it
enjoys great popularity there today. The various Islamic styles are
a strong competition to juju music in Nigeria's Yoruba territories,
sometimes even reaching higher sales figures than those of the juju
kings.

Thus far, fuji is the latest Islamic dance music in Nigeria. Alhaji
Sikiru Ayinde Barrister is credited with having created the style.
Fuji is above all a continuation of older traditions utilizing the
technical perfection possible today. Percussion instruments are recorded brilliantly, but no electric instruments are used—though
naturally, those instruments that are used are amplified electroni-
cally.

Alhaji Chief Kollington Ayinla and His African Fuji 1978 Organization is another of the great fuji bands. He incorporated the
Yoruba bata drums (which were traditionally reserved for the god
Shango) into fuji, and thus created the "bata-disco-fuji" style. The
texts of this music are similar to those of juju: they may be songs of
praise or more philosophical compositions. A record by Alhaji
Sikiru Ayinde Barrister, released before the election of 1983, im-
plored the Nigerian people to keep peace among themselves. It
was intended to defuse a very tense and heated atmosphere. Barrister commemorated the death of Bobby Benson in 1983 on this
LP; Benson's *Taxi Driver* text had been modified by Barrister to be
"If you love Bobby Benson, God bless you."[37] New Fuji styles do
appear from time to time and carry fancy names like Barrister's
"Fuji-Garbage" in 1989.

### IGBO MINSTRELS AND IGBO HIGHLIFE

In the eastern region of Nigeria, there existed an active and creative music scene before and after the Biafra war. Oriental Brothers International is one of the modern bands of Igbo Highlife in the guitar band style that dominates the market. Oliver de Coque and His Expo '76 and their Ogene Sound Super of Africa is another popular group. Charles Iwegbue and His Hino Sound, Chief Ngozita and His Ngozi Brothers, and Joe Nez are only a few names among many. The late Joe Nez was mainly loved on account of his beautiful voice. On the record released after his death he may be heard singing alternately with an electric organ, which reminds us of one of the roots of Highlife: Christian hymns. Chief Osita Osadebe comes from the Igbo region west of the Niger river. He is one of those Highlife musicians who have held on to traditional Highlife style even today.

As soloists or with a few accompanying musicians, Igbo minstrels recite texts in which they comment on questions of everyday life and formulate the hopes and concerns of the population. The emphasis of their tests is modified to correspond to the occasion or situation. If a singer is invited to a baptism or funeral, he will accordingly sing about the future life of the newborn or the past life of the deceased.

The minstrels (this designation remains provisional) were not, for a long time, in particularly high esteem within Igbo society, due to their poverty and the candid manner in which they expressed opinions in their songs. A song of the modern minstrel Prince Morocco Maduka refers to the despised position of the minstrels:

> Whoever says that the music is not good,
> he shall not call the minstrels when his mother dies.
> Whoever says that the music is not good,
> he shall not call the minstrels when his father dies.[38]

Hence a modern minstrel can act confidently today and tell the people a thing or two: "Then they shouldn't come in the first place!"

Akunwafo Ezigbo Obiligbo of Nteje sings in one song about the recently deceased Onyekwelu, the founder and owner of a record label that had become famous in the 1950s, Nigerphone—

CTO (standing for Christopher Taagbo Onyekwelu). He praises the record producer affectionately as "the breast that nourishes the child," suggesting that C. T. O. was not one of the worst wheeler-dealers. Perhaps he had rather been a kind of sponsor or patron of his musicians.[39] The following commentary by E. Chpalo appears on the record jacket:

Chief Akunwafo Ezigbo Obiligbo was born on August 10, 1904, in the city of Njete. He began his musical career with an inspiration given to him in a dream. Akunwafo's fame grew slowly but steadily and reached its first highpoint with his maiden recording on Nigerphone, *Njenje Amaka-Nma*. On this record, Akunwafo sings his obituary for the late C. T. Onjekwelu, in whose studio he made his early recordings.[40]

Bewildering to us, but also refreshing is the open manner in which the question of payment of an honorarium or salary for performance is dealt with in the song commemorating C. T. Onyekwelu, the first part of which (with annotations) is given below. Ezigbo Obiligbo was supposed to perform at a reunion of politicians from the first days of the independence movement. Before he was willing to enter the hall, he inquired about payment. The amount he asked for surely is an expression of recognition and appreciation of his artistic ability. After the performance, the money was counted and acknowledged. The concert was successful, above all because he contrived to create unity among the mixed assembly, which is indicated in one line of the song: "and the audience agreed!"

The functional aspect of music has a prominent place in this song. Every single word and line, even all the names mentioned in the song, embody the richness of traditional Igbo culture. Here the Igbo minstrels resemble the griots: they are masters of the word, and beyond pure eloquence, power, and ability of speech, they are philosophers, poets, and historians. Even if we annotated each verse of the song, our understanding would still remain rudimentary. Only intensive review of the entire Igbo history and society would yield a deeper comprehension. The following translation was intended to be used as an interlinear translation in order to demonstrate the structure of traditional song poetry.[41]

*Akunwafor Ezigbo Obiligbo: The Death of C. T. Oneykwelu*
The day this drive came over Onyekwelu in his compound
CHORUS: Onyekweli, great person
I was there the day this urge befell Onyekwelu beyond anything

5    Came back from abroad to his people
     They told us that black people should rule themselves and we
          agreed
     And said that they had a conference at Fegge
     And told me that they had a conference at Fegge
     I went and brought my friend Okpaelo
     A short elephant that put a herd of elephants to flight, Imanuel
10   I went and brought my friend Melody Okpaelo
     They said that the buffalo sprouted horns in their ground
     Then they went to confer at Fegge
     Then he said to go and bring Obiligbo and his musicians for him
     They came with a car and carried Obiligbo
15   I came in and he said to me, Obiligbo, sing the songs that you sing
     It was Onyekweli that the black people used for the conference to
          agree
     Onyekweli, the white man
     My man Onyekweli, breast that nourishes the child, Onyekweli
     CHORUS: Onyekweli, white man
     Onyekweli, breast that nourishes the child
20   He said who accepts that his fellows are surpass him
     A young man and his fellow are equal in word of mouth, Onyekweli
     Then he said to me, come into the house
     Then he said, Obiligbo, come into the house
     Onyekweli, how much will you pay Obiligbo, you will pay Obiligbo
          how much?
25   He said that he would pay two bags and four hundred units
     I led my musicians into the house
     I sang two times, the atmosphere charged
     I just sang two times and the audience agreed
     Your friend Ezigbo Obiligbo and his musicians
30   He counted two bags of money and four hundred shillings
     Told them to take Obiligbo home, to start carry home Obiligbo that
          he should go
     Take a pleasure car to carry home Obiligbo that he might go to his
          house
     Not quite two *izu* I landed at his house
     As I approached started hearing as wailing resounded and I cried
35   I asked the people of Nnofia, what is this, what has happened?
     Then they told me that Onyekweli had died
     My friend Onyekweli, breast that nourishes the child, tragedy has
          hit me
     I led my musicians and entered the house
     His wife, spouse that knows the husband's mind, she was crying
          away

40    Stop, let me sing Obiligbo song for all to hear
      Tragedy has befallen me, tragedy has befallen me in this music
      Tragedy has befallen me, tragedy has befallen me in this music
      I said that the death that killed Onyekweli did not act rightly
      I said that the fire that burnt Onitsha market made the town weep
45    Fire that burnt Onitsha market is not good
      Children of Iboland are crying that fire burnt their wealth
      Divination that *dibia* performs for the ne'er-do-well and he rejoices
      Divination that *dibia* performs for the ne'er-do-well and he rejoices
      Death is not good in this world, death is mighty
50    Death, tragedy had befallen me, tragedy has befallen me on this
          world
      Children of the world, look at Ezigbo Obiligbo and his musicians
      Children of the world, look at Ezigbo Obiligbo, I am saying this
          thing
      A person that is distinguished is not so in the eyes of his community
      CHORUS: Children of the community, the king is not subject to
          prohibitions
55    A person that is distinguished is not so in the eyes of his community
      A child born into well-being is not reluctant towards the
          community
      Who is that person that will make as much money as Onyekweli,
          people of enjoyment
      He that gathered wealth without spending it has carried poverty in
          going.[42]

Annotations to *The Death of C. T. Onyekwelu*
The numbers of the annotations refer to the text lines.

1. "Akunwafor" is a title. Within Igbo society, there exists a whole culture of assuming titles. On the one hand, it serves to distribute wealth since the ceremonies connected with it swallow up immense amounts of money. On the other hand, it establishes a certain social hierarchy in an otherwise almost egalitarian society. "Akunwafor" literally means "wealth child of the womb." It indicates that Obiligbo was already rich at birth, thus, he came from a well-to-do family.

2. The name Onyekwelu means "he who assumes that another person will surpass him." The chorus is repeated after each verse.

3. "Onyekweli" is a local dialect variant of "Onyekwelu."

5. The verse refers to those Nigerians returning from studies abroad in Europe and America who founded the first political groups. Later, these groups developed into the first parties to negotiate the independence of Nigeria.

6. The independence movement indeed did not emanate from the people, but rather from members of the elite educated in the West.

9. A pictorial characterization of his friend Okafo.

10. "Melody" Okpaelo was an aide to C. T. Onyekwelu, who founded his own record company, Melody Sound Studio, after Onyekwelu's death. This company released the "obituary" for Onyekwelu by Obiligbo, as MSLP 1! Okpaelo literally means "somebody who gets good ideas and can give good advice."

11. An allusion to preparations for political struggles.

17. Onyekwelu, on the one hand, had a light complexion and, on the other hand, he was a man who, on account of his Western education, was well respected by people not trained in the Western system. Any negative connotation regarding the "white man," which we perhaps immediately suspect, is not applicable.

25. In counting modern money, old customs of counting that were used in calculating cowry and other currencies are still utilized. The standard unit of the British shilling is used even today as the accounting basis for modern currencies by market women all over the former British regions.

27. "Two times" does not mean two songs, but rather two larger sections that were sung through.

32. In the original Igbo text, Obiligbo refers here constantly to "pleasure" without "car." But a "pleasure car" is meant, a luxury car in contrast to a commercial car.

33. An *izu* is the traditional four-day week of the Igbo.

41. Obiligbo has lost his main patron, hence "in this music."

44. Onitsha is one of the largest market places in this part of Africa. It is situated at the Niger river and, thus, is also an important emporium of commercial goods.

56. A wealthy member will not turn his back on the demands and concerns of his community.

59. "Going" here means "death."

In another song, Ezigbo Obiligbo addressed the question of hunger and blamed it on the population's declining interest in agriculture.[43]

> I say some should go to college, the others to the farm.
> The number of thieves surpasses the farmers.
> The number of tradesmen surpasses the farmers.
> The number of swindlers surpasses the farmers.
> That is why famine has overcome us.[44]

Ezigbo Obiligbo plays ubo, the Igbo variant of the hand piano. (The ubo is played by plucking metal lamellas fastened to a wooden board closing off half of a calabash.) Most often he performs with three other musicians. One plays a rattle of fruit shells tied-together, which sometimes may give a rather shrill sound. The second musician plays a small wooden slit gong, and the third beats the opening of a clay pot with a kind of fan. Solo singing constitutes the foreground, and to each text line a refrain is added at the end—which changes only three times in the song given above. Musically, however, the minstrel pieces are entertaining as well. The tempo may accelerate and then decelerate again. The rattle is handled skillfully and in various ways. Often, it is recorded as a musical foreground, sounding shrill through the loudspeakers—mixed quite differently from our ideas of acoustic balance. That

Record label of C. T. Onyekwelu, "Bottom Belly."

The Ubo, instrument of the Igbo minstrels, is a kind of hand piano.

demonstrates how important the rattle is in this kind of music, and
how popular a virtuoso approach to the instrument is. In Western
contexts, a rattle is perceived only marginally.[45]

### AKWETE AND OZZIDISM

Sir Victor Uwaifo comes from Benin City, the capital of the former
great empire of Benin and of today's Nigerian Bendel state,[46]
where he runs his Hotel Joromi. He began as a Highlife musician
and then developed his akwete style. His first hit, *Joromi,* sold one
hundred thousand copies. That happened in 1969, and he has remained a successful and popular star ever since.

The band Sonny Okosun and Ozzidi built their style on Ishan
culture and enriched it with two further specialities, creating an
unmistakable sound: Okosun adopted calypso as well as reggae.
Together with calypso as a musical style, he also took up its criticism of social and cultural characteristics. Thus, we find texts
concerned with questions like "Why don't taxis in Lagos have
taximeters?" or questions of a more general nature, like "What is
all that running around in space about?"—if there remains
enough to do here on earth.[47] With reggae he also addressed the

political problems in southern Africa. He produced an LP with the title song *Fire in Soweto,* and another song entitled *Oh Namibia.* As a consequence, he is probably one of very few West African musicians to be represented on the single-record market in Zimbabwe.

## AFRO-BEAT

Fela Anikulapo-Kuti counts as the founder of Afro-beat. At first he played Highlife, but he changed his style after a visit to the U.S. and after becoming acquainted with jazz. He reached the conclusion that it should not have been necessary to play jazz in order to play African music. Hence, he developed his Afro-beat. Fela recorded numerous records in this style, which was picked up in one or another form by quite diverse African groups. Practically all of his records are dominated by discussions of political events and cultural questions, which he approaches as a follower of Nkrumah's African or, rather, pan-African ideas. The idea of African unity is at the center of this conception. Fela's criticism is primarily directed against corrupt elite groups. In one of his texts he criticizes the blindness of the leaders; on another record he assails the hypocrisy of many Africans. The attacks launched against him by successive Nigerian governments became subjects of his songs, too. His position against the military regime of General Gowon has caused him much trouble. His record *Zombie* became a most popular hit ("zombie" here refers to soldiers). Though even officers of the Nigerian army danced to the record in their clubs, the soldiery took revenge with a bloody assault on Fela's house.

For many years Fela was one of the few African musicians known all over the world. He sings his songs in Pidgin English, which makes them accessible to a worldwide audience. At first he was known as Fela Ransome-Kuti. He discarded his family name, however, since it originated in the days of slavery and meant "ransom." His present name, translated from Yoruba, means approximately "he who has an arrow in his quiver"—which he can shoot. This, in short, sums up his self-set task and program. In 1984, Fela was sentenced to five years in prison for an alleged currency violation. Finally the Nigerian elite had reached its goal, which had eluded them for many years, and sent one of their most important critics to prison. After nearly two years he was finally released.

Mural of Felix Lebarty "Lover Boy," by Amigo, a bar painter in Freetown, Sierra Leone.

Before its destruction by the military, Fela owned a large estate in Lagos, called Kalakuta Republic. He created a sensation all over the world when he made a show of marrying twenty-seven women at the same time. All of the women have their responsibilities in the band Africa '70 (later, Egypt '80) as singers and dancers. The band itself consists of numerous saxophonists, trumpeters, drummers, percussionists, and, of course, many guitarists. Live performances of the orchestra are a convincing show, and it is a pleasure to hear the slowly unfolding compositions, which always extend through complete LP sides.

The interesting record covers for Fela's music ought not be forgotten. The first series was designed by the artist Ghariokwu Lemi, who reinforced the songs' political content with his drawings and cartoons.[48]

### SWEET MOTHER

Prince Nico Mbarga, born of Nigerian and Camerounian parents, lives in Nigeria. His song texts are almost exclusively in Pidgin English. *Sweet Mother,* a title he recorded with the Rocafil Jazz Band, became his biggest success. In addition, it is believed to be the biggest hit ever in Africa. Thirteen million copies of *Sweet Mother* were supposedly sold in Africa and the international market.[49]

Nico Mbarga releases his records on the Roger All Stars label. His music lies between traditions of east Nigerian Highlife and Congo jazz.

*Sweet Mother* is one of a few examples of African music that have enjoyed great popularity outside of their native boundaries— and for many years at that. *Sweet Mother,* it is said, originated in Kenya. It was re-introduced there in Prince Nico Mbarga's version by Slim Ali.

### WOMEN IN NIGERIAN POP MUSIC

Neither in classical Highlife or juju Highlife have there been any female singers or musicians who made a big name for themselves, with the possible exception of juju singer Lady Ola Balogun. There are, however, many female singers and composers in many other areas of popular music. Most women may be found in pop, disco, and funk styles. Many recording artists well-known in

Nigeria could be listed here. Most important to note is that they reach an international, especially a U.S.-American or British audience. Of course, there are differences in standards among them. Some only copy the international repertory; others still have connections to African music, however vague they may be. Nelly Uchendu, for instance, is among the latter.

Some of the more famous female pop stars are Christie Essien Igbokwe, Dora Ifudu, and Onyeka Onwenu. The Lijadu sisters occupy a special position. Their music follows traditional Yoruba music, the Afro-beat of Fela, and reggae, but also international pop music.

Women are especially well represented in religious music, Christian as well as Islamic. A great number of women's choirs are maintained by different independent African Christian churches in the country. One of the most important is the Good Women's Choir of the C.A.C. (Christian Apostolic Church) of Ibadan, which has recorded numerous LPs.

## Brass Bands and Double-Decker Busses in Freetown

The musical development in Sierra Leone took a course similar to that in Ghana and Nigeria. One aspect, however, distinguishes Sierra Leone: the history of its capital Freetown. It was founded by English philanthropists in 1787 to repatriate liberated slaves of African origin. After slave trading had been banned in the British Empire in 1807, the British captured slave transport ships and relocated the freed slaves in Sierra Leone; thus Freetown received its name. Since the former slaves came from all over West Africa, the most distinct cultures and languages met in Freetown and its surrounding peninsula ("the Colony") and formed a new independent culture and society. From a predominantly English vocabulary and a grammar based on African languages, a new language developed, Krio. The "Creoles" were christianized and educated by British missionaries and became for many years the backbone of the colonial administration. With independence approaching and with the growing influence of the population from the interior country (called "upcountry" by the Creoles), the dominance of Creoles had to be reduced, especially in the political sector.

Even today, popular culture in Freetown is characterized by

Record covers of 10-inch 78 RMP shellac records with "exotic" illustrations. The store, Records Palace, is no longer in existence.

Creole influence, which has become enriched, supplemented, and diversified by inhabitants of different provinces of the country relocating in Freetown. At "Thanksgiving" (the anniversary of the foundation of certain schools), brass bands march through the streets of the inner city on Sundays. I witnessed one such day: first came the band of the school celebrating Thanksgiving, then the pupils in their school uniforms, followed by the teachers, and, finally, the "old boys," dressed in old English tradition in straw hats, carrying walking-sticks and charmingly frolicking to the music of the marching band. Reminiscences of New Orleans! Coming next—corresponding to the reputation of the school—were more bands from schools more or less well known. The instruments were, naturally, not the newest. There hardly was a trumpet that had not been through many adventures. The procession was interrupted for a service at a church and, as a concession to Freetown's newer residents, at a mosque.

A dance band of female police officers played modern Sierra Leonean dance music in the garden of the State House: a mixture of Highlife and Congo rumba to reggae, with pleasant-sounding brass choirs and guitars. On the lot in front, army and police bands performed a tattoo in British fashion. The police dressed in blue jackets and the army in red coats; it was a colorful show.

Late in the afternoon, a funeral procession moved through the streets of Freetown. A woman, 103 years old, had died, and after

The maringa singer and guitarist Ebenezer Calender at the door of his house in Free-
town in 1984. This costume, which included a long black wig, was reserved for special
occasions.

the service in church, Calender's Band was playing. Calender himself was not present. Instead, the trumpeter "Locomotive," who normally played with Prison's Dance Band, had joined in. In addition, there were two drummers in the band: one played the big drum carried in front and beaten from the side; the other played a smaller drum. Finally, there was a musician playing cymbals. Leading the procession were the chaplains, in robes similar to academic gowns and hats, playing simple percussion instruments. Women participating in the funeral procession sang and danced exuberantly in high spirits.

Ebenezer Calender, it was said, had pains in his knee and could not march in the procession that day. The following day, however, he sat in the studio of Sierra Leone Broadcasting System (SLBS) with six musicians and recorded *en bloc* four shows, each half an hour long. Each show proceeded according to a certain principle: Calender told a story in Krio, and a pivotal sentence became the first line of the next strophe or its refrain. The band played percussion instruments, among them three drums, a triangle, a milk-can scraper, and a rattle. Calender played his guitar, still in maringa style; his band, on the other hand, played in gombe style, according to Chris During.[50] Gombe (or gumbe) music is a sort of "proto-Highlife," as John Collins wrote.[51] Calender himself played gombe music before he developed his maringa style.

From the 1940s to the 1960s, Calender was popular and famous for his maringa music. Shellac records on Decca, HMV, and the local label Bassophone originated in those years. Calender was something of a moral institution to Krio society, since he performed at births, weddings, and wakes. For decades, he had broadcasts scheduled regularly on the radio, and later on television as well. Nevertheless, he remained a modest person to his death on Good Friday of 1985. He began as a trained joiner and earned his living as a coffin maker. His music and songs enriched many others, yet he never made his fortune.

One of his songs took up the maiden voyage of double-decker busses in Freetown in January 1951. A singer like Calender is also a historiographer of popular events:

> Welcome to Sierra Leone, double-decker bus.
> Welcome to Sierra Leone, double-decker bus.

Mr. Stobbat, Mr. Gorman, and the citizens had a party at . . .

My grandfather and my grandmother
Refused to go to the top stairs.

Welcome to Sierra Leone, double-decker bus.
Alleluia. Welcome to Sierra Leone, double-decker bus.

The driver was Mr. Abdulai Bah
Who drove the governor round the town
. . . at Oxford Street, oh happy meeting . . .

Welcome to Sierra Leone, double-decker bus.
Alleluia. Welcome to Sierra Leone, double-decker bus.

The manager is Mr. Stobbat.
His assistant is Mr. Garmon.
They are trying to do their level best
By sending the double-decker.

Welcome to Sierra Leone, double-decker bus.
Alleluia. Welcome to Sierra Leone, double-decker bus.

Mr. Stobbat, Mr. Gorman, and the citizens
Had a party in east to west.
My grandfather and my grandmother
Refused to go to the top stairs.

Welcome to Sierra Leone, double-decker bus.
Alleluia. Welcome to Sierra Leone, double-decker bus.[52]

At night in Freetown, one may have the opportunity to attend a performance of probably the best-known band in Sierra Leone: Afro National Band, under the leadership of Sule and the singer Patricia Koroma (by now married to Sule). Afro National plays old numbers and popular titles by other musicians. The band released LPs in the United States and Great Britain, and some titles, like *Money Palaver* (available as a single in Sierra Leone), had great success.

Afro National, however, has not released any records for a long time. The reason is that the record trade in Sierra Leone has collapsed, and record production does not exist anymore. There are no more records or record players to buy. On the sidewalk, perhaps, it is possible to purchase a few old singles, but that is all. Records found in so-called "recording studios" are not for sale! They are only used for copying to cassette tapes and constitute the

Inside one of the so-called "recording studios" which produce pirated copies.

capital of the store, as it were. If one wants to obtain this or that music, it can be ordered and, against down payment, it will be copied by the next day (if that is not hindered by power outages). Even favorite single titles may be copied by themselves on demand. True service! But not for the musicians in Sierra Leone and elsewhere. Institutions like these recording studios are the end of any music production. No band, no musician, can sell a record in Sierra Leone under these conditions. Probably for that reason, Afro National hardly performs any new titles at live concerts in order to avoid new pirated tapes being sold. Sule sees this as the only chance for Afro National and other groups to release their own tapes at a price lower than pirated ones (whose price was about eight dollars in 1985).

The profits of this business go to the owners of recording studios. This situation has progressed so far in Sierra Leone that even the broadcasting system is dependent on the recording studios.

These have to import only one copy of a record or cassette tape which will then be copied in any number. The broadcasting system does not even have the funds to buy one new record. Consequently, they play pirated tapes as advertisements for the recording studios. Otherwise, there would not be any new and current "record" on the radio, a truly macabre situation.

One positive aspect of the recording studios is that, in a few cases, local musicians can occasionally circulate their music relatively well despite the lack of a functioning record industry. Thus, the Mende accordion player Salia Koroma (who is now over eighty years old and formerly recorded many 78 RPM shellac records) can distribute his current songs on tape.[53]

Many musicians, however, go abroad. Most musicians of Super Combo, for instance, have retreated to London; others went to the

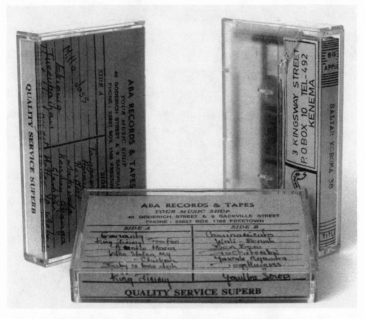

Pirated cassettes are sold at markets. ABA Records & Tapes in Freetown has its own stores and prints its own labels.

United States. Super Combo was once the leading band next to Afro National. Bunny Mack had great success in Nigeria with a fusion of Afro-beat, reggae, and calypso. A small dance band discovered another possibility: Jehpeh Londo, under the direction of

Bunny Mack, painting by Amigo in Freetown, Sierra Leone.

Abou Whyte, played for tourists on the Canary Islands, and recorded and released a number of singles in Spain. At least something! Naturally, these records cannot be purchased in Freetown, but many recording studios own copies.

Mural by Amigo in the O.T.S. (On the Spot) bar at Freetown.

# 4

# GOURD TRUMPETS AND
# GUITAR MUSIC

■

## Beni Ngoma, Danzi, Tarab: Tanzania

### THE BENI NGOMA

At the end of the nineteenth century, associations, called beni ngoma (*beni* = band, *ngoma* = music), had formed in the cities on the East African coast. They organized dance festivities that on first sight simply looked like copies of European military drills. Often in uniform-like clothing, the participants marched in different formations. A beni ngoma had a hierarchical structure with ranks and honorary titles. During these festivities the commanders were honored in order of their rank. The senior ranks were entrusted with the administration of the group and had to look after the well-being of the members.

The beni ngomas continued an old tradition of coastal culture: dance competitions, which included exhibitions of military proficiency. Characteristic was the appearance of two competing groups facing each other. In the colonial situation, these unions offered an opportunity for employees and military personnel of the colonial rulers to define their own domain in life outside of areas of influences controlled by Europeans. Here they had their own hierarchies, their own pride, and their own amusements.

The following song is an excerpt from a beni ngoma song of

118

1918. It was recorded in Nairobi but supposedly is part of Tan-
ganyikan song tradition. It is a post-war song that apparently
incorporates the perspective of the Askari (black colonial soldiers). *Arinati* is a word describing one side of the competing beni
ngoma formations, literally meaning infantry. The other half is
called *marini,* standing for marines.

> Lend me a guitar;
> let the Arinati dance;
> let me set the troop dancing.
> When the guitar is sounding may it beguile me,
> let not this solitude last.
> We think of a maiden so black and so slim;
> her mother bore her and God adorned her.
> Let us please her to see her silvery teeth.
> If she fails to laugh she shows us no silver.[1]

For all that, the beni ngoma was above all a musical event. In
Bantu-speaking regions, "ngoma" stands for dance, music, and
singing. The collective term is an indication that these factors
hardly ever occur independently. Something like absolute music—
without singing and dancing—rarely happens in Africa.

Just as the division of the participants of a beni ngoma was a
reflection of military order, the instrumentation imitated that of
military bands. Besides the big drum, it included various wind instruments. Missing brass instruments were replaced with gourd
trumpets. Adequate manipulation of growth allowed control over
the shape of a gourd. Even gourds with multiple coils could be
grown. It did not altogether sound like a brass band as we know it,
but it was still quite impressive. The calabashes were blown like
kazoos and produced a polyphonic sound pattern, as can be heard
on a very rare recording.[2]

## DANZI SUPERSEDE BENI NGOMA

The beni ngoma tradition continued under British rule even after
the end of German colonial times. Only at the end of the 1940s
did the beni ngoma begin to disappear. At the time of independence it had completely vanished. While the events of World War I
manifested themselves even in its home country and allowed the
beni ngoma to reflect these events, World War II dealt the final
death-blow. The young men who had fought for the British (in

Burma, for instance) had seen the world and had experienced new music, new dances and new living customs. What they brought back home were mostly current European social dances, which fell into the category of "danzi."

Danzi, that is, ballroom dancing, already had been known in East Africa in the 1920s. Indian traders had brought the first record players and 78 RPM records into the country, playing Indian music to attract customers.[3] Dance styles like the danzi employed accordion, harmonica, and guitar.[4] Differing from beni ngoma, danzi were not community oriented.

But even beni ngoma groups attempted to adapt to changing circumstances. Groups in Mombasa (apparently equipped with real brass instruments) renamed themselves in the 1940s and 1950s, for example, Kingi Jazz Band and Scotchi Jazz Band. ("Kingi" = king, and "Scotchi" = Scotsman, constituted opposing pairs of competing groups in Mombasa.) They had cornets, bugles, and flutes. Soon the music was called brass band jazz, or simply "brasso." Dancing clubs had emerged in the 1930s: these, too, were a form of modernized beni ngoma. But all these endeavors did not help, and new music and social changes led to the ultimate disappearance of beni ngomas.

The new music was represented, on the one hand, by the so-called "urban jazz" or kwela, which reached the east from South Africa, and, on the other hand, by Arabic music and Congo jazz. Yet, even in modern dance orchestras of the late 1960s, like Dar es Salaam Jazz Band or Morogoro Jazz Band, vestiges of beni ngoma may be found. The Dar es Salaam Jazz Band, for example, had a steady audience of fans, similar to a soccer fan club, that accompanied the band to all performances.

"Tanzania's pop music fans today are solo crazy," wrote *Now in Tanzania* in April 1969.

Every song played at the various city halls these days has a solo . . . A solo is an instrumental piece performed by one person, usually the guitarist . . . It is the solo that makes or breaks the song, since it is the piece that evokes the most spontaneous reaction from the floor. Often a song with a good solo is greeted with shouts, whistling, howls, or claps. Dancers will shout "encore" four, five, or maybe six times depending on what the solo does to them. All dancing becomes uninhibited during a solo . . . The musicians themselves are happy when a solo "kills" . . . Many times a group of young men would dance in a line or circle, and during the solo,

Military instruments such as the bugle were among the first Western musical influences.

arouse themselves to a state of great excitement. "It is an act of faith dancing a solo played by your favorite band." Tanzania's favourite solo players are in Nuta, Dar es Salaam, and Morogoro Jazz Bands . . . These bands, notably those of Dar es Salaam, have a hard-core following of about one hundred people who attend every dance at which their favourite band plays.[5]

### CULTURAL POLICIES IN TANZANIA

After independence (*uhuru*) in 1961, new cultural policies emerged step by step. A so-called "Consciousness Campaign" began on the radio in 1964 as part of nationalistic efforts. The Arusha declaration of 1967 propagated Tanzania's own approach to socialism. In 1973, Radio Tanzania decided to air no more foreign music (with the exception music of Zaire) on national programs. International pop music only appeared in programs broadcast to foreign countries, primarily to southern Africa.

In contrast, to the broadcasting systems of other countries once under British control, which customarily take into consideration the various African languages, the Tanzanian broadcasting system transmits only in the national language, Kiswahili. Since 1970, even English may be heard only in international programs. All that corresponds to the declared policy to create one nation. The fact that multiple languages may exist even within one nation, and that these have a right to be considered, is officially disregarded. The politics of language are reflected not only in the broadcasting system, but in the educational sector and in literature as well. I do not know, however, whether music groups sing exclusively in Kiswahili, or whether they may sing in other languages as well.

The establishment of a new Department for National Culture and Youth Programs in 1974 placed the entire cultural field, and especially music, under one bureaucratic administrative structure. A national music council (Baraza la Muziki la Taifa =

This picture by Adeusi of Tanzania shows a recording from the microphone directly to the record. Technical processes come to pass magically. "Square paintings" of this kind, so called because of their format, were encouraged by western technical advisers. Local murals were transferred to hardboards with lacquer paints.

BAMAUTA) was created, appointed to oversee planning and execution of governmental musical policies. A vast network of cultural agencies was set up in the districts. BAMUTA was closely associated with Tanzania Film Company (which has a monopoly on the publication of records), Radio Tanzania, and the Household and Bicycle Agency, which holds the only permit to import music instruments. Furthermore, BAMUTA is responsible for licensing dance halls, discotheques, night clubs, etc., to music groups and producers.[6]

Tanzania's economic problems and resulting shortages of foreign currency meant that many musicians and groups could not obtain the necessary equipment through official channels. Hence, an unofficial private market emerged that illegally imports music instruments and also sells tapes with Tanzanian music to Nairobi. In Tanzania, there exists no recording industry and no facility to press records. Yet there are records by Tanzanian groups as a result of the illegal trade. Radio Tanzania speaks of pinched tapes in this context: how else could a series of records have appeared under the Moto-Moto label of the Kenyian company A.I.T. It is obvious that the situation of royalties is not exactly satisfactory. Besides, Tanzania has not joined in any international copyright agreement.

The lack of a recording industry and production facilities caused the broadcasting system to become the central promoter of musicians and bands. It is responsible for an exceedingly active local music scene. According to Wallis, 6,000 traditional music and dance groups (*ngoma*), 120 Swahili "jazz" bands, 60 tarab groups, 50 choirs, and 30 brass bands existed in 1979.[7]

Radio Tanzania uses an archive that contained in 1980 about one thousand five hundred tapes with recordings of fifty-six different orchestras. To my knowledge, Radio Tanzania makes weekly recordings of at least two electric bands as well as choirs and traditional groups, often far away from the capital. Only one music and dance group with traditional orientation and three police brass bands are directly supported by the government.[8]

The choirs are so-called *kwaya,* a term derived from the English "choir." They reach back to early missions, but today they do not necessarily have a direct connection to the church. Musically they are characterized by four-part harmony of Western origin sung over traditional percussive rhythms. Parallel thirds and sixths can also be discerned often but, as ethnomusicologists tell us, they are also part of local music traditions.[9] The traditional scheme of responsorial singing—lead singer and choir—is common.

Under the influence of music from Congo and especially guitar playing, the previously dominant brass instruments were pushed completely into the background. In the 1950s it was the guitar style of Mwenda Jean Bosco and other guitarists from Katanga (today's Shaba). Among other languages, they sang in an inland Kiswahili, which was used as a lingua franca in Congo. In the 1960s, Congo jazz from Kinshasa and Brazzaville became the dominate music. It opened the door for many musicians from the former Belgian Congo who left for East Africa during the conflicts after independence. These musicians were popular and much in demand.

Groups like Cuban Marimba Band showed strong Congolese influences during the 1960s, together with Arabian elements from the Islamic coastal regions.[10] The Nuta Jazz Band were celebrities during the seventies. NUTA stands for National Union of Tanzanian Workers: apparently all eleven musicians were members of that union. Bands like this one conveyed political content and created fashions.

Nuta Jazz Band included three electric guitars, an electric bass, a rattle, a tambourine, a set of trap drums, and a cow bell. One of the three guitars played the leading melody part, the second played a melodic ostinato figure, and the third—the "high guitar"—played a clear embellishment over the leading melody, all throughout the piece. The bass stressed the rhythmic component rather than the harmonic, yet, without denying its harmonic function. Of the percussion instruments, the rattle and the tambourine were constantly present. The trap drums performed cross rhythms against almost all of the rest of the orchestra. The drums were employed rather like an African drum, and not like Western drums. The use of the cow bell was limited. Its function was to enrich the rhythm and to underscore outstanding moments of the performance. In addition, it was used to indicate to the rest of the ensemble when to proceed to the next piece.[11]

One Tanzanian group, Orchestra Makassy, which came originally from Zaire, has become known in Europe through a record recorded in Nairobi and sung in Kiswahili that was released by a London-based company.[12] One of the most famous Tanzanian artists, Mbarako Muinshehe died in a car accident in 1979. The orchestras Mlimani Park and Orchestra Maquis Original are both highly ranked in Tanzania.

## TARAB MUSIC

Through sailors and immigrants, the coastal regions of East Africa came under Arabian and Indian influence in the course of the centuries. At times, Islamic sultans and emirs ruled the East African

Alley in the old section of Mombasa, the great seaport on the Indian Ocean with Arabic characteristics (1964).

coast. Thus, Swahili culture experienced a strong influx of Arabian elements. Oboes, harmoniums, rattles, drums, and nowadays also the electric fiddle, as well as a certain singing style are distinctive to tarab music. ("Tarab" is derived from the Arabic word for music.) At first tarab seems to sound rather Arabian, and only after extensive listening do African rhythms become discernible. The music is performed at various family festivities, to which famous musicians and female singers are invited. In the meantime, the music also exists on records, both ethnological and commercial. There are distinct dances corresponding to particular occasions, and the instrumentation varies accordingly. The old oboe (*sumari*) is often replaced today by the trumpet.

Modern tarab music has been influenced by Indian film music. The sentimental Indian films, which include lots of music and singing, are shown all over Africa, if only because they are cheaper to obtain than European and American productions.

Yassen Mohamed and Party is one of the groups recording tarab. Others are Hafusa Abbasi and the Yahoos Band, Saida, and ASP Youth Musical Club (from Kenya). Siti Binti Saad (1880–1950) was among the first female tarab singers released on record.[13] The texts of her songs, too, relate to love, politics, work, education; in short, all subjects that affect people's lives.

## Stars and Producers: Kenya

In Kenya, unlike Tanzania, there are no officially determined cultural policies. Instead, local musicians face a strong presence of international recording companies. Since Polygram owns the only record press in the country, demands for a second press are heard again and again, for instance, from Adam Kutahi. Kutahi established the first Kenyan recording company under African ownership in 1965: Mwangaza Music.[14] There is, however, no second press thus far. On the other hand, Kenya has a local performing rights society for musicians (MPRSK), an exception in Africa.

By international standards, the sales figures for Kenya are still quite insignificant. If Kenya sells 2.5 million singles a year, that is comparable to one sales week in Great Britain or a single day in the United States, where it may even happen that one million copies of an album are sold within an hour of release.[15] By comparison, the Kenyan musician Slim Ali received a "Silver Record" for thirty thousand copies sold.[16]

Phonogram is the second largest record company after AIT. According to its own account, it dominates the music market from Zaire and Tanzania. It also produces records for the African market outside of Kenya. EMI is a relative newcomer to Kenya. A manager of the company, Graham Shepherd, in 1977 remarked in astonishment that there is absolutely no interest in Kenyan artists by the general population: the native musician has such an absolutely low status that nobody asks him for autographs, nor is he beset by fans; musicians are considered drunkards and lazy, and as such they are judged. It is obvious that where certain phenomena do not correspond to those of the European or American pop busi-

The Maroon Commandos were a pop band from Kenya.

ness, the sympathy of the manager ends. In the meantime, EMI has left Kenya again.

Besides foreign record producers, there are a great number of independent African producers who also collaborate, however, with one of the great international companies. P. Oluoch Kanindo, for instance, worked with EMI. Formerly he worked for *Drum*[17] and was employed as a radio announcer. Ethnically he belongs to the Luo people, which is relevant inasmuch as he attends to the music of his native region. He produces mainly Luo bands and songs with Luo texts. Kanindo sells his records in Malawi, Zambia, Nigeria, France, Madagascar, and The Gambia. Benga-beat, the Luo version of modern dance music, sells particularly well. Benga-beat supposedly is built on traditional drum rhythms of the Luo.

Kanindo shows himself in a Mercedes with a chauffeur, and he flies from Nairobi into his region. That is where he gets *his* bands and *his* musicians. The best known are Shirati Jazz Band and Victoria Jazz Band. In his self-portrait, the problems facing Kenya's musicians became clearly visible. He presents himself as the prototype of an ice-cold manager of the American school: "When a band becomes hostile, I break them! I choose the best men and mix them and give them instruments." This means they are nothing without him. No musician could afford the expensive instruments. A complete LP is recorded in a single day. Ironically, one of Kanindo's labels is even called "Angel: Music of the People, for the People, by the People." Often the bands earn only a fixed amount for recording a single, no matter how high the sales may be. Contracts including royalties are only offered at later recordings.[18]

CBS promoted Daudi Kabaka as a local celebrity and recorded singles with the Orchestra Maquis du Zaire of Tanzania. Eagles Lupopo Band (featuring Daudi Kabaka and Sarah Abukutsa) developed Kenyan reggae, sung in Kiswahili.

### DANIEL KAMAU

Daniel Kamau, likewise, is a producer who brings out primarily bands from his native Kikuyu region, but he is himself also a musician. According to his own statement, he visits the old men of his people to learn from them more about old "deep" Kikuyu in conversations, so he may use it again in his songs. Proverbs are naturally a part of it. Kamau owns a number of record stores and controls the distribution of his records.

An LP by RCA comprises twelve of his single titles. The record jacket contains the following biographical information about him:

Daniel Kamau was born on February 2, 1949, in Murang'a, in central Kenya . . . Daniel was only nine years old when his father died in the fight against colonial rule. He continued to go to school while his brothers pursued various activities. They also played guitar, and young Daniel listened and watched carefully how they drew magic tones from their self-made box guitars.

But Daniel was not allowed to play his guitar. His brothers said that he was too young and should be concerned about school. So there was nothing left but to take a brother's guitar secretly, and, soon skilled in magic tones, he released his first record, *Mami Tiga Guthura,* while he was still a student. And thus began his ascent to become one of Kenya's top musicians . . .

His inspiring manner of phrasing and his beautiful lyrical love songs earned him thousands of fans, and he never disappointed them. He released one hit after another.

In 1970 he was on top again: he established his own label and made his own recordings. *Koruo Ni Ndoi* was his first independent production, and ever since then his label has become stronger and stronger. There is hardly any week in which a D.K. record is not on the charts. That prompted Kenya's music critics to celebrate D.K. as the irrevocable Number One in Kenya.

In 1976, Daniel felt that he had to broaden his musical experiences, and to set about it, he made for London. On his return, he decided to record an album . . . He talked to AIT records who made the recording and put D.K.'s first LP on the market. Number one for Number One.[19]

## SLIM ALI

Slim Ali sings mainly in English, Western mainstream pop, but also reggae and African pop pieces. On his LP *Sweet Mother,* he sings a slightly altered version of Prince Nico Mbarga's original; he has some problems, however, with Nigerian Pidgin.

The cover text addressing Slim Ali's biography makes clear that great value is put on international musical experience:

Slim was born in December 1947 in Mombasa, where he also attended school. Relatively late, at Hamisi Secondary School, he began to take music more seriously and played in the school band. He sang the current popular standards.

After graduating from school, he moved to Nairobi and initiated steps that became the basis for his subsequent full engagement in music. After briefly playing with Tusker Band and Kitale Hotel band, Slim joined the Hodi Boys in 1968. At this point, the Hodi Boys were still young and copied songs that had made Otis Redding and Percy Sledge famous.

But Slim longed to travel, and his voice served as a vehicle. He went to Addis Ababa, Djibouti, and Aden and toured the whole Middle East. He played with the most diverse groups, but he always intended to settle down and record seriously. And so it happened that Slim returned to Nairobi in 1976 and again joined the Boys. Here he translated all the experiences gained on his world tour into music.

In late 1976, Slim Ali and The Hodi Boys recorded *You Can Do It*. It

A Kenyan single with printed cover.

turned out to be the crucial record that established Slim Ali, as well as The Hodi Boys, as one of the international bands in Africa on account of their distinctive sound.[20]

## THE CASE OF MALAIKA

*Malaika* is one of the few songs of African origin that has been disseminated throughout the world. Like no other song, the history of *Malaika* (more exactly, *Malaika Nakupenda,* translated "Angel, I Love You") demonstrates the problems and questions of copyright. A case in point is that nobody ever speaks about the composer Lukas Tututu of Frere Town near Mombasa.[21] Fadhili Williams of Nairobi is generally considered the actual owner of the copyright. He first released the song on record, a ten-inch 78 RPM shellac record by Equator Sound.[22]

Miriam Makeba included the song in her repertory and had great success with it. Not enough: even outside of Africa a variety of performers took up the song and made it a hit, among them Boney M., Harry Belafonte, Pete Seeger, Benny Andersson, the Saragossa Band, and the Les Humphries Singers.[23] If international copyright agreements had been observed, Fadhili Williams surely would be a rich man today. Nobody questioned the sevenfold division of copyright claims for *Malaika*. Yet even Miriam Makeba, who once had recognized Fadhili Williams's copyright, today collects for herself. All are pocketing money and Fadhili Williams—not to mention Lukas Tututu—is the loser. Fadhili Williams mentioned sometime in 1976–77 that he once received £1,000 from the United States after fifteen years! And that even though Kenya is a member of the International Copyright Convention.

## WHAT THEY ARE SINGING ABOUT

The texts deal with all possible themes, anything that affects the people in the streets. There are social commentaries and moral considerations: unemployment, the rent, alcohol, prostitution, and lazyness were taken up as subjects. Addressing everyday problems should also be seen as a continuation of the traditional function of African music.

In respect to political themes, John Mwale composed a song full of optimism about the East African Federation that was contemplated but never realized.

*African Federation (Shirikisho la Afrika)*

African Federation—
we all have mixed in together;
come on you fellows,
let's rejoice at African Federation.
In East Africa we have all united—
Kenya, Uganda, and Tanganyika, all you people of Africa.
Let's honor our leaders who drafted federation:
Kenyatte, Obote, and Nyerere.[24]

The twist is the subject of the following song, whose author has remained anonymous.

*Twist of the Young People (Twist ya vijana)*

Listen, brothers, hear—today
we tell the newest from Nairobi:

There are many people in the city of Nairobi
who enjoy dancing the twist.

On the way you meet children
continuously singing and dancing the twist.

The women, too, are leaving their houses
to go idle and twist.

The pupils, too, forget their lessons
because they like the twist.

The twist is beautiful, and the boys love it;
but the parents don't like it.

Listen, brothers, hear—today
we tell the newest from Nairobi.[25]

The following song is composed by an anonymous poet as well:

*Poverty (Umasikini)*

If I were rich, I would be happy.
I would built myself a city, a beautiful one.
Poverty is a very bad thing.
It has ruined my life.
Take it easy, boy in the city.
The fortune of your friend is not yours.
Look, I have come from far away because of money.
Now I sleep far away from home because of money.
Now I leave you, God, because of money.
Now I leave the children because of money.[26]

The significance of the last lines becomes apparent only if we consider the importance of children in Africa. Children represent the continuation of family and community, and they support parents in old age. A household with many children is still considered a rich household.

## DRY GUITAR

Kenya's early guitar style, like that of Tanzania, was influenced by guitar playing of Katanga (Shaba) musicians. Mwenda Jean Bosco even spent several months in Kenya in 1959 to advertize Aspro, the pain reliever. John Storm Roberts captured the beginnings of recorded guitar music in Kenya on his collective LP *The Nairobi Sound*. It contains magnificent pieces from the sixties and seventies. The acoustic guitar is called "dry guitar": most often one or two guitarists perform together with a percussionist, who beats two Fanta bottles.

### THE LIBERTY OF LISTENING TO BONEY M. AND ABBA

A revaluation of East African pop music in Kenya even caused great problems to the Department of Information: in March 1980, it decreed that, starting immediately, 75 percent of all music in regular (English-speaking) programs had to be of Kenyan origin. In view of Tanzania's procedure, this appeared to be a cautious solution, and it occurred primarily in competition with Tanzanian broadcasts that were very popular in Kenya. For Kenyan conditions, however, it was asking too much. The directive was issued so suddenly that it was practically impossible for Voice of Kenya to comply. They were accustomed to playing the softest pop from Abba to Boney M.: now the disc jockeys were asked to put on local titles. Voice of Kenya had neither the resources nor the intention to do that. The Kenyan disc jockeys made their living by presenting international stars, and they identified themselves with that music. They looked upon local music with contempt. Imagine a comparable situation here in Germany, if German disc jockeys were allowed to play only German productions.

A disc jockey from Voice of Kenya expressed his sentiments as follows:

I am under-payed. I am over-worked. The local music sounds so terrible that nothing I could say between numbers comes to my mind. It is com-

Mural by Ringo Arts of Nairobi (1985).

pletely different if one puts on Abba or Boney M. I don't understand why they want us to play Kenyan music, which the people don't want to hear.[27]

The question here probably is this: Which people do not want to listen to local music, and which people would prefer it? That is the crucial point. After only two weeks, the ministerial directive was withdrawn. Musicians and small record companies suspected that the employees of Voice of Kenya and international record companies had sabotaged the government resolution. The management of Phonogram, in turn, suspected a lobby of small African companies behind the new direction. The affair started a big debate to and fro. The two opposing positions, however, remained: one side advocated a stronger consideration of Kenyan music, the other wanted to accept only Western music as the only possible form of entertainment.

How important it can be in Africa to have the right music available at the right time is suggested by the example of a failed coup against President Moi on August 1, 1982. Instead of the gentle rolling sounds of Jim Reeves, Kenyans woke up to East African pop.[28] "An employee of Voice of Kenya who 'survived' the coup attempt argued whether the Kenyan Air Force—supposedly responsible for the coup attempt—did not make a tactical mistake in its selection of music. Marching music should accompany any coup attempt, not African pop."[29] On the other hand, a song by Joseph Kamura (recorded by the City Sound Band) is said to have been responsible, as the singer expressed it himself, for having "brought Kenya back to normal"—that according to a CBS staff member.[30] The song praises the government and expresses hope that it will succeed in restoring order. The record aptly begins with gun shots!

# 5

## MUSIC OF LIBERATION

■

### From Kalela to Kalindula: Zambia

[Q] The women of the beer hall have stolen my husband. School girls in ruffled petticoats constantly hang about the place and oblige him for money or beer. If I stay home, I will loose my husband forever. So I go with him and we drink together, and then we quarrel. We have a sad home, and I am ashamed. Perhaps one day, someone will turn the beer halls into schools for our children. But what can I do to preserve my marriage until that day?

[A] I understand your situation, but your participation in such wicked undertakings will not help your marriage. Enroll in cooking classes conducted by welfare agencies. Then learn how you can do up your home nicely. Perhaps your good cooking will lure your husband home.

Ask his permission to buy beer for him and serve it at home when his friends visit. Suggest inviting his friends occasionally for dinner so he may feel encouraged to seek his diversion at home.[1]

This letter and response were printed in the 1950s in the Northern Rhodesian newspaper *Central Africa Mail*. It appeared in a section entitled "Tell me, Josephine." Yet not only women, but men, too, sought advice from Josephine. The following letter is an example:

[Q] A woman once married has taken it into her head to win me over, that is, only if she is drunk. When she is not loaded with beer, she doesn't take notice of me and doesn't molest me. But usually she is drunk, and that is the reason why her husband chased her away.

136

I hardly have fun any more going out and enjoying my can of beer, because as soon as I sit at the table, she steers towards me and embarrasses me with tendernesses and loud talking. My heart sinks when I see her approaching. What can I do without giving up my beloved beer?

[A] Hide under the table until she has passed.[2]

Especially in the Copperbelt,[3] municipalities had built beer halls where beer was sold in gallon-size "cans." The halls and the life in and around them were an expression of industrialization and its social consequences. Workers from all parts of Zambia— the former Northern Rhodesia—and neighboring countries as far as South Africa were hired for the season and housed in company-owned settlements. A great number of them stayed for many years. They took wives without traditional marriage practices, in so-called town marriages. Women mostly came from the vicinity seeking their luck with the workers: workers earned cash money, which in turn could buy the many new imported wares from Europe. Guitarist and singer Alic Nkhata recorded a song describing the sad case of a man finally going home and leaving his wife behind:

> Good-bye. Now I go back to my home where I come from.
> I'm tired of waiting.
> It seems you cannot change your ways.
> Go! Die alone.
> Now I go back to my home where I come from.
> Do not forget your duty: look after your children.
> Even though I go, I will help you support them.
> It is you who have made the mistake.
> You want too much wealth which I can never possess.
> I, poor man, must return to my home.[4]

This song was sung in Cibemba, which serves, mixed with English expressions, as a lingua franca in the Copperbelt.

The workers brought their own musical culture from their countries of origin, thus creating new urban traditions. Corresponding to the beni ngoma dance in East Africa and the malipenga in Malawi, here the kalela dance emerged. Again, dancers participated dressed rather in European style and uniforms, including a ranking order and arrangement in groups. Dancing and singing was accompanied by drums, that is, large barrels covered with cowhide beaten with bent drumsticks.[5]

This mural at Ndola by Green K. Kaosah depicts a mining complex in the copper belt where the artist had worked as a miner.

The urban industrial culture of workers in Zambia's copper belt was not much different from that in neighboring Shaba (Zaire). A musician like Mwenda Jean Bosco, therefore, was a well-known entity in Northern Rhodesia as well. His records and those of Losta Abelo had been sold since the early 1950s, as well as cheap wind-up grammophones known as "talking machines."[6] Even today, the traces of Bosco have not yet disappeared. Guitarist Alfred Kalusha from Luapula province in northern Zambia included two of Bosco's compositions on his LP *Kakonko* (the title refers to a traditional dance).[7]

## ALICK NKHATA, "DREAMER OF SONGS"

Alick Nkhata was probably the best-known musician of Northern Rhodesia especially in the 1950s. A blind minstrel, unfortunately unknown, dubbed him a "dreamer of songs" in one of his songs of praise because of his charm and his showmanship. Alick Nkhata has been described as a very sensible man by his white friends, having been especially sensitive in questions concerning the relationships of blacks and whites. It is important to note that British

Lino-cut of a beer hall by the Zambian artist David K. Chibwe (1981).

Alick Nkhata's quartet: "Good-bye, my love. Go, die alone."

Rhodesia at the time was characterized by an out-and-out racist white predominance. White settlements in the north were not as numerous as in the south (now Zimbabwe), but the aura of supremacy was just as present there. At the time, exception was still taken to addressing an African as "Mister" on the radio.

Before World War II, Alick Nkhata was a teacher. His apparent great talent for playing guitar, singing, and composing was noticed while he was serving as a sergeant in the army during the war. After the war, he received a stipend as an ex-serviceman to further his musical knowledge. He was fortunate to be referred to Hugh Tracey, then director of the International Library of African Music. With him he undertook some recording trips throughout central Africa. After his training, Alick Nkhata was employed by the Central African Broadcasting Station (CABS).[8]

At the station, he attended especially to traditional music. Under his direction recordings were made everywhere in Zambia. But supposedly Alick Nkhata only felt truly at home in his job when he made music himself, playing the guitar with his quartet. His songs dealt with a variety of subjects, often full of humor, even when he pursued educational and moral intentions. Here is an example: the song deals with cooks working for Europeans who had apparently made a name for themselves as "Romeos" (the text was sung in Cibemba; the italicized verses were in English in the original).

> Some young men of today have no sense.
> When they see a girl with painted lips
> they lose their heads.
> Then they speak in English:
> *Yesh, good,*
> alas my beauty,
> come live with me in the yards.
> *You're gonna get bread an' butter*
> I have everything.
> *New look in plenty.*
> You'll have so many dresses
> You'll be changing clothes all day.
> And every morning you'll be taking
> *Morning coffee, toshta an' butter*
> if you live with me
> You'll grow very fat.
> If we two appear in public,
> young men will be shaking their heads
> because of your beautiful clothes.[9]

Alick Nkhata did not know much about the theory of music. He also did not progress very much in being able to read music. Supposedly he made a few attempts in vain "to improve his guitar-playing technique." Probably, these were the results of well-intentioned encouragements by white colleagues at the station. We may assume that Alick Nkhata performed in a style corresponding to those of other African musicians, which was just perfect for the realization of his music. His European friends were in all likelihood not aware of that. How else could he have become the best-known guitarist and the most popular singer in the sphere of influence of CABS with his "simple technique" of playing?[10] He was able to sell records by the thousands.

As a division of the radio station, the quartet was enlarged to the Lusaka Radio Band: the vocal group with guitar was joined by a piano, drums, double bass, and maracas. In order to produce a sufficient number of programs for the radio, recordings of traditional music were searched and suitable pieces were arranged for the new orchestration. Sometimes, that led to extreme contrasts, as Fraenkel reports:

In one [song] the drums and maracas had taken over the rhythm originally provided by maize-pounding pestles, and Nkhata's quartet in smart evening dress sang the plaint of bare-breasted Nsenga women about the drift of men to the centres of European settlement:

> Kalindawalo is a good chief. Oh! Oh!
> Kalindawalo is a good chief. Oh! Oh!
> Only one thing is wrong with his reign,
> The loss of his people.
> They drift away.
> His people sing:
> "I want to see the railway line before I die.
> Before I die I want to see the line of rail."[11]

In addition, Fraenkel remarks:

My favorite among Nkhata's songs was one with a haunting melody like that of a gypsy violin, so sweet and full of suffering. It was a deep allegorical song that he had adapted, but when the allegory was unravelled to me, it turned out to be mean: "Wait until I get that woman into bed. Man, the things I'm going to do to her." . . . I never did understand the African musical conventions![12]

Eventually, Alick Nkhata advanced at the radio station to Deputy Director of Broadcasting and then became director of Zambian Cultural Services.[13] In November 1978 he fell victim to a raid on an alleged camp of Freedom Fighters from Zimbabwe by Southern Rhodesian paratroopers and bombers.[14]

### OUT OF THE SAUCEPAN: WAYALESHI

After the war, in 1945 in Lusaka, the Central African Broadcasting Station was established to broadcast exclusively for Africans. The station for whites was located in Salisbury (today called Harare), the capital of Zimbabwe. Suitable radios that could be powered by batteries, however, were lacking, and only the larger cities in Northern Rhodesia had electricity. At first, Lusaka only had wired radio, and a line could be rented for two shillings, sixpence per month. Starting in 1950, the battery manufacturer Eveready sold a radio set encased in a cooking pot called "The Saucepan Special." It cost five pounds—relatively little compared to the price of one pound, five shillings for the batteries. Surely the cost of batteries was a financial burden much too high for many, but broadcasting had made a breakthrough.

The English "wireless" became the "wayaleshi." Many letters

addressed to the station prove its enormous popularity. Here are two examples:

Many people—men, women, and children—came in large numbers as if they were entering a church, all desirous to hear the news . . . Then they

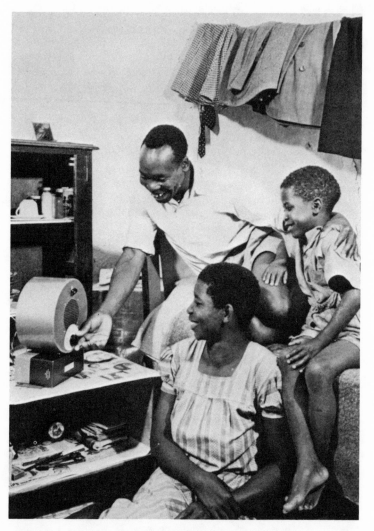

"I feel proud when I switch on my Saucepan Special and have the whole world in my hut."

said: "These Europeans are wonderful people and the wisdom which God gave them is incomparable."

I thank you very much for your work of making our country progress. Through your help we learn many different kind of things by hearing them through our wireless set . . . Therefore I am thanking you and the Government who chose you to work for us we Africans. And you do your duty heartedly for love for Africans.[15]

CABS made many recording trips and then broadcast local music, but it also aired the newest records from America, South Africa, and Southern Rhodesia. That, in turn, stimulated record sales and the development of modern popular music as a whole in Zambia. The Lusaka Radio Band gave the booster charge, as it were, to dance bands in all the larger cities of Zambia. Most bands were purely African, but there were also a number of mixed and white bands.

New dance styles were imported to Zambia, in the first place by migrating workers coming to the Copperbelt from South Africa and Southern Rhodesia—or, reversely, by Zambian workers returning from work in Johannesburg or in the Southern Rhodesian mines. Thus the newest fashions were disseminated relatively quickly. The styles discussed below reached Zambia—sometimes overlapping, but approximately in this chronological succession—and with them, of course, came the corresponding music, transmitted on record or as performed music:

Makwaya; a choral style accompanied by dancing, was especially popular with school teachers and pupils. Some of Alic Nkhata's compositions had makwaya characteristics as, for instance, *Filamba*. Tsaba-tsaba is derived from the Zulu word for "to separate," and the name describes the process of the dance; just before the partners met head-on, they exclaimed "*tsaba*" and again danced apart. Pata-pata and kwela, often also interchangeably called jive, followed—altogether South African dance styles. In the early 1960s, simanje-manje, twist, and sinjonjo came along. After independence, music from Congo was in vogue. It became more easily accessible, especially through East African productions from Nairobi, but also directly across the border.

During the late 1960s, Western rock music exercised a strong influence on modern Zambian music. A particular Zambian variant emerged: zamrock! The various attempts to emulate European and American models (for example, the Beatles, or Jimi Hendrix) demonstrate some basic problems, for instance, (1) a general lack of instruments, and especially good instruments and instruments owned by the musicians; (2) bad recording conditions (that has improved somewhat only in the 1980s); and (3) insufficient musi-

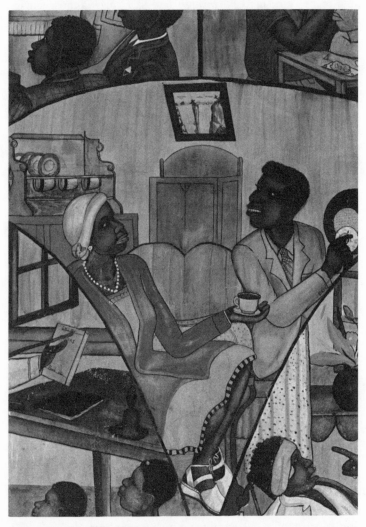

Mural by Ranford Sililo, probably from the 1950s, showing the Saucepan Special. Livingstone Museum, Zambia.

cal education, particularly as far as these emulations are concerned.

In order to record under satisfactory conditions, Zambian groups had to migrate to Kenya. After an eight-channel D.B. studio became available in Lusaka, Keith Mlevhu, for instance, was able to produce his LP *Through Fire to Heaven* almost single-handedly by playback. For the singer and musician Sheleni Shanyinde it was now possible to record a whole string of singles in Lusaka as his own producer, after having recorded an earlier single in Nairobi.[16]

Some additional Zambian musicians ought to be introduced. The band Madzi-a-Moyo ("Water of Life"), which emerged from Mosi-o-Tunya (the Lozi word for the Victoria Falls of the Zambezi river) in 1981, plays Afro-rock and some reggae. In view of the relative isolation of Zambian music, it is important to note that this band was able to tour Mozambique in 1982. Rikki Ililonga even has recorded a record in Denmark, with four Danish musicians and a conga player from the Caribbean. Finally, The Blackfoot should be mentioned, a group that was able to record an LP at the Malachite Film Studio in Chingola *The Foot Steps* (1978).

<h2>KALINDULA</h2>

Thomas Mambo, music columnist of the Zambia Daily Mail, calls kalindula the music that may become as characteristic of Zambia as Highlife is of Ghana:

During colonial times, we had no recording possibilities in Zambia. Musicians went as far as South Africa to record, as Alic Nkhata did, for instance. We mainly imported Congolese records without being able to produce anything ourselves. We received everything from West, East, and South Africa. Simply, we didn't have the time to sit down and contemplate who we were. Yet that tradition is still present. But kalindula, that is a thing that hit like a bombshell.[17]

Where does kalindula come from? Kalindula originated in rural northern Zambia with the Bemba people. It is "festive music" to dance to at "beer parties." It is not a traditional music in a narrow sense, but rather a neo-traditional music. The orchestration consists of acoustic guitar, a two-string bass, drum(s), and percussion. The characteristic sound of kalindula arises from the

Posters from Ndola, the largest city in Zambia's Copperbelt.

bass, for which a long wooden staff, mounted on a double-headed drum, serves as a neck. Kalindula has a continuous rhythm over which the voice sings. The drum has to adjust to the voice; thus, it does not play a central role.

Spokes Chola, together with his Mansa Radio Band (or Mansa Kalindula Band), is one of the famous kalindula performers. Appropriately, one of his singles is entitled *Kalindula.* Here is one of the verbose texts of a Kalindula song by Spokes Chola, *Kapwepwe:*

Mr. Mansa Kapwepwe, your death is terrible. It is a long way to Chinsali, from where you came. You wanted to go off and visit your daughters Sampa in Chilalama. You died in a hospital, here in Chibuluma. It was Saturday at 10 A.M. when you died. Oh, Mr. Kapwepwe, we are sad. I don't even have a car. If I owned one, I would have come to the funeral. If I could see, I would have come to the funeral, too.[18]

In 1981, Spokes Chola's Mansa Kalindula Band was awarded a price for the best "rural" band in Zambia in connection with the distribution of prizes of the National Music Industry. The same occasion resulted in an important breakthrough for kalindula style: The zamrock band 5 Revolutions, a band typical for the ur-

ban music scene received first prize for the best song for its
kalindula adaptation of *Mukamfwilwa*. With this hit, a music
originally limited to a region gained nationwide popularity for the
first time.

Banjo by the Siamucando Brothers Jazz Band (1981).

Yet kalindula has not only developed "upwards," but has also spread within Zambia, down into the south, into the region of the Tonga people at Kariba Lake. There, kalindula pieces are played by juvenile banjo bands, though with different instrumentation. Banjo players and bands, who build their instruments from old motor oil and floor polish cans, may be encountered all over Zambia. A thin wooden board serves as a fingerboard for these banjos, and wire and nails are used for strings and their mounting. Frets are also easily constructed: notches are cut into the fingerboard at adequate distances which are then filled with pieces of wire. All sorts of pieces and music styles are played on these simple instruments. The group Siamukande Brothers Jazz Band of Siamukande, near Nkandabwe is an example. They listened to records by Nashil Pichen (Kazembe),[19] which they then emulated—with all the trimmings.

Why exactly Nashil Pichen? On the one hand, he played Zaire rumba. More important, however, is apparently what a soldier at one of the many road blocks once told me: he loved him for what he was singing about. "His songs mean something to me." That is one of the most important points in understanding African music in general: the song text is of supreme importance to the African listener. For us, however, the texts of certain favorite songs may remain unintelligible.

This also explains why most Africans are not at all interested in songs from another country if they are sung in a language different from their own. There are, of course, exceptions—music from Zaire, for instance. In the 1950s, Bosco was heard with enthusiasm even in Sierra Leone without anybody being able to understand what he was singing about. But it did not take long before something was interpreted into the song: it had to make some sense.

The music of Siamukande Brothers Jazz Band was oriented toward Zaire bands, especially the rumba groups and the banjo styles common all over the country. To a lead banjo and one with bass functions, various percussion instruments were added according to the playing situation. Even a retired petroleum stove could serve the purpose.[20]

Siamukande Brothers Jazz Band hardly adopted any texts, but composed their own songs that reflected their own experiences, local events, and things that appealed to them. Here is an example:

This year we plant.
This year we plant.
This year we have more money than the workers.
We, this year we have more money than the workers. (4x)

Let's try very hard.

Koka!

Let's make it up (to play more).
We are from very far away.
To be full (to make the guitar sound very well),
The guitar only.[21]

### MANDALENA KASAMA/MANDALENA MAZABUKA

Smokey Haangala is one of the few Zambian musicians from the Tonga region who has produced singles and LPs. He, too, developed his present style in a roundabout way. He began his musical career in a rock band, X-Ray. They picked up Beatles songs and then, during the "underground" period, Jimi Hendrix.[22] Haangala still plays acoustic and electric guitar, and sings to it. Today, however, he usually takes a traditional composition and adopts it for guitar. This results in a fascinating yet unassuming expression of his songs, almost always gently flowing along without becoming boring, even if the text is not understood (as in our case). Sometimes even a bit of English is present, which immediately enforces the association with rock music.

In the song *Mandalena Mazabuka* he tells a story about a trip to Mazabuka, where he meets a woman so fantastic that he does not want to leave again. The song was released on a single, sung in Cibemba on side A, and in Citonga on side B. The names of places have been filled correspondingly: Mazabuka for the Tonga listeners, changed to Kasama for the Bemba. This is an attempt to accommodate the manifold structure of the country and, at the same time, to extend the limited market of Tonga buyers with the much larger Bemba market.[23]

## Music and Research: Malawi

Commissioned by the German Africa Society, the Austrian musician and ethnologist Gerhard Kubik in 1967 traveled through Malawi (the former British colony Nyassaland) in order to prepare an account of traditional and neo-traditional music of the country. He met two musicians who impressed him so much that he immediately looked after them. A relationship developed that still flourishes today. Daniel Kachamba (1947–1987) and Donald Kachamba (born 1955) played South African kwela music accompanied by various musicians. When Kubik met the group for the first time in Blantyre, Daniel played guitar, Donald played penny whistle, and a third musician played rattle. Later they were joined by Moya Aliya. Whenever somebody gave the band a three-pence piece, a "tickey," a song was played: "a tickey per record," it was called.

Kubik improved his relationship to the musicians, and, rather

Record cover of an LP by Smokey Haangala (RAK-1). He sings about an recurrent theme in African songs: it is money that matters, especially if one wants to keep a woman. With money you can even get a Mercedes . . .

by accident, he became part of the band. He succeeded in having the two brothers perform at a music festival organized in Nairobi in 1972 by the Goethe Institute. The rattle player was missing, however, and so Gerhard Kubik stepped in as a helper-in-need. In the same year the band traveled to Vienna, now with three members. Besides guitar, penny whistle, and rattle, a tea-chest bass (with one string) was part of the standard instrumentation of the band. Kubik, however, also introduced the clarinet, which he played himself, and which fit perfectly into kwela music.

It was simply standard practice in Malawi in 1967 that the band emulated kwela, simanje-manje, and twist by South African bands. It is unique in Africa, however, that they are still playing this music even today.[24] Original kwela has died out and modern electric styles have replaced it, even in Malawi. Besides, Congolese dance bands flooded all of eastern and south-eastern Africa and, additionally, the influence from the south has diminished.

It was solely and entirely owing to Kubik that these musicians were secured the prospect of a means of support. Thus, they were able to survive by means of their music and did not have to share the fate of most bands, which had to stop making music because of financial difficulties. Kubik remained part of the band. Daniel, however, established himself as a solo guitarist and ever since called himself "Dr." Daniel Kachamba. He died in Malawi in 1987. The Kachamba Brothers' Band became Donald Kachamba's Kwela Band. Today it is probably one of the best-studied neo-traditional bands in Africa.[25] Their playing techniques were photographed by the Institute for Scientific Film in Göttingen.[26] The compositions, compositional techniques, and the texts, as well as the ideas of the musicians, their listening habits, and the range of musical terminology have been analyzed. Today the band has turned into something of a research team itself. They who were once analyzed are by now ethnologists themselves. Moya Aliya Malamusi had worked together with Gerhard Kubik in Zambia and Malawi. It is certainly to their great advantage since African musicians in their research have much better access to many things than Europeans do.[27] Lidiya Malamusi, Moya's sister, joined the band in the late 1980s and was part of the research team until her sudden death in 1989.

When Donald Kachamba's Kwela Band performs today, time seems to have come to a standstill. The gripping, fast rhythm and

"Dr." Daniel Kachamba at a concert given in Tübingen (1984).

the speedy, high playing of the penny whistle everywhere meets the greatest excitement.

The history of popular music in Malawi has not been written either. Here are a few pieces of the yet unfinished puzzle. Mbumba music[28] is among the most popular styles since independence. It is often sung by women at political events. Women sing *a capella,* or a women's chorus accompanied by drums performs in a responsorial game of question and answer, as it were. The best singers are broadcast by Malawi Broadcasting Corporation (MBC).[29]

MBC also maintains its own band, which performs all styles from pop to rumba, mbaqanga, dance music from Zimbabwe, and traditional Malawian music in modern arrangements. The radio also releases its own records on the label Ngoma. In addition, there are the Nzeru Record Company and the Lakeside label, yet these are small companies with little production capacity. Consequently, there is no opportunity for many groups and singers to record a single. On a visit to Zambia in 1979, Malawi's best-known female singer, Maria Nkhoma, complained about lacking chances for advancement in her country. At the time she performed under a four-week contract in a hotel in Lusaka (Zambia). After graduating from school, she began her career as a singer with the radio orchestra in Malawi. She continues to go without producing a record, however, and now fears having to retire from singing.[30]

Among banjo musicians, who form the core of modern musicians in Malawi, the blind Michael Yekha has made a name for himself. The musical spectrum of bands and musicians also includes a number of jazz bands (such as Ndingo Brothers Band, Mulanje Mountain Jazz Band, Nzeru Zatha River Jazz Band, Alan Namoko & Chimvu River Band, etc.) and the so-called Afroma (Afro = rock = Malawi) groups, which include Love Aquarius with Maria Chidzanja and Ed Manda, New Scene A, Chenasau Roots, Super Kaso Makusa, etc., and the heavy metal group Gas Machine Head.[31]

## Chimurenga Requests: Zimbabwe

The traditional music of Southern Rhodesia has disappeared to an alarming degree. Christian missionaries, recognizing the close relationship between heathen religion and music, ensured a fast

decline in traditional culture.[32] White Rhodesian society, which
took its bearing from principles of apartheid, further advanced the
contempt kindled among the black population for their own
culture.[33] Only emerging nationalism during the 1960s (at the
time, other states in West, Central and East Africa became independent) and world-wide recognition of black culture, including
the Black Power movement in the United States, led to a recon-
sideration of their own traditions. The mbira players were
recognized again and valued more highly.

The mbira is the classic instrument of Zimbabwe. An entire
musical genre developed around it, within which instrument
types, customs of playing, styles, song texts, and functions may be
discerned. Great skill and artistic ability is required to express the
melodic and rhythmic wealth of mbira music to its full extent.

The mbira has been in use by the Shona people[34] for a long
time. It has been documented at least for the Monomotapa dynas-
ty of the sixteenth and seventeenth centuries. The instrument
usually consists of twenty-two metal lamellas, which are fastened
at one end with a wooden resonator body. The free protruding
ends are then plucked with the thumb of the left hand and the
thumb and index finger of the right hand. A musical analysis of
mbira playing reveals many properties also characteristic of the
rest of black Africa: the artistic technique of interlocking (as it is
called by ethnomusicologists) of parts undertaken by individual
players is one basic principle. An audio picture emerges from
which individual parts may not be separated out: together they
form a totality. From listening alone, a mbira composition could
not be transcribed for performance. That has remained unnoticed
for a long time, since the "motional" aspect of African music has
been disregarded (see also chapter 2, on Zaire).

Among the most important features of mbira music is its cyclic
character: a formula is repeated again and again. That easily gives
an impression of monotony to one with our Western expectations
and listening habits. Actually, each repetition introduces slight
variations that are almost indistinguishable to the untrained ear. A
virtuoso player is also judged by how skillfully he incorporates his
variations into the repetitions.

The different types of the instrument all have their own names,

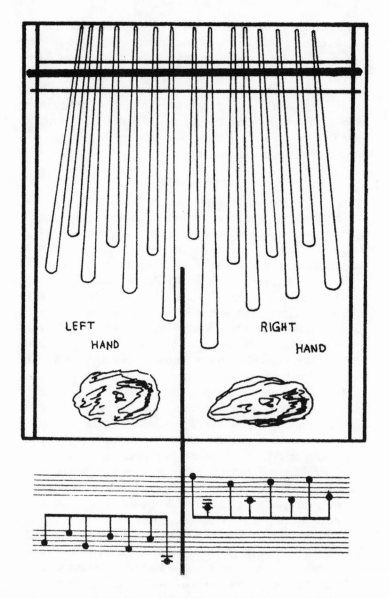

Mbira set-up with a transcription of the individual lamellas to relative pitches.

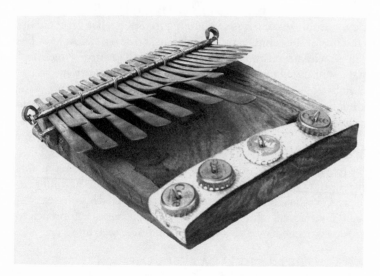

Mbira. Photo by Ralph Thomas.

but musicians refer to all of them as mbira to simplify matters. The great mbira dzavadzimu—meaning as much as "mbira of the ancestors"—receives its name by being employed at religious functions, where it contributes to communication between the living and the deceased. Though it may be played as a solo instrument—at entertainments, for instance—it is always played in an ensemble at religious or other formal festive occasions: two or three mbiras and a gourd rattle, called *hosho*. A *bira* (plural: *mapira*), a spiritual ceremony, without a mbira group is unthinkable. Its function is to play in such a manner that the medium may go off into a trance, and that a direct link to the ancestors may be established.

Formerly these ceremonies were held on the land on which the ancestors had lived. It is one of the crimes of white colonialists, however, that Africans were driven away from agriculturally valuable soil and were forced to relocate in so-called TTLs, Tribal Trust Lands (more precisely, reservations), reserved for Africans. Here *mapira* are still performed today in special buildings constructed specifically for the purpose, or at larger estates.

The ancestors are mediators between God (*Mwari*) and humans. In important matters (such as fertility), the Shona people address spirits that emerged from Mwari himself and are very close to him. Mwari, it is said among the Shona, has accepted the presence of the white people. That was, however, before they began to violate custom and heritage. Subsequently, a modified statement circulated that became of great importance in the national struggle: Mwari recognizes white people as part of mankind, but they will only belong to the land once they recognize its laws and the political responsibility of Africans.[35]

Corresponding to the revival of mbira music, a greater interest in experimentation may be observed among mbira players. Since the player normally is the instrument builder as well, it is obvious that he may wish to alter the instrument according to new musical ideas. Gweshe is one of the artists who constructed his own experimental mbira deviating from the norm. This creative approach to music instruments led to an advance in traditional music.

## THE MUNICIPAL AMUSEMENT CENTERS:
## THE BEER GARDENS

The beer gardens in worker's settlements, at the outskirts of white cities, were the meeting places of blacks, comparable to the beer halls in Northern Rhodesia. In addition, municipal administrations erected roofed structures that serve as stages for traditional performances, drumming and dances. As still today in South Africa, the policies of the whites aimed at preserving such elements of traditional culture as were seen as useful factors in maintaining order. Thus, drumming and dancing were encouraged as outlets for aggression and as a bond to maintain disrupted social relations, at least on a rudimentary level. The development of these guided amusements took a different direction, however: despite its limitations, it became an expression of a new self-confidence among Africans.

Besides events officially approved, it also happened that travelling mbira players or guitarists gathered people together and proceeded to one of the many private *shebeens* (illegal bars). Members of the South African broadcasting system recorded such musicians when they came to Salisbury (today called Harare). Shorty and Jacob Mungu were two guitarists who became known beyond the borders of their country in that manner.

During the late 1940s, so-called entertainment halls, a sort of dance hall, spread in the cities. Music groups came into being who performed in the halls. The Epworth Singers, a quartet with piano accompaniment, were the first band in Salisbury. The D. Black Evening Follies—with an instrumentation of a double bass, two or three guitars, saxophone, and drums—came into being soon after. Thus a beginning was made, and bands like Mashonaland Melodians in Salisbury, Wood Woodpeckers as well as the Gold Rhythm Crooners in Bulawayo, and Jazz Revelers in Umtali followed shortly. The groups were, of course, the first to be recorded when broadcasting commenced in Cishona in 1954, which considerably enhanced their influence.[36]

After the founding of the Federation of Rhodesia and Nyassaland in 1953, alcoholic beverages formerly reserved for Europeans (whiskey, gin, etc.) became accessible to Africans in the townships. Night clubs were established, and Rhodesia suddenly became attractive to musicians from Congo and South Africa. One group—more appropriately, an enterprise—came from Congo, calling itself O.K. Success. A name, a program! Approximately sixty to seventy musicians were dispersed among the larger cities of Tanzania, Zambia, and Southern Rhodesia. The branch in Salisbury picked up Shona music and enriched it with Congo elements.

Still today the instrumentation of dance bands follows conventional Western patterns: three electric guitars, drums, saxophone, trumpet, voices, and, in exceptional cases, an electric organ. The repertory was wide-ranging, and South African jazz, American jazz (in the style of the mid-1940s), Congo jazz, Western pop-rock, and also traditional Shona music had to be mastered. The new developing Shona music employed traditional rhythms and melodies arranged for the standard instrumentation. Such groups included bands like Granford Jangano and the Harare Mambos. Elias Banda and his Great Sounds Band indicated that they preserved the qualitative properties of traditional music in their adaptations.

Additional bands popular in Rhodesia in 1971 were: Springfield Rifle in Salisbury and Bulawayo, The Valley Association, The Eye of Liberty, and Jupiter.[37] Hardly any of these groups existed ten years later.

Since independence in 1980, the newly-gained liberty made itself felt in the enthusiasm of musicians: the fight was won, no songs were banned anymore, and new tasks and themes appeared.

### CHIMURENGA

The chimurenga, the armed uprising against rule in Zimbabwe in the 1970s, was conceived in the tradition of the first struggle for liberation in 1896/97. At that time, the liberation attempt was brutally suppressed by colonial troops. As a public warning, the two most famous Shona mediums, NeHanda and Kagubi, were convicted as ringleaders and hanged. Songs disseminated by choirs of the liberation movement for agitation and encouragement again and again referred to *mbuya* (grandmother) NeHanda:

> We sing your praises mbuya NeHanda.
> Chorus:
> We take our inspiration from you.
> We sing your praises mbuya NeHanda.[38]

During the war, Radio Moçambique broadcast a program by the Voice of Zimbabwe every day at 8 P.M. The program was put together by the Zimbabwe African National Union (ZANU). Radio Zambia, Radio Tanzania, Radio Cairo, and Radio Moscow broadcast programs of the Zimbabwe People's Revolutionary Voice—a branch of the Zimbabwe African People's Union (ZAPU)—in English, Shona, and Ndebele to Southern Rhodesia. Thus, media control could be circumvented and the propaganda of the white regime of Ian Smith could be countered with ZAPU's own voice. The liberation movements were able to define their fight as a struggle against white rule by portraying the disclosures from Salisbury as threats against Africans. The broadcasts served as education and recruited new fighters.

In interviews with freedom fighters, the Voice of Zimbabwe reported on the progress of the resistance, which existed officially only as "terrorist attacks." The program "Chimurenga Requests" maintained contact between the fighters and those who remained at home by transmitting greetings, answering questions, and playing resistance and revolutionary songs. Many musicians not actively participating in the fight sang songs that more or less covertly supported the struggle for independence. In doing so they constantly had to fear being arrested by security police.

Nevertheless, it is astonishing how openly many hits released on singles commented on the war for liberation and asked for understanding and support. Since the songs came on the market

Thomas Mapfumo and the Black Spirits (drum set) in Zimbabwe (1981).

exclusively in African languages, the authorities apparently had difficulty seeing through the deeper meaning of many a text. Often the apparatus of censorship only began to work when it was noticed that one song or another enjoyed popularity on the guerilla side. Dissemination by the Southern Rhodesian broadcasting system was thus excluded, but the records continued to be sold, even if it was more or less under the counter. Thomas Mapfumo, one of the best-known singers of chimurenga songs, maintained the highest sales figures even though he was banned from the radio: The ban had the opposite effect from what was intended.

Security forces also called on Tony Rivet of the TEAL Records company (today called GRAMMA):

Thomas's music! Whew! If you only knew what the words were before— we had to change some of the words . . . to a certain extent, and let the meaning be understood through innuendos, though everybody knew what was going on. We had to change words so the songs would be acceptable to the government. I remember they came along to me and said, the *terrs* are getting all the tribes-people to sing *gook* songs. The one they really didn't like was *Tumira Vana Kuhondo,* which means "Send your children to war." I told them it was a bloody RAR [Rhodesian African Rifles] marching song, an old military marching song.[39]

> ### We Are Sending Our Children to War
> ### (tumira vana kuhondo)
> ### by Thomas Mapfumo
>
> We are sending our children to join the struggle;
> Children to war, children to war.
> Fathers, mothers, send your children to war,
> We are all sending our children to war.
>
> We may be eliminated,
> But our children are fighting;
> This year we shall send our children to war.
> Look, the enemy will be destroyed;
> To the war, children!
> Children, to the battlefield!
> Boys, to war, girls!
> To the battlefield, children!
> We shall continue to send children to war.[40]

Thomas Mapfumo said this about the song: "You see, the soldiers thought the song was meant to support them, that was the whole trick. They sang the very same song themselves; they just meant it the other way. We pulled their leg and, at the same time, encouraged our people to fight."[41]

The example of Mapfumo makes clear how difficult the position of a politically committed musician was and still is. Mapfumo was arrested by security police; shortly after, he suddenly performed at an event organized by Bishop Muzorewa. Muzorewa was a black politician who was supported by the white racists as a moderate. If Mapfumo performed for him—so the propaganda specialists hoped—he would become a traitor to the revolution. Though it did not work out that way, a certain taint on Mapfumo's reputation remained, even though he emphasized that he only performed revolutionary songs at the event.

Still more confusion ensued when white Rhodesians blared Mapfumo's songs from loudspeakers mounted on helicopters. It was part of a strategy to divide the black population. The strategy also included the assassination of clergy members, for which the guerillas consequently were held responsible.

The great success the music of Thomas Mapfumo and other

Thomas Mapfumo in Hamburg (1984).

groups from Zimbabwe enjoyed is only partly due to partisan
texts: it is also based in the music itself.[42] Mapfumo's band—then
called Acid Band, later Blacks Unlimited—usually had an instrumentation of three guitars, drums, saxophones, and trumpets.
The music they made, however, was modeled on traditional mbira
playing. Even though it is electric guitar music, it is still called traditional in Zimbabwe. Here we are at an end with our pigeon-

holes: what we would classify as modern music from a technical point of view, the Africans call traditional. Yet, many traditional styles of singing and playing have indeed been maintained in this music. Mapfumo's singing resembles that of mbira players, including yodeling, which compares to the huro yodel phrase. The guitar style imitates the technique of plucking the lamellas: thus, the rhythm and voice leading of mbira music become apparent.

The first year of independence, 1980–1981, became the year of chimurenga-pop. The most successful musicians were Thomas Mapfumo and Oliver Mutukudzi. Compared to Mutukudzi, Mapfumo is an austere musician rooted in the chimurenga. Oliver Mutukudzi, on the other hand, was able to adjust quickly to the

Singles from Zimbabwe can be recognized immediately by their covers, which are made of wallpaper samples.

new situation. Playing songs in pop character posed no problem for him. Thomas Mapfumo could break with his partiality to chimurenga only with difficulty, which is understandable. But this also resulted in criticism: after all, the war was over. Now even he plays a reggae now and then but, as he maintains, "only for variety." Apparently, it is still difficult for him to adjust to new themes.

Reggae had been important already during the war, since Bob Marley had addressed the fight for liberation in one of his songs. He was invited to the independence festivities in Zimbabwe and performed with his group in Harare. Today, the Pied Pipers are considered one of the foremost reggae bands of the country.

The production of records experienced a tremendous boom after independence. It was limited only by severe currency regulations, which originated in times of Rhodesia's economic isolation but are still necessary for Zimbabwe today. Polyvinyl chloride, needed for manufacturing records, has to be imported, mainly from the Federal Republic of Germany.

Local African music previously had been produced mainly on singles, the reason being the limited spending power of workers. Now, however, Zimbabwe has been gripped by an "LP craze." It is an absolute must for any self-respecting group to have made an LP or, even better, to release one after another, like Devera Ngwena. Thomas Mapfuno laments that there is still too little done for the development of local music. It is his opinion that too much sunguru music is being produced by recording companies, that is, music under international copyright and music from Zaire that has been supplied with Shona texts, a procedure that corresponds to the world-wide policies of record companies.

Today, two main directions of musical development are discernible: first, the further development of traditional music through the modification of instruments and, second, the adoption of elements of traditional music by popular dance bands in modern orchestration.

## From Prohibition to State Production of Entertainment Music: Mozambique

Sam Mangwana of Zaire performed in Mozambique in 1983 and shortly after, released the LP *Sam Mangwana canta Moçambique*. Its first composition is entitled *Vamos para o campo (Let's go to the countryside*). Hereby he addresses the central thesis of political maxims of independent Mozambique, which suffers from rural exodus as do all African countries. Maputo, the former Lourenço Marcques, kept growing despite all administrative measures. Sam Mangwana, however, is no dry political ideologist. His call to move back to the country became one of the most fascinating musical compositions produced in recent years in Africa. Sung in Portuguese, the piece presents a play on the words Mozambique, Maracuene, and marrabenta. A simple text:

> When we arrived in Mozambique
> We visited a district called Maracuene, Maracuene
> Maracuene, Maracuene
> Maracuene, dance Marabenta
>
> I'm through with amusing the town all the time
> Now I go to the countryside fight against hunger
> Anti-hunger operation
> My love, let's go to the countryside
> Maracuene, Maracuene, Maracuene
> Dance Marabenta[43]

Here Sam Mangwana uses a popular music form that originated in colonial days, the marrabenta. It is dance music as it developed similarly everywhere in Africa's Portuguese colonies: a synthesis of Portuguese dance music with Afro-Brazilian and African elements.

On the second side of the LP, Sam Mangwana celebrates the independent Mozambique, as it were, in catch words, dates, and the most current slogan, "The fight continues." Yet, even the words describing the armed struggle here sound light, even inspired and sweet, almost bordering on kitsch. Melody and rhythm, interjected with full-sounding brass sets, are very catchy.

With composure, the *cantor zairense* stepped into a rather tense musical discussion in Mozambique, which was conducted in 1981 in the weekly journal *Tempo* and among experts. In the cities, there existed a music for the Portuguese and the better-situated Africans (who were not numerous in Mozambique, though) as well as a music of the quickly growing urban African population. The situation of this popular music—*música legeira*, as entertainment music is called in Portuguese—was problematic from the beginning, since it could be seen as an expression of colonial culture. On

Record cover of the LP *Sam Mangwana canta Moçambique.*

the other side, there was an independent tradition of anti-colonial songs—often working songs—which had developed from traditional music in the country.[44]

After the intensification of the anti-colonial struggle on September 25, 1964, the beginning date of the official armed fight, the choir of the FPLM[45] was founded. In the opinion of Frelimo, revolutionary music could be characterized as a music that expressed the suffering of the suppressed and exploited, and intended to establish unity between peasants and workers. The song texts were correspondingly instructive. The singing of the choir, based on traditional responsorial schemes, strongly resembled that of Christian choirs of southern Africa, which spread so widely due to existing African choral traditions. This makwaya tradition is decidedly popular. During a visit to Mozambique in 1981, I heard men's choirs of various local companies sing makwaya in the streets of the capital during lunch break.[46]

In Zimbabwe, the music of the resistance could be found also in the area of popular music, but that apparently was not the case with dance bands in Mozambique's capitalistic-colonialistic era. It is not surprising, then, that Frelimo first outlawed all *música*

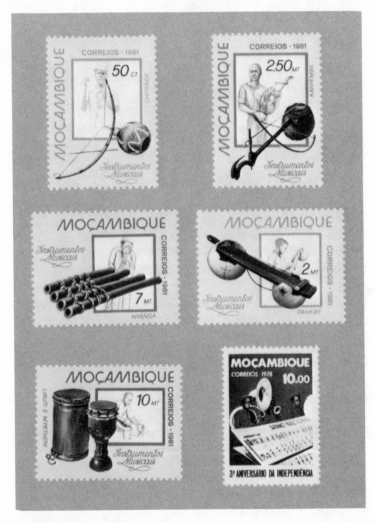

Traditional instruments as postage stamp designs.

*legeira* after independence as a bourgeois reminder of the past era. This resolution, however, was doomed to failure from the beginning. Basically it was a scandalous action. Dance orchestras, after all, had become part of popular urban culture, though a few years would pass before this realization won recognition. At any rate, the prohibition was withdrawn, and, in 1979, record production was initiated even by the government. By 1981, forty titles had been released on the label Ngoma by the Instituto do Livro e do Disco (INLD), mainly singles of various singers and bands. Ten thousand copies of singles and six thousand to seven thousand copies of LPs were pressed.

The INLD formed a commission to decide on titles to be produced. The expediency of this commission, in which no musician is represented, is naturally questioned, especially by musicians. The allocation of vinyl (not only to INLD, but two other existing record companies, Teal and Somodisco, as well) is decided by the government. As in other African countries, vinyl is available only in limited quantities; it must be important at a high price. Another problem hampering a successful record business is the lack of available hi-fi sets. Record players and amplifiers are practically unavailable for sale, except in stores similar to Intershops in the German Democratic Republic, where they can be purchased against hard currencies.

Recordings are made in the country either at the broadcasting studio or at one of the smaller studios. The master disc, however, cannot be cut in Mozambique. That is done in South Africa, even at times of greatest political struggle and conflict, an expression of Mozambique's dependence on its neighbor.

The ideological precariousness of Frelimo in regard to modern music and the resulting policies led to insecurities among musicians; not a few of them moved to Portugal. The party put its emphasis on traditional music and choirs of agitation. In 1981, the Primeiro Festival Nacional de Canção e Música Tradicional took place. The musicians of dance bands tried to adapt to the new situation, the Brazilian music critic Martino Lutero told me. They began to incorporate political texts into their songs. We may call this lip-service. It went so far that a talented musician, for example, incorporated excerpts from each of President Samora Machel's speeches into his compositions in order to demonstrate that he was a revolutionary! Revolutionary music cannot, of course, be developed in this manner.[47]

Barber shop on the road to the Maputo airport.

But this is not the only reason why musicians of dance bands have been criticized. Too much is expected from the musicians. According to Frelimo's opinion of a necessary development of culture, they were not in close enough contact with the populace: they were living in a vacuum, so to speak. Now they are expected to go into the country to experience there the people directly, in order to create their new music based on that experience. That may all be very well, but this departure ought to change not only the content. In order to develop a new music corresponding to changing social circumstances, the heritage of both traditional music and *música legeira* should be studied. Only then may a new tradition of Mozambiquian music perhaps be founded.[48]

In 1981, no music schools existed in Mozambique. Awendila Bikili, one of the few musicians who has completed an academic musical training (in the German Democratic Republic), laments the lack of theoretical and practical training among his colleagues.[49] Even Pedro Ben, singer of the radio band, confirms: "Somos analfabetos da música," "We are musical illiterates." The result, according to these critics, is that popular music persists in

This cloth, made for women's wrap-around skirts, commemorates the First National Festival of Traditional Song and Music.

Marrabenta rhythms, and no break-throughs in other directions may be noted. In order to improve the situation, musicians should organize and stand up for their rights. Copyright laws should be passed, and the country should join international copyright agreements. At the same time, a better supply of musical instruments and better music education must be striven for. Music is too mediocre. "The crisis of music is only a reflection of the crisis of society in general."[50]

Sam Mangwana's performance—his hymn of praise on the decried marrabenta music almost being an affront—perhaps had a relaxing effect. The official fear of "marrabentizing" music shows too little confidence in the creativity of musicians. It runs parallel to a deliberate attempt to revolutionize music based on a theoretical concept that will never be realized in this manner. Mangwana has shown at least that marrabenta can be modernized. The technical conditions of production, the quality of studios, and a musical climate as they may be found in Ivory Coast or Kinshasa, for instance, cannot be realized in Mozambique for the time being, due to an economic and political situation determined by civil war and famine.

# 6

# MARABI CULTURE AND
# BACKYARD STUDIOS:
# SOUTH AFRICA

■

Nkosi sikelel' i-Afrika
Maluphakanyisw' mphondo lwayo
Yiva nemithandazo yethu
Nkosi sikelela, Nkosi sikelela
Woza moya, Woza moya, oyingcwele
Nkosi sikelela
Thina lusapho lwako

Lord Bless Africa
Let its horn (of hope) be raised
Listen also to our pleas
Lord bless, Lord bless
Come spirit, come spirit,
Lord Bless Us
Us, thy children[1]

Like no other song, *Nkosi sikelel' i-Afrika* is representative of
South Africa, even beyond the actual Republic. The national an-
thems of Tanzania, Zambia, and Zimbabwe, at least, have been
composed to this song. After it had always been sung by the African National Congress (ANC)—the largest political party of
Africans in the Republic of South Africa—to conclude their meet-

ings, the song assumed the character of a national anthem: the national anthem of a South Africa liberated from the apartheid regime that the ANC intends to call Azania.

A teacher from the eastern cape province, Enoch Sontonga, was the composer of the anthem. He had settled in the township of Nancefield near Johannesburg. Although the song was composed in 1887, it was first performed in 1899 and was sung in 1912 at the founding assembly of the South African Native National Congress.[2]

It was a deeply religious song that became the national anthem of the Africans in southern Africa. It shows that despite colonialism and the destruction of traditional culture, a deep religiousness remained, readily assuming Christian content. It should be taken into account that christianization in South Africa had begun already in the nineteenth century. Thus, Christianity among South African blacks looks back at a relatively long tradition. It comes as no surprise, then, that a large portion of music is determined by religious music even today.

Corresponding to southern Africa's exceptional political situation within Africa, the music occupies a special place as well. The absolute rule of the white minority over the black majority naturally made itself felt in all areas of cultural life. This holds true not only for the Republic but for the neighboring countries as well, since thousands of laborers working in the mining regions come from the bordering states. The industrialization in connection with discoveries of diamonds and gold at the end of the nineteenth century had grave consequences for the resident black Africans. They were needed as workers in the mines. Huge workers' settlements, like camps, were established at the outskirts of towns and mines. That was the beginning of the townships, living areas assigned to the blacks. In these living conditions, determined by industries of the white minority, lies the main distinction between South Africa and the rest of Africa. Here a music emerged that was referred to as township jazz.

Contract workers introduced their own musical traditions into the townships. The coincidence of such diverse elements proved be fruitful: a new music could develop corresponding to the new living conditions of the new industrial workers. The mining concerns erected dance arenas, in which workers could rehearse their dances and hold competitions after work and on weekends. That was not, however, pure charity: it is one of the cynical sides of apartheid representatives, who supported certain aspects of traditional culture in strict racial segregation. It is an expression of the fundamental attitude that the "savages" should continue to beat their tom-tom: thus they will be content, and the old "war dance" will become an escape valve for accumulated aggressions. Such a course of action had also been taken in Rhodesia. The film *Rhythm of Resistence* shows a clear example of that—during work hours, however. One scene in the movie shows a crew of road construction workers singing during work. A white overseer strolls around them. The commentary in the film translates the text of the song as "the whites be damned." With each stroke of the pick, aggression is turned into profitable work, for the whites. This is, however, only one side: organized dances are an important means of preserving identity in apartheid even today.[3]

The dances of the mine workers are fascinating. They are characterized by stamping motions and a collapsing motion of the body at the hip. The legs are thrown full force towards the ground—a great display of force and strength, tamed and transformed into gentleness.[4]

Various peoples have their characteristic dance processes. Hugh Tracey distinguished eight groups:

1. Stamping dances of the Ngumi group
2. Shaking dances of the Xhosa
3. Fife dances of the Pedi and Sotho
4. Striding dances of the Sotho
5. Pacing dances of the Tswa, Zulu, and Ndau
6. Acrobatic and tumbling dances of the Twa and Ndau
7. Mimic and singing group dances of the Shangaan
8. Orchestra dances of the Chopi

Of course, Hugh Tracey notes that there are many more dances in southern Africa: for instance, those in which women participate. But since mine workers mostly did not have their wives living with them, these dances were excluded from the above account.[5]

Today, the decoration of dancers in the mining settlements is a mixture of traditional dance costumes and so-called substitutes. The basic necessities cannot always be found in the industrial regions. Instead of braided rattle-bands, for instance, Coca-Cola caps may be strung together.

Even though they are "rural bring-alongs," the dances of the mine workers are also an expression of urbanization. Originally associated with traditional customs, the dances are now performed outside their functional context. Thus, they have developed into what we commonly call "folklore."

A new music arose in the urban culture: a music not holding on to a continuation of traditional dances, but, on the other hand, also unable to deny its connection to them. This music, which later became known as marabi, was played in the *shebeens* (illegal taverns selling alcohol in private houses). In the twenties and thirties, one danced to more-or-less Western influenced rhythms played on battered pedal organs and milk-can rattles.

African brass bands became wide spread through the activities of missionaries, who promoted music groups in order to win blacks for the Church. The bands marched through the streets at all possible occasions, for instance, at weddings. As a result, the most varied grades in performance quality could be discerned: bands closely associated with the institutions perfectly reproduced the pieces put before them; more independent musicians retained their traditional scales and thus were able to include traditional songs in their repertories.

Men's choirs are among the most impressive experiences of South African music culture. *Rhythm of Resistance* documents such a concert evening: a men's choir—polyphonic, powerful, rhythmically breath-taking—is shown entering a men's hostel, while stamping their feet. The men appear in uniform dress: red jackets, black trousers, and white gloves, which clearly emphasize the movement of arms and hands. While being folded in front of the chest, while the men are walking, the hands are pulled from left to right, in rhythm, of course. One troupe in red, another in blue European-tailored suits with ties sing in the course of a competition: one group after another sings all through the night until early morning. Their pieces are distinguished by text, rhythm, melody, and a specific style of performance. Some groups rather swing, others emphasize especially their acrobatic tricks—all that in a fine presentation.

We would completely misunderstand these events if we interpreted them superficially as a typical "parrotism" of white customs by blacks. The succession of performances is determined by lot. As a referee, the workers of a hostel call upon a white "just having been released from prison." That has become the norm at such presentations. The referee must be white, thus outside of African culture, because that is the best guarantee of, and qualification for, an objective judgment. In addition, any possible family relationship is excluded. No white is permitted to function as a referee twice. Facing the competitors, he is not allowed to turn around so that he may not be influenced in any form by the audience. He is kept awake all night with coffee, and his judgment is irrevocable.

A goat is set as a price. It represents traditional values and content. The competition is given in a dreary-looking hall, but the music revives everybody. The voices of the men, singing *a capella*—at most hand clapping is added—touches everybody deep inside.

The choral tradition in South Africa—called makwaya just as in east and central Africa—is so strong because choirs already existed before the arrival of Europeans. Thus two traditions, European church singing and traditional African choirs, merged together. Choirs are a wide-spread spare-time occupation, and almost a school sport. Vocal groups of popular music ought to be delimited as off-shoots located at the margin of the choral tradition. Ladysmith Black Mambazo and Mahotella Queens, two such groups, emerged from the makwaya tradition and impress with their fast music and presentation.

In many aspects, the choirs strongly resemble black American vocal groups such as singers of spirituals. Surely that is not so far from the mark since musical and social parallels can be demonstrated. Similarities between South African choral music and Afro-American variants cannot be explained as simple adoption by the South Africans. The influence of American music on the black population was and is to this day especially strong: white South Africa saw to it that modern American music was heard on the radio, and the records could be bought in stores. Surely the interests of industry and business were influential here.

During the thirties and forties, jazz from the States could be heard by the African population in South Africa. In his book *Black music of Two Worlds,* John Storm Roberts lists various reasons why American jazz was so well received. He mentions, for instance, that riff figures used by soloists in big-band jazz style have an equivalent in South African vocal techniques.[6] This analogy, of course, is vague and inaccurate. What Roberts simply wants to suggest is that there are corresponding moments and ideas in South African music and jazz.

As a result of the enthusiasm for jazz music from the States, first ragtime and later swing was copied. Boys on the street, who could not afford expensive instruments like saxophones, imitated these instruments on cheap tin flutes, generally called penny whistles.

Workers at Durban companies form dance groups and organize competitions on weekends, like the choral competitions shown in the documentary *Rhythm of Resistance*. Here the leader of a Zulu dance group bows to a white referee, a cultural outsider.

Pennywhistle players.

These cheap tin flutes became the distinguishing mark of a musical
movement: penny whistle music. During its heyday, the West German company Hohner of Trossingen sold more than one hundred
thousand of these flutes to South Africa! Together with guitars and
a tea-chest bass, the result was a kwela band.[7]

In one of the few relevant film documents of the 1950s, *Pennywhistle Boys,* we see three boys, one guitarist and two flutists, as
they set out one morning by bus from their township, located at
the outskirts of Capetown, for the white inner city. They wander
the streets playing, sometimes in a jive step, sometimes remaining
at one location. Their audience is mostly white. The pieces they
play were arranged from records, even coming to a close with a
played "fade-out." Unfortunately, the film sound in this case is not
always synchronized.[8] In two other films from the fifties, the various musical styles of the townships may be seen very well. One film
is *The Magic Garden* (1952) by Donald Swanson, which has also
been released under the title *Pennywhistle Blues.* The penny whistle player Willard Cele is featured in this film. The other film is
much better known: Lionel Rogosin's *Come Back Africa* (1959).[9]
These black-and-white documents present a cross-section of the
entire contemporary black music: drum and fife bands marching

through the streets; boys playing their flutes at street corners; a guitarist sitting under a tree with his sweetheart.

Accusations of township romanticism were heard. But life in the African living quarters consists not only of suffering and protest; or, to look at it from the other side, the black population of South Africa do not let their spirits be determined by the whites twenty-four hours a day. It is, then, no escapism if people in the ghettos meet to make music and dance to be cheerful. It is rather a sign of autonomous self-determination and obvious independence when Africans enjoy themselves.

It is almost impossible to find any records with penny whistle music as it was played by the boys on the street, since it did not correspond to the standards of the recording studios. As soon as the musicians came to the studio, they were given completely different instruments in order to raise the standard of the music. The tea-chest bass unavoidably became a conventional double bass, necessary by Western conceptions. The penny whistle even became a saxophone or clarinet, despite the fact that it was a characteristic of this music to imitate saxophones with tin flutes. Studio norms thus deprived the original songs of their specific charm. In Miriam Makeba's recording of the famous click song, a double bass sounds in the background! These remarks should not to taken to suggest that Africans should retain their "primitive" instruments. Rather, they submit that a classical double bass sounds decidedly different than a chord tightened on a tea chest, and the sound evokes certain associations.

Miriam Makeba sang with the Manhattan Brothers and in the musical *King Kong,* which had its premiere in 1959. *King Kong* was produced by a white South African, Leo Gluckman, and the music was composed by an African, Todd Matshikiza. Besides some penny whistle interludes, *King Kong* stands essentially in the tradition of the American musical. *King Kong* was brought to London, where it became a great success and played for a year.

Miriam Makeba, a South African black who has lived in exile in Guinea for many years, is undisputedly the most important female singer in South Africa, if not in all of Africa. After a showing of *Come Back Africa* at the film festival in Venice in 1959 she went to the United Sates. Harry Belafonte looked after her and helped her secure a place in the international pop music market. For several years she was married to the Black Power leader

Stokely Carmichael. While living in Conakry, the capital of Guinea, she made some recordings with Guinea musicians who played her South African compositions. It is self-evident that the result was not quite the South African music desired.

Already in South Africa Miriam Makeba had become famous for her jazz singing. The record *Something New from Africa,* released in 1959, features her with a wordless vocal part in a version of Duke Ellington's *Rockin' in Rhythm.* That was her métier. In exile she had her greatest successes with "African children's and wedding songs," which came as a surprise to many blacks back home in South Africa.[10] Children's and wedding songs were, however, only part of her success. Popular pieces of township jazz were at least as significant and were the basis of her world-wide fame, even though these pieces were played and performed in polished form and with technical perfection. *Pata-Pata* is probably the best-known example. This song (a whole style is named pata-pata in southern Africa) has been played for many years even by West German radio stations. Supposedly, pata-pata was a dance style that emerged from penny whistle music. According to Coplan, it was an individualized, sexually suggestive form of the jive dance styles of young people, in which the dance partners alternately touched each other's bodies with their hands to the rhythm of the music. Pata-pata does not mean "touch-touch" without reason.[11]

The dancers often also called out "kwela, kwela," meaning "come on, up!" in Zulu, to encourage those sitting about to dance. The expression, however, more likely seems to originate with paddy wagons of the police, also called "kwela-kewla," since the police chased prisoners into them with the words "kwela, kwela," Kwela music is characterized by a fast, continuous rhythm, which presses ahead and pushes one downright forward. The chord sequence usually is C–F–C–G.[12]

Lemmy Special and Spokes Mashiyane were two of the greatest kwela penny whistle musicians, and Aaron Lerole was another star of the 1950s. The musical basis of kwela was not only American swing, but also the preceding popular music styles of the twenties and thirties, all of which are comprised in the collective term "marabi culture."[13]

Marabi is seen as the result of cultural urbanization and a synthesis of various local musical currents in a new context.

Growing out of shebeen society, marabi can be defined as (1) a syncretic style of instrumental (and secondarily, vocal) music with a distinctive rhythm based on the Western three-chord, tonic-dominant-subdominant harmonic system; (2) a variable individual or couple dance emphasizing sexuality and accompanied by this music; (3) an extended social occasion where liquor was consumed, marabi music and dance performed, and general social interaction was a focal activity; and (4) a category of people who derived their identity from regular attendance at these occasions and who enjoyed a low social status and a reputation of immoral behavior.[14]

The instrumentation of marabi music was rather variable. It depended primarily on what instruments actually were available at the time. The pedal organ was an essential instrument, but kazoos, guitars, acoustic bass, drums, or even instruments by chance borrowed from a brass band were incorporated. The musicians were no professionals and performed on weekends at these festivities. They were payed with "gas," a slang term for alcohol.[15]

The South African journalist and musician Todd Matshikiza correctly emphasizes that marabi was more than the hot, strongly rhythmic, repetitive, and monothematic dance melodies of the late 1920s: marabi is also the name of an era.[16]

Marabi pieces marketed by the recording industry were developed further as *mbaqanga,* a term actually denoting the corn bread of the Africans. It was applied to music to indicate authentic African music. Local music critics, however, defamed this music also broadcast on the radio as *msakazo* ("radio"), that is, as a music that sold itself out to the whites.[17]

The general criticism of popular music disseminated by the recording industry has continued until today. It is joined by criticism of the structure of the industry, which is completely in white hands. Music produced by white producers is obviously always suspected of presenting a music tailored for Africans. Today there are, however, a number of small labels producing recordings in so-called backyard studios under simple technical conditions. The sellout of tradition in favor of profits for the record industry certainly is a fact. At the same time, however, it is true that interesting new currents and styles find their way through the recording industry.

The derogatory term *msakazo,* in addition, is partly due to the fact that all music broadcast on the radio is censored. The South

African broadcasting system only airs music produced in advance. Each program has to pass the censorship authorities. Each record that is integrated into the broadcasting archives is first tested for its content. The South African Broadcasting Corporation (SABC) employs a team of experts, mostly linguists, in order to detect the most hidden suggestions in idiomatic expressions that in any way could have a political character. As a consequence, the recording studios subject themselves to self-censorship in order to keep losses resulting from a possible ban of songs at a minimum. Record stores, however, are allowed to sell records containing political allusions, as long as they do not go too far.[18] In Jeremy Marre's film *Rhythm of Resistance,* a disc jockey of the South African Broadcasting System explains that banned records are scratched with a sharp object to make them unplayable.

The recording industry thus is involved in a constant struggle with, and a demarcation of, its domain against the censorship authorities. Records of "Dollar Brand" Abdullah Ibrahim are pressed even in South Africa despite the fact that in exile he openly advocates the armed resistance of the ANC. As long as his texts do not explicate any propaganda for the ANC or any other African liberation movement, they pass censorship.

In individual cases, ironic circumstances may occur. Boney M.'s version of *Rivers of Babylon,* pinched from the Jamaican group The Melodians, was brought on the South African market in local languages. The song deals with the liberation of the Jews from the Babylonian captivity. For black listeners the Babylon of the song was reflected in Johannesburg. Surely the text was understood by the black population quite differently than the censors had anticipated.

Lefifi Tladi, a drummer living in exile for years, once said the following in an interview about the situation of the recording industry and the broadcasting system:

[Q] So you say the government, the radio stations, and the producers have a common interest to water down black music originally of high quality to a purely commercial music, and to stultify it to gumba-gumba music.

[A] Exactly. Besides, this gumba-gumba music! It is a special music conceptualized and created particularly for the slum. It is unbelievable how people are being cheated with this kind of music. It goes so far that the slum becomes an ideal. It is then overlooked that the slum is a product of industrialization under the special conditions of apartheid. This idealized slum has even become to some degree part of our musical culture. By its nature, gumba-gumba is not our culture. Rather, it is a culture that people have been conditioned to by constantly being frustrated culturally. In the end, it forces them to swallow this replacement culture. Thereby, gumba-gumba music even receives some creative elements. The musical potential exists anyway, but it has no means of expression—except in officially ordered gumba-gumba music. That is why the system has such an interest in gumba-gumba; it is the creator of this music.[19]

Puristical pretensions cannot be missed in this criticism. It may be replied that commercialism is not simply commercialism and consequently damned to begin with. In one current case, commercialism has struck in such a manner that the remarks made above appear to be inoffensive. The Duo Juluka became known years ago as the only racially mixed duo in the South African Republic. It consisted of Sipho Mchunu, a Zulu musician and guitarist, and Johnny Clegg, a former ethnology teacher, born in 1953 in England, who learned to master traditional Zulu instruments and dances—besides playing guitar—and was able to sing in Zulu. In 1978, the Duo still had to perform in clubs to some extent illegally since black and white on stage were not tolerated by the apartheid regime. Today the situation is much more relaxed. In performances at the time, Sipho Mchunu played guitar and Johnny Clegg played Zulu mouth bow. The result was a music obligated to tradition, yet new. The recording industry seized the opportunity, world-wide. Adding some musicians, the Duo became the group Juluka. Juluka dissolved when Sipho Mchunu decided in 1985 to return to the countryside. After one solo LP, Johnny Clegg put together the Savuka band. Savuka stands for "Awakening" and comprises three white and three black musicians from South Africa. Being marketed by EMI-Pathe Marconi in France, Savuka was having a lot of success and even reached the top of the charts in the late 1980s. At the 1990 world tour the band appeared with a female singer and dancer. Township pop as well as standard international rock music belong to their repertoire.

When Philip Tabane, for instance, plays music that does not take its bearing from developments in international pop music, but rather attempts to present traditional themes in new arrangements for guitar and malombo drums, it may happen that he attracts a limited predominantly white audience of enthusiasts in South Africa. For the majority of Africans, however, he will be too

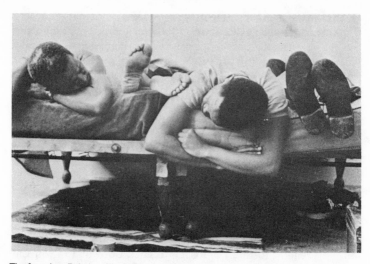

The four Jazz Epistles: Kiepie Mocketsi, Jonas Gwangwa's feet, Hugh Masekela, and Dollar Brand's boots.
Jonas Gwangwa, a famous trombone player from South Africa, also arranged songs for Miriam Makeba. Likewise living in exile, Dollar Brand, who has called himself Abdullah Ibrahim since his conversion to Islam, is today one of the great jazz players. Primarily a pianist, he also plays saxophone and flute. His compositions are founded on South African township jazz. Hugh Masekela, while living in the United States, became the most popular of these three musicians-in-exile. Louis Armstrong gave him his trumpet, which indicates Masekela's close connection to American jazz.

"academic" and experimental. Popular in South Africa are groups that are quite different: Steve Kekana, or Brenda and The Big Dudes, for example. Steve Kekana performs a modern version of the musical style that began with kwela. After kwela, it turned into simanje-manje, which translates into something like the "music of 'now, now.'" Basically, it is an electronic continuation of kwela. Simanje-manje nowadays is followed, for a second time, by mbaqanga. Surely, the blind Steve Kekana is especially popular because of his voice and texts. Muff Anderson describes Steve Kekana at a concert in Soweto:

I barely could [hold back my tears] when I saw Steve at a concert in the rain at Jabulani Stadium in Soweto.

He had been announced at the top of the mbaqanga festival that also featured the Soul Brothers and Juluka.

Ten thousand people must have been there, despite an incredible thunder storm that practically destroyed the sound system. The people waited for Steve until it was almost night. They shouted "Ke-ka-na" with the same vehemence at other times applied to shouting "A-man-dla" or "So-we-to," and pushed further and further towards the stage. It appeared to be too much to ask of a blind man to come onto stage under these conditions. Even the Soul Brothers, who had performed before Steve, had shortened their part.

Yet still, Steve performed. He wore a red satin suit in pyjama style, his hair in orderly dreadlocks, and his customary sun glasses. He stepped onto the stage and performed; fearlessly he danced in his peculiar androgynous manner. He slipped and almost fell several times, but he continued until the rain had washed away all of Jabulani Stadium.[20]

The Jazz Epistles were the first jazz group in South Africa to record a 33 RPM LP. In exile, Hugh Masekela had great success with records oriented toward and produced for the American market. Since 1982 he has been living in Botswana's capital, Gaborone, close to his original home. On his LP *Techno-Bush*, Masekela presents himself as an international musician: a medley of famous South African pieces such as *Wimoweh, Smokian*, and *Grazing the in Grass* is set in a modern arrangement.

The Soul Brothers are the big competition for Steve Kekana on the South African market. The four leading members of the group share equal parts of all proceeds; they are a true team, even in writing texts, etc. Yet, even though they have sold millions of records—singles and LPs—they still do not earn much more than they once made working together in a factory.

Finally, a quotation from John Blackling, which emphasizes again how important music is for black South Africans:

South African musical systems reflect both the different societies and cultures in which they thrive, and they have a transcendental function: in the shared experience of music itself, of humanly significant form in tonal motion, there is the possibility of reaching beyond the constraints of words and social role and cultural time, by extending tonal and harmonic structures in a special world of musical time. Recent developments in South African music reflect the growth of a collective African consciousness. This should help to generate the energy and imagination required for black South Africans to transcend the confines of a white-dominated settler colony based on the values and institutions of an alien culture and to build a new African state with the same confidence and ability that they have shown in creating their own black South African music.[21]

# APPENDIX
# Some Music-Theoretical
# Explanations

■

For further reading, the reader is referred to the collection *Musik in Afrika*, edited by Artur Simon, especially to the following articles contained therein: Gerhard Kubik, "Musikgestaltung in Afrika," "Verstehen in afrikanischen Musikkulturen," and "Kognitive Grundlagen afrikanischer Musik;" and Alfons Dauer, "Kinesis and Katharsis." The following notes are taken from that collection.

Actually, there is a risk involved in using the term "African music," because one African music does not exist, only many African music types. Each ethnic group has its own music, and the astounding wealth of musical creativity in Africa is not easily reduced to a common denominator. (Kubik, "Musikgestaltung in Afrika," p. 27.)

Traditional African music is not always distinct in all aspects from European musical forms. For instance, one may sometimes be tempted to ascribe certain harmonic reminiscences too quickly to European influences. That, however, is not necessarily so.

One of the many peculiarities of African music creation are various scales not identical with Western scales. "African tone systems may contain five, six, seven, or more tones." (Kubik, "Musikgestaltung in Afrika," p. 27.) Hugh Tracey offers a comparison between an European twelve-tone scale and the scale used by the timibila xylophone of the Chopi in Mozambique (quoted in Kubik, "Musikgestaltung in Afrika," p. 27):

European Scale: C  D  E  F  G  A  H  C

Timbila:

The scale indicated here is heptatonic and is only one example.

*Polymeter, polyrhythm, cross rhythm,* and *fundamental rhythm* are further characteristics of African musical cultures.

*Polymeter* is described as follows: "Several distinct meters, as a rule, proceed simultaneously . . . The simultaneous occurrence of distinct motional events—often complementary, often contrasting—is the most important condition for a realization of African music sentiment." (Dauer, p. 169). As a graphic example, Dauer gives a transcription of music for three instruments (p. 169):

| | ♩ = 108 | ∞ |
|---|---|---|
| iron bell | 6 | ‖: ſ  ſſ  ſ  ſ  :‖ |
| mid-size drum | 6 | ‖: ſ  ♩  ♩  :‖ |
| small drum | 6 | ‖: ſſſſſſ  :‖ |

Dauer refers to *polyrhythm* as "simultaneous use of various distinct rhythms. The music . . . has a single, clearly audible and discernible fundamental beat, from which the respective rhythms may be distinctly perceived. The effect is not a flowing or gliding to and fro, but an impetuous tension and propelling drive, as it is called in jazz. The music is also transformed into body motion, likewise split up, since perception registers a stratification of procedures and reacts to them on different levels of perception." (Dauer, p. 170f.)

Dauer supplies a clear example (p. 171; it is a transcription of a recording made about 1949 in West Africa by Alberts; Alberts 1950, Album I, p. 3, No. 1).

| iron bell | 16‖: ſ  ſ  ſ  ſ  ſ  :‖ ∞ |
|---|---|
| small drum | 8‖: ſ  ♫ſ  ♫‖ſ  ♫ſ  ♫  :‖ ∞ |
| mid-size drum  A | 8‖: ſ  ſſ  ſſ  ‖ſ  ♪  ♪  ♪  :‖ 4x |

Each instrument produces its own rhythm based on a four beat meter. "First the iron bell again begins beating and establishing the meter. The small drum 'listens' its way into the beat. Having found the right point of entry, it introduces its drumming formula, which is very simple and from there on serves as 'the beat' and a point of orientation." It is followed by the entry of the mid-size drum, "and we finally perceive three distinct rhythms simultaneously in the same meter." (Dauer, p. 171.)

*Cross rhythm* occurs in the following example: "The drum formula of mid-size drum conflicts with that of the other instruments." (Dauer, p. 172.) While iron bell and small drum share the same main accents, the mid-size drum moves its main accent one beat ahead. "Thus we will refer to cross rhythm as those forms of African rhythm, in which the motion of main accents of given meters or rhythms conflict with each other in simultaneous stratification." (Dauer, p. 172.)

Dauer points out that we should not immediately infer syncopations when hearing such cross rhythmic structures. "The moment of displacement is so short that it will almost not be noticed. The mid-size drum becomes the center of attention, and its beat, perceived as 'syncopated', captures the interest completely. Not so for the African listener! Here, the meter established by the introductory instruments remains at the center of attention and continues to carry the whole experience of motion, even at the entry of the mid-size drum, the actual main drum of the piece." (Dauer, p. 172.)

*Fundamental rhythm* is "the result of polymetrically, polyrhythmically, or cross-rhythmically staggered simultaneous beat successions." Thus, "it is a compounded motion formula of considerable complexity," not to be confused with the fundamental beat! "The [fundamental] beat, on the other hand, is nothing but the permanent substrata of all rhythmic movement and the controlling pulse of the entire performance, often only implicitly perceptible at the very bottom of the structure." (Dauer, p. 174.)

# NOTES

■

## 1. The Griot Style

1. Junior 1979, 114f.

2. Junior 1979, 114; Schachter 1958, 675; UNESCO 1979, 34.

3. Jahn 1972, 131.

4. UNESCO 1979, 74.

5. Kaba 1976, 215, quoted from Ahmed Sékou Touré, *Poèmes Militants* on syliphone SLP 13.

6. In May 1980, a grenade exploded during a play in the Palais du Peuple demonstrating that this institution was considered especially representative of Sékou Touré's regime. Compare *Verschwunden in Guinea,* Bonn: Amnesty International, 1982), 6.

7. Kaba 1976, 213.

8. *Ballets Africains de la République de Guinée,* Syliphone SLP 14.

9. UNESCO 1979, 81f.

10. Excerpts of a conversation of the author with Marcellin Momo Bangoura (Directeur Technique des Formations Artistiques Nationales), Momo Soumah Wandel (saxophonist of the Formation Nationale Kélétigui et Ses Tambourinis), and Barry Mamadou Aliou (Chef du Orchestre Kaloum Star) held May 1984 in the Palais de Peuple, Conakry.

11. ". . . the European inspired dance orchestras and chamber music ensembles such as La Douce Parisette, Les Joviales Symphonies, L'Africana Swing Band, La Habanera Jazz, Le Guinea Jazz, L'Etoile du Sud, Le Harlem Jazz Band and L'Etoile du Nord . . ." UNESCO 1979, 80.

12. Laye 1966, 150–51. Originally published in Paris, 1953. Historic references—and the fact that the novel is largely autobiographic—suggest

that the scene described above occurred in the late 1940s or perhaps the early 1950s. After 1964, Camara Laye lived in exile in Senegal and died in 1980. In 1978, he published a volume of reports on the Malinke groits under the title *Le maître de la parole.*

13. Laye 1966, 162.

14. Conversation with M. M. Bangoura. See note 10. The extent of state-organized promotion of culture only becomes clear if we consider the structure of this enterprise more closely: The Department of Youth, Art, and Sport includes an Office of Art. There was an art group in each of the 2422 local revolutionary administrative branches. On the level of the 236 *arrondissements* just as many art groups existed, and the regional area included 24 such groups. Eight national orchestras, three national ballets, and one national instrumental ensemble worked on the national level. This framework encompassed yearly competitions at the local level. Each group could enter one theater play (with didactical content, of course), one choral work, one ballet, and examples of its traditional folk music. The best productions qualified to participate in a two-week cultural festival in Conakry. The modern dance orchestras were only included from the regional level on. The best groups could then take part in the national festivals held every other year. The national groups were all employed by the national government, and the regional groups were supported in part by the national and regional authorities. (UNESCO 1979, 73f).

15. *Folklore et Ensembles Instrumenteaux,* Syliphone SLP 43, cover text.

16. Bembeya Jazz National, *Special Recueil Souvenir,* Syliphone SLP 44, cover text.

17. Ibid. Transcription and translation into the French by Diapy Diawara.

18. "Guinea's most important political prison is Camp Boiro in Conakry. It is the largest and most notorious prison camp of the country, overcrowded with more than fifteen hundred prisoners. Most of the well-known prisoners are held in detention here." See *Guinea* (Länderreihe: Amnesty International, 1978), 8.

19. The manner in which the radio operated as a driving force at the beginning of the new government was unique in Africa. Radio broadcasting, which began as a colonial institution, was a rather inflexible and slow establishment which operated somewhat timidly, especially considering its importance. The open manner in which RTG broadcast demonstrates impressively the quality of free life that the military was striving for after years of restrictions. Live telephone interviews, listeners calling in, all that without censorship: that is amazing, especially when politics are involved.

20. Kebendo Jazz de Gueckedou; Niandan–Jazz de Kissidougou;

Nimba Jazz; Kaloum Star; 22. Novembre Band; Palm Jazz; Tele-Jazz de Telemene; Tropical Djoli Band de Faranah; Sorsornet Rythme de Boke; Simandou de Beyla.

21. Bembeya Jazz National, *Regard sur le Passe,* Syliphone SLP 10.

22. Bembeya Jazz National, *Djanfamagni,* Syliphone SLP 4.

23. Bembeya Jazz National, *Parade Africaine,* Syliphone SLP 39.

24. *Les Amazones de Guinée,* SLP 76; Sona Diabate des *Amazones, Sons de la Savane,* SLP 77; M'Mah Sylla, *Le Rossignol de Guinée,* SLP 78.

25. *Kandia,* SYL 12; Kandia, *L'Epopee du Mandingue,* vols. 1–3, SLP 36–38.

26. Zemp 1964, 375.

27. Junior 1979, 22.

28. This saying is ascribed to the philosopher Amadou Hampaté Ba of Mali.

29. From an enclosure to the record, *Kora Music from the Gambia* by F. M. Muso, FW 8510. Notes by Roderic Knight.

30. *Kora Manding-Mandinka Music of the Gambia* by F. M. Muso, ER 12102. Notes by Roderic Knight, p. 6.

31. Examples are found on these records, among others: *Nigeria: Hausa Music I and II* (Bärenreiter) and *UNESCO Collection: An Anthology of African Music,* BM 302 2306/2307.

32. E. T. Mensah and His Tempo's Band, WAL 1022. Transcription: Margit Hawelleck.

33. *Mali: Epic, Historical, Political, and Propaganda Songs of the Socialist Government of Modibo Keita (1960–1968).* VPA 8326/8327 Vol. 2, 1.

34. Cutter 1968, 77.

35. Voss 1962, 30.

36. *Mali: Epic, Historical, Political and Propaganda Songs,* LLST 7325.

37. See Bärenreiter series.

38. *Bingo,* no. 242, May 1988, 42.

39. The name Biton is a reference to Biton Kulubari—one of the great figures of Mali's history, from the eighteenth-century kingdom of the Bambara of Segou.

40. *Afro Music,* no. 5, May 1976, 4f. In this issue, Fanta Damba was elected the female singer of the month ("La Vedette du Mois").

41. *Afro Music,* no. 5, May 1976, 5.

42. *Afro Music,* no. 7, July 1976, 5.

43. Djeli Madi Cissoko and Sidiki Diabaté played kora, Bourama Kouyaté, balafon, Modibo Kouyaté and Solo Dianaté, guitar, and Ali Wague played flute.

44. Mokontafe Sako, *Farafina Moussou,* SAF 50012.

45. Mokontafe Sako, *Les Aigles du Mali*, SAF 50033.

46. *Afro Music*, no. 7, July 1976, p. 5.

47. Fanta Sako, *Musique de Mali*, BM 30L 2551, commentary.

48. Bazoumana Sissoko, "Le Vieux Lion I and II." *Musique du Mali*, BM 30L 2552/2553.

49. Sow 1981, 64f.

50. Senghor 1963.

51. Konté, *Chant du Nègre . . . chant du monde*, ARN 33395.

52. Rejholec 1984.

53. Beaumier 1968.

54. In many aspects the musical culture corresponds to that of the neighboring countries. The griots (called "*jewel*" in Wolof), for instance, use the same classical instruments: kora, khalam, balafon, and different types of drums.

55. Diallo 1975, 15.

56. *Bingo*, no. 374, March 1984, 65.

57. Another group with a long tradition is the Orchestre Baobab. L'Orchestre N'Guewel de Dakar, Cosaan Orchestre de Dakar, and Super Jamano de Dakar originated in the second half of the 1970s.

58. *Bingo*, no. 376, May 1984, 53.


## 2. Francophone Connections

1. *Bingo*, no. 290, March 1977, 69.

2. Compare Bemba 1984. This book presents a comprehensive history of music of Congo and Zaire in view of sociological and cultural developments with many examples of lyrics.

3. Out of love for, and interest in, Katanga guitar music, the English guitarist John Low visited musicians such as Bosco, Abelo, and Masengo in 1979. In his charmingly written diary, (Low 1982), rich in interesting and important observations, he stresses again and again that it would be misleading to consider the guitarists named as individual cases. Rather, they should be seen as representatives of contemporary guitar music: only then may they be appreciated properly.

4. Rycroft 1961, 81–98; and 1962, 86–102.

5. Low 1982, 26. He refers to a release on Kaleidophone KMA 6.

6. Low 1982, 26, 36.

7. *Ile Wakati ya Pension* was part of Bosco's repertory on his 1982 tour.

8. Low 1982, 20–22.

9. Kubik 1982, 33, 36.

10. Kubik 1983g, 340.

11. Kubik 1983g, 341.

12. Kubik 1983e, 202–216.

13. See also Low 1982, 43.

14. Low 1982, 19.

15. Low 1982, 103.

16. Low 1982, 103f.

17. Low 1982, 104.

18. Low 1982, 17.

19. Low 1982, 82.

20. Low 1982, 33f.

21. Bosco in a conversation with the author in Bayreuth, June 1982.

22. Ibid.

23. Bosco performed at the opening ceremony of a conference at the University of Bayreuth, which was instrumental in the realization of his tour.

24. Thus far, I do not know how the historic events after independence influenced the music scene. It is surprising that civil war and Katanga's separation under Tshombe apparently had no effect on music. I have not found any texts that deal directly with the civil war, except some referring to the assasination of Patrice Lumumba. Yet perhaps the reason is that I had access only to texts in translation.

25. Low 1982, 31.

26. Ibid.

27. Lonoh 1984; Bemba 1984.

28. OTRACO, today called ONATRA, has been Zaire's most important carrier in internal navigation since colonial days.

29. Lonoh 1984, 68.

30. Balbaud 1971, 28f. Besides Balbaud, M. Lonoh (already cited) is the source for the biography of Tabu Ley.

31. Balbaud 1971, 28.

32. Lonoh 1984, 67ff.

33. Balbaud 1971, 30.

34. This piece has also been released on John Storm Roberts's record *African Dances,* Authentic 001.

35. *Bingo,* no. 311, December 1978, 63.

36. Lonoh 1984, 69.

37. Unwelcome intruders at assemblies are called "vampires."

38. Dzokanga (ca. 1984), 141.

39. At the concert, Tabu Ley performed with a band that included, among others, five trumpets, three trombones, and five guitars (Balbaud 1971, 28).

40. Monga 1983, 68f.

41. *Africa Now,* February 1985, 42.

42. Graham 1988, 195.

43. May and Stapelton 1988, 148.
44. Ibid., 169.
45. *Jeune Afrique Magazine,* no. 21, Novembre 1985, 21.
46. *Amina,* no. 172, October 15, 1985.
47. *Akoua,* December 1982, 16.
48. *Jeune Afrique* no. 18, July–August 1985, 19.
49. I follow here the presentation of Kazadi 1971, 25–27.
50. The Orquesta Aragon is a Cuban group.
51. *Bingo,* no. 333, October 1980, 52f. Adam Gaye spoke with Sam Mangwana.
52. Dzokanga (ca. 1984), 223–5.
53. Surely, Kinshasa, Brazzaville, and Douala are centers in this sense as well. Yet since the rise of Abidjan, they have decreased greatly in importance. In respect to record production, Brazzaville may again gain ground since there now exists a recording studio equipped with the latest technology.
54. *Akoua,* no. 143, September 1984, 11.
55. *Bingo,* no. 392, September 1985, 47.
56. Imfeld 1980, 216f.
57. Manu Dibango in an interview with Adam Isaacs in *Melody Maker,* September 8, 1984, 34.
58. Bebey 1963, 1975.
59. *Melody Maker,* September 8, 1984, 34.
60. *Afro Music,* no. 15, May 1977, 18.
61. Kala-Lobe 1982, 2881–2883.

## 3. West African Highlife

1. Lynn 1967, 121f.
2. Collins 1979, 2041. Collins 1976, 62. King 1966, 3f.
3. Sprigge 1961, 89.
4. Collins 1973; Collins 1976b.
5. Collins 1976a, 52f. Alain Ricard's movie *Le Principe d'Asihu* furnishes an especially clear picture of the tradition of slapstick comedies still alive in the 1960s. The example of the Happy Star Concert Band demonstrates how a group of actors and musicians together conceived and performed a piece, and toured Togo.
6. Collins 1973, 17.
7. *West African Review* (no. 337, October 1955): 888.
8. Horton 1979, 96.
9. Horton 1979, 32f.
10. The Afro Cubans, The Red Spots, The Rhythm Aces, The Sham-

bros, Dan Tackies Band, The Planets, Sawaaba Soundz, etc. (Compare Collins 1973).

11. Geest 1982, 31.

12. Geest 1982, 32f.

13. Asante-Darko 1983, 253f.

14. Asante-Darko 1983, 254.

15. Geest 1980, 155.

16. Geest 1980, 156.

17. *Soul to Soul,* Atlantic ATL 40290, 1971.

18. Collins, in verbal communication, July 1983.

19. The Niger Company was a semi-governmental trading company that exercised British interests before the establishment of a colonial administration.

20. Fiofori 1983, 26.

21. *West African Review,* 29, (no. 373, October 1958) 808.

22. Ita 1984, 18. In the following account of Benson's life I also draw on the book listed.

23. Ita 1984, 19.

24. *Catchy Rhythms from Nigeria,* Vol. 1, Philips P 3400 R, Side B: 4.

25. Ibid., Side A: 1.

26. Alhaji (Chief) Sikiru Ayinde Barrister and His Supreme Fuji Commanders, *Nigeria,* Siky Oluyole Records SKOLP 022, 1983.

27. King 1966, 3–8. Bruce King is himself a musician and performed Highlife in London and Nigeria.

28. Achebe 1961, 112–113.

29. "Juju" customarily refers to magical practices or medicines of a magical nature. Another theory suggests the use of the term "juju" in connection with music as an onomatopoetic imitation of the "joo-joo" sound of the talking drum.

30. The agidigbo—a large-framed variant of hand pianos with three or four lamellas—was included in early Juju bands. Today, these lamellas may consist of sawblades or (a highly suggestive symbolism!) of parts of springs of old wind-up gramophones.

31. Chief Obafemi Awolowo was the leader of Action Group. Its followers came mainly from western Nigeria and, thus, were Yoruba. Awolowo felt that Nigeria's partition, devised by the British, and the consequent representation of his people in parliament permitted only marginal participation of his people in political life. His party split up and a significant number of followers joined one of the large parties. Only two years after independence, in 1962, Awolowo was charged with high treason for supposedly attempting to overthrow the government by force.

32. I. K. Dairo, *Awolowo,* Alowonle Sound Studio, 45 rpm, 7"; transcribed in Okagbare 1969, 22; translation by Fatai Salau.

33. I. K. Dairo, *Ashiko Music,* Vol. 2, DECCA WAPS 34, 1972.

34. It is one of many independent Christian churches in Nigeria and other African countries that combine Christian and traditional African elements.

35. Among the other bands are Dr. Orlando Owoh and His African Kenneries Beat International, General Prince Adekunle and His Western Brothers, Sir Shina Adewale and His Super Stars International, Admiral Dele Abiodun and His Top Hitters Band, Emperor Pick Peters and His Seidormatic International. "Admiral," "Emperor," or "King" are all self-conferred, grandiose-sounding titles that permanently became part of the musicians' names. Even self-elevation occurs: with increasing success, "Pastor" Rex Lawson became "Cardinal" Rex Lawson.

36. The Biafra war of 1967–71 was an attempt by the eastern region of Nigeria to become independent. One source of the conflict was the colonial foundation of states that united two hundred fifty different people under one government. The Igbo, one of the three or four largest population groups in the country, lived in the eastern region. Since the Igbos had been missionized and trained in the Western educational system early, the British preferred to appoint them as railway officials and the like in the Islamic north of the country. The retail business was in the hands of Igbos as well. Thousands of Igbos were killed or mutilated at pogroms instigated by local politicians in the North. The survivors fled back east. Frictions about distribution of oil money (oil was produced in the territory of the eastern region but also benefitted the north) finally led to political severance of the east under Colonel Ojukwu. Great dissatisfaction with the policies of the corrupt government dominated by the north existed in the east and south of Nigeria. The situation in the country had become gradually worse, and the government had neglected to provide for broader prosperity after independence.

Supported by the governments of Great Britain, the USSR, and the USA, the central Nigerian government did not tolerate the separation. In turn, independent Biafra received aid from France, South Africa, China, and Tanzania. France had an interest in the oil resources since it had come off short in the allocation of concessions. In the Western hemisphere, the war in Biafra was falsely portrayed as a religious war of Islamic Nigerians against Catholic Igbos. Two million died in the three-year war. It ended with the capitulation of the Biafra army and the re-integration of the east, divided into several regions in a Nigeria of nineteen states.

37. Sikiru Ayinde Barrister, *Nigeria,* Siky Oluyole Records SKOLP 022, 1983.

38. Enekwe, Udechukwu, and Okafor Forthcoming, typescript p. 13.

39. Enekwe, Udechukwu & Okafor Forthcoming, typescript p. 13. (Onyekwelu encouraged some of the earliest minstrels by giving them the

opportunity to record and paying them decently.) Regarding patronage, see p. 12.

40. Obiligbo Ezigbo of Nteje, *Egwu Odegbodu*, Melody Sound Studio, MSLP 1, cover text.

41. Transcribed from Ibiligbo Ezigbo of Nteje, *Egwu Odegbodu*, Melody Sound Studio, MSLP 1.

42. Achebe and Udechukwu 1982. The text was transcribed and translated into English from Ezigbo Obiligbo's record *Egwu Odegbodu* by O. Udechkwu and edited and annotated conjointly with the author.

43. Compare Enekwe, Udechkwu, and Okafor Forthcoming, typescript pp. 6f.

44. Enekwe, Udechkwu, and Okafor Forthcoming, typescript p. 7; Okafor 1980, 157–58.

45. In Europe, unacquainted engineers recording touring African bands often eliminate rattles at the mixing console or drop them into the background: the first falsification of the music occurs!

46. The empire of Benin—which is not identical with the present country Benin, the former Dahoméy—encompassed vast parts of Nigeria and neighboring territories to the west. Benin was destroyed in 1898 by a British "punitive expedition." Earlier the British had ignored a request to refrain from visiting the city since the king had religious obligations and could not receive visitors. They came anyway and were killed for their sacrilege. The punitive expedition destroyed the whole city, and the king was sent into exile. Captured bronze castings from the palace and shrines were sold all over the world and today are among the treasures of many ethnology museums, even in West Germany.

47. *Sonny Okosun Meets Lord Superior (Bleech People)*, EMI Pathe Marconi, 2 C 062-82 425, 1978, side B, 2, "Lagos Taxi."

48. Bender 1980a.

49. See the cover text of *Sweet Mother* on the Rounder Records release.

50. Chris During is probably the best authority on the history of modern music in Sierra Leone. He recorded radio programs for years. He was also the bandleader of the legendary Rokel River Boys and, later, the Versatile Publicans. He made a comic radio program with "Chris Na Case," which was cancelled for political reasons.

51. King 1966, 3–4.

52. Bender 1984, 15, 17.

53. Salia Koroma was represented on Nugatone, a label owned until his recent death by Adenuga, a Yoruba living in Freetown. He produced hundreds of 78 RPM records.

## 4. Gourd Trumpets and Guitar Music

1. Lambert 1962/63, 20.

2. The Columbia World Library of Folk and Primitive Music, Vol. 10, 91 A 02017. The piece represented here is actually no beni ngoma, but it is a recording of a related malipenga from Malawi.

3. Kubik 1981, 90f.

4. Ranger 1975, 15f.

5. Ranger 1975, 155; from "Solos Kill Jazz Lovers," in *Now in Tanzania*, no. 7, April 1969, 1–15.

6. Wallis and Malm 1984, 225.

7. Ibid., 227.

8. Ibid., 225.

9. Martin 1982, 158f.

10. Roberts 1973, 254.

11. Martin 1982, 158f.

12. After a few productions of bands, Virgin Records soon lost interest again. In the typical manner of international record companies, groups were contracted; but instead of looking after distribution, the company dropped them like hot potatoes if they did not reach the projected sales figures within a certain amount of time.

13. Graebner 1990 (forthcoming).

14. Wallis & Malm 1984, 145.

15. *Afro Rock: Sweet Sound of Honey,* 1977. Produced by BBC, directed by Richard Taylor.

16. Slim Ali and The Hodi Boys, *Sweet Mother,* WE A Reprise Records SKRLP 02.

17. *Drum* (including an irregularly appearing music enclosure *Drumbeat*) is a monthly magazine published in local editions in East, West, and southern Africa. To my knowledge, *Drum* is owned by South African capital.

18. *Afro Rock: Sweet Sound of Honey.*

19. Kamau, *Flying High,* cover text.

20. Slim Ali and The Hodi Boys, *You Can Do It,* cover text.

21. Kubik 1981, 83.

22. A detailed account can be read in Wallis and Malm 1984, 186.

23. Wallis and Malm 1984, 186.

24. Roberts 1965, 202.

25. Graebner 1984, 106.

26. Ibid.

27. Wallis and Malm 1984, 258.

28. Ibid. 258f.

29. Ibid. 259.

30. Joseph J. Kamaru, *Safari ya Japan,* parts 1 and 2.

## 5. Music of Liberation

1. Hall 1956, 143.

2. Hall 1956, 143f.

3. The border between Zambia and Zaire (Shaba province) stretches through an area rich in mineral resources. It is one of the largest copper mining areas in the world.

4. Fraenkel 1959, 54.

5. Mitchell 1956.

6. Mensah 1971/72, 127.

7. Alfred Kalusha, *Kanunko,* pieces A, 1 and B, 4.

8. Regarding Nkhata in general, refer to Fraenkel 1959; here, see p. 51. The song "Some young men" appears in Fraenkel, 51–52.

9. Fraenkel 1959, 51–52.

10. Peter Fraenkel, also on the CABS staff, here has his limitations, despite his great sympathy for Nkhata. The estimation of the African musicologist Atta Anan Mensah appears to be much more sensitive. He wrote that Nkhata picked up traditional compositions from various corners of Zambia, set them in "four-part harmony" and let them swing to the beat of one or the other current pop style (Mensah 1971/72, 130).

11. Fraenkel 1959, 53.

12. Ibid. 54f.

13. Mensah 1971/72, 130.

14. Mapoma 1980, 80.

15. Fraenkel 1959, 20.

16. The single still has priority in Zambia, which is reflected in sales figures. Not more than three thousand copies are sold. Since Zambia is a poor country, the music industry has its limits.

17. Interview in *Ndola,* March 1981.

18. Spokes Chola, *Kapwepwe.* Kindly translated from Bemba by Mrs. Agnes Lucheya.

19. It is also interesting to note here that Nashil Pichen's song *Vamahala Vinatha* received a prize for the best-selling single (51,000 copies were sold) at the award ceremony described above.

20. Recordings of Siamukande Brothers Jazz Band may be found in the archives of the ethnological division of the Museum for Ethnology in Berlin, as well as in the author's collection.

21. Translated from Tonga by the singers themselves. "To plant" here refers to cotton cultivation propagated by the government. The miners

from the Gwembe valley were the only ones up to that time who had money, in contrast to the farmers. Planting cotton, the farmers now made money, too. "Koka!" is a verbal insertion that recurs whenever the banjo plays without vocal accompaniment.

22. Th. Mambo, see note 17 to chapter 5.

23. Haangala, *Mandalena Kasama, Mandalena Mazabuka.*

24. There are, however, revivals at other places as well. The music of Congo Retro Band, for instance, resurrects pieces by the late Leon Bukasa; or the English-African band Orchestre Jazira picks up old High-life pieces. Mostly there are modern instruments and recording techniques involved, leading to a new quality in sound. The case of solo guitarists appears to be different. Some of the older musicians, like Bosco, indeed are still playing the old songs of the 50s and 60s.

25. Kubik used the term "neo-classical" to indicate that this is indeed modern music, but it is still deeply rooted in the tradition of its own musical culture.

26. The films: *Daniel Kachamba's Guitar Songs,* IWF E 2136, and *Daniel Kachamba's Solo Guitar Music,* IWF E 2137.

27. Malamusi 1984, among others.

28. It corresponds to a purely vocal style known in South Africa as *mbube.*

29. Harlow 1985, 26f. Harlow gives a current overview of the music scene in Malawi.

30. *Sunday Times of Zambia,* September 16, 1979.

31. Harlow 1985, 27. Program notes: First Festival of the Arts, University of Malawi, 1983; Second Festival of the Arts, University of Malawi, 1984.

32. Axelsson 1971.

33. Kauffman 1975, 138.

34. The term *shona* originally was an invective for the linguistically and culturally closely related ethnic groups living between the Zambezi and Limpopo rivers. It became the recognized denomination propagated by the colonial administration.

35. During Chimurenga, the war of independence in the 1970s, the guerillas moved a medium to one of their bases for consultation in their fight and to receive the necessary support in their just cause "from above."

36. Kauffman 1975, 132f.

37. Ibid., 140f.

38. Pongweni 1982, 54.

39. Frederikse 1982, 108.

40. Ibid.

41. Ibid., 109.

42. Some other groups also have contributed to the development of

Zimbabwe's new music style, though perhaps not to the same degree: Oliver Mutukudzi and His Black Spirits, Elijah Madzikatire and His Ocean City Band, and the Green Arrows. These are only the best-known groups.

43. French and English texts on the inner jacket of LP SAM 004.

44. See also Vail and White 1978, 1–25; also Vali and White 1980.

45. The FPLM was the armed branch of the Frelimo, the party that took up the fight for liberation.

46. Canti Rivoluzionari del Mozambico, La nostra lotta è populare; Coral das F.P.L.M.

47. Lutero in a conversation with the author in 1981.

48. Tembe and Tinga 1981, 12–17.

49. He released an LP, *Wansanti: Awendila, Wili & Anibal* on the label Bayla of Somodisco, LMB 004 1978 (1979 on the cover).

50. Ibid.

## 6. Marabi Culture and Backyard Studios

1. Andersson 1981, 31. English translation by Todd Matshikiza.

2. Kirby 1959, 39; Emig 1980, 10–11; Coplan 1980, 114ff.

3. It is one of the paradoxes of the South African apartheid state that it is home to what is almost the only institute for traditional African music. Hugh Tracey was its founder and also the founder of the International Library of African Music, which is associated with it and is so far the only specialist journal in the field. Having devoted his life to African music, he died in 1977 at age 74. Starting in 1932, he worked for the former African Broadcasting Company in Durban as director of the recording studio. Much of the music he was able to record at that time is still in the archives of the South African broadcasting system. "After World War II, he was able to gain support from Eric Gallo. It was a double-edged situation. Tracey was able to record traditional musicians, though he was not interested in stars or money. Gallo, on the other hand, received the rights to any potential hit" (Andersson 1981, 19).

Tracey founded the International Library of African Music in 1954. Step by step he was able to become independent from Gallo through outside sponsors. They continued, however, to release his records. He recorded in all countries south of Zaire and Uganda, except Angola. During the eighteen years he recorded, he released almost three hundred LPs. He did not limit himself strictly to purely traditional music. He also recorded, for instance, many beautiful pieces by migrating guitarists and accordion players. Today, his son, Andrew Tracey, continues to lead the ILAM.

4. Dauer 1977, 8.

5. Tracey 1952, 3.

6. Roberts 1973, 159.

7. Kubik 1983a, p. 31.

8. *Pennywhistle Boys*, Lala Sana, no publication date. Producer and director: Ken Law, Capetown; camera: Charles B. Frater; sound: London Studios; music: Robert Sitole, Isaac Ngoma, Joshua Sitole; 16 mm, black-and-white, approximately 20 minutes.

9. *Come Back Africa* was shot officially as a music film in South Africa, even though it is actually a political film against apartheid. Miriam Makeba was seen and heard for the first time—in a shebeen, as described above.

10. Coplan 1979, 146f.

11. Ibid., 342.

12. Ibid., 343; quoted from Kubik 1974, 24.

13. Coplan 1979/80, 49–75.

14. Ibid., 52–53.

15. Ibid., 72.

16. Ibid., 73; quoted from *Drum*, December 1959.

17. Ibid., 152–3.

18. Ibid., 148.

19. Weimer 1980, 20.

20. Anderson 1981, 131.

21. Blackling 1980, 212.

# BIBLIOGRAPHY

■

Achebe, Chinua. 1961. *No Longer at Ease.* New York.

Achebe, Chinua, and Obiora Udechukwu, eds. 1982. "Aka Wetu. Egwu Aguluagu Egwu Edekuede." *Okike Magazine.* Nsukka.

Alaja-Browne, Afolabi. 1985. Juju Music: A Study of its Social History and Style. Ph.D. dissertation, University of Pittsburgh.

Andersson, Muff. 1981. *Music in the Mix: The Story of South African Popular Music.* Johannesburg.

Anikulapo-Kutis Musik. *Tendenzen* 132 (Oktober–Dezember): 50–57.

Asante-Darko, Nimrod, and Sjaak van der Geest. 1983. "Male Chauvinism: Men and Women in Ghanian Highlife Songs." In *Female and Male in West Africa,* edited by Christine Oppong, 242–55. London.

Axelsson, Olaf. 1971. *African Music and Christian Mission.* Thesis, University of Uppsala.

Balbaud, René. 1971. "Profile: 'Signeur' Rochereau's Swinging Sounds." *Africa Report* (April 1971): 28f.

Beaumier, Lucien. 1968. *African Ballet.* Program notes for the third tour.

Bebey, Francis. 1963. *La radiodiffusion en Afrique Noire.*

———. 1975. *African Music: A People's Art.* London.

Bemba, Silvain. 1984. *Cinquante ans de musique du Congo-Zaire: (1920–1970): De Paul Kamba à Tabu Ley.* Paris.

Bender, Wolfgang. 1980a. "I be no gentleman at all, I be african man original—Musik, Kunst und Politik in Nigeria: Die Schallplattencover von Ghariokwu Lemi zu Fela.

———. 1980b. *Moderne Afrikanische Musik auf Schallplatte: Ein kommentierter Katalog.* Institut für Ethnologie und Afrika-Studien der Universität Mainz.

———. 1982. *Musik aus Äthiopien: Ein kommentierter Katalog zu einer Auswahl traditioneller und moderner Musik aus Äthiopien.* Kommentierte Kataloge zur afrikanischen Musik, Nr. 1. University of Bayreuth.

———. 1983. *Waka—Sakara—Apala—Fuji: Islamisch beeinflu 56bte Musik der Yoruba.* Kommentierte Kataloge zur afrikanischen Musik, Nr. 2. University of Bayreuth.

——— (editor). 1984. *Song Texts of African Popular Music,* No. 2. Bayreuth: 1984. (Therein: "Songs by Ebenezer Calender in Krio and English from Freetown, Sierra Leone. Transcription and Translation: Alex Johnson.)

———. 1988. Notes to *Sierra Leone Music: West African Gramophone Records recorded at Freetown in the 1950s and early 60s.* Zensor ZS 41, Cass. ZS 43.

———, ed. 1989. *Perspectives on African Music.* Bayreuth African Studies Series No. 9.

———. 1989. Ebenezer Calender: An Appraisal. In *Perspectives on African Music* W. Bender, ed., 43–68. Bayreuth African Studies Series 9.

Berliner, Paul F. 1978. *The Soul of Mbira.* Los Angeles.

Blacking, John. 1976(1973). *How Musical is Man?* London.

———. 1980. "Trends in the Black Music of South Africa, 1959–1969." In *Music of Many Cultures,* edited by Elizabeth May, 195–215. Los Angeles.

Bloom, Harry, (book) and Pat Williams (lyrics). 1961. *King Kong: An African Jazz Opera.* London.

Cathcart, Jenny. 1989. *Hey You!: A Portrait of Youssou N'Dour.* Witney.

Chernoff, John Miller. 1979. *African Rhythm and African Sensibility: Aesthetics and Social Action in African Musical Idioms.* Chicago.

Collins, John E., ed. n.d. *My Life by Sir Victor Umwaifo: The Black Knight of Music Fame.*

———. n.d. *The Jaguar Jokers: Comic Opera in Ghana.* Unpublished typescript. University library, Bayreuth.

———. 1976a. "Comic Opera in Ghana." *African Arts:* 9, no. 2 (1976): 50–57.

———. 1976b. "Ghanaian Highlife." *African Arts:* 9, no. 2 (1976): 62–68.

———. 1977. "Post-War Popular Band Music in West Africa." *African Arts:* 10, no. 3 (1977).

———. 1979. "Sixty Years of West African Popular Music." *West Africa:* 16 (October 1979): 2041–44.

———. 1985. *African Pop Roots.* London.

———. 1985. *Musicmakers of West Africa.* Washington.

———. 1985. "Pop Profile of Liberia." *African Music:* 24 (March–April 1985): 10f.

———. 1986. *E. T. Mensah: The King of Highlife*. London.

Conrath, Philippe. 1988. *Johnny Clegg: La Passion Zoulou*. Paris.

Coplan, David. 1979. "The African Musician and the Development of the Johannesburg Entertainment Industry, 1900–1960." *Journal of Southern African Studies 5*, no. 2 (April 1979): 135–64.

———. 1979/80. "Marabi Culture: Continuity and Transformation in African Music in Johannesburg, 1920–1940." *African Urban Studies* 6 (Winter 1979/80): 47–75.

———. 1980. *The Urbanization of African Performing Arts in South Africa*. Ph.D. dissertation, Indiana University.

———. 1985. *In Township Tonight! South Africa's Black City Music and Theatre*. Johannesburg.

Cutter, Charles H. 1968. "The Politics of Music in Mali." *African Arts 1*, no. 3 (Spring 1968): 38f, 74–77.

Dargie, David. 1988. *Xhosa Music: Its techniques and instruments with a collection of songs*. Cape Town and Johannesburg.

Darkwa, Asante. 1974. *The New Musical Traditions in Ghana*. Ph.D. dissertation, Wesleyan University.

Dauer. Alfons M. 1977. "Südafrika, Transvaal, Tänze der Arbeiter von Johannesburg—Roodeport." Commentary to film E 1417, Institut für wissenschaftlichen Film, Göttingen.

———. 1983a. "Musiklandschaften in Afrika." *Musik in Afrika*, edited by A. Simon, 41–48. Museum für Völkerkunde. Berlin.

———. 1983b. "Kinesis und Katharsis." *Musik in Afrika*, edited by A. Simon, 166–86. Museum für Völkerkunde. Berlin.

———. 1985. *Tradition afrikanischer Blasorchester und Entstehung des Jazz*. Graz.

Diallo, Nafissatou. 1975. *De Tilène au Playeau: Une Enfance Dakaroise*. Dakar.

Dikobe, Modikwe. 1980. *Der Marabi-Tanz*. Olten.

Dzokanga, Adolphe. (no date, ca. 1984). *Bikolongo, Nzembo mpe Masapo ya Lingala: Proverbs, Chansons, et Contes Lingala*. Paris.

Enekwe, Ossie, Obiora Udechukwu, and Richard Okafor. (Forthcoming). "Minstrelsy in Igboland." *Studies in Igboland*, edited by G. E. K. Ofomata.

Erlmann, Veit. 1987. Cover notes to *Mbube Roots: Zulu Choral Music from South Africa, 1930s–1960s*, Rounder Records 5025.

Eshete, Aleme. 1979. *Songs of the Ethiopian Revolution*. Addis Abbaba.

Ewens, Graeme. 1986. *Luamba Franco and Thirty Years of O. K. Jazz: A History and Discography*. London.

Fiofori, Tam. 1983. "Bala Miller: Developing Music and Musicians in Nigeria." *Spear* (July 1983): 26–28.

Fraenkel, Peter. 1959. *Wayaleshi*. London.

Frederikse, Julie. 1982. *None But Ourselves: Mass vs. Media in the Making of Zimbabwe.* Johannesburg.

Gaye, Adama. 1980. Interview with Sam Mangwana in *Bingo* 333 (October): 52f.

Geest, S. van der. 1980. "The Image of Death in Akan Highlife Songs of Ghana." *Research in African Literatures* 11, 2 (1980): 145–73.

Geest, S. van der, and Nimrod K. Asante-Darko. 1982. "The Political Meaning of Highlife Songs in Ghana." *African Studies Review* 25, no. 1 (March 1982): 27–35.

Graebner, Werner. 1984. *Urbanes Leben in Afrika: Dargestellt an ausgewählten, volkstümlichen Texten des swahilischen Raums.* Masters thesis. University of Mainz.

———. Forthcoming. "Tarabu: Populäre Musik am Indischen Ozean." *Populäre Musik in Afrika: 16 Beiträge zur neuen afrikanischen Musik,* edited by Veit Erlmann. Museum für Völkerkunde. Berlin.

Graham, Ronnie. 1988. *Stern's Guide to Contemporary African Music.* London.

Hall, Barbara, ed. 1956. *Fragen Sie Josephine: Afrikanischer Alltag in Leserbriefen.* Hamburg.

Harlow, John. 1985. ". . . and all that Jazz." *Africa Beat* 3 (Summer 1985): 26f.

Harrev, Flemming. 1989. "Jambo Records and the Promotion Of Popular Music In East Africa: The story of Otto Larsen and East African Records Ltd. 1952–1963." In *Perspectives on African Music,* edited by Wolfgang Bender, 103–37. Bayreuth African Studies Series No. 9.

Haydon, Geoffrey and Dennis Marks, eds., *Schwarze Rhythmen: Von den Ursprüngen der afro-amerikanischen Musik zu Jazz und Pop.* München.

*Hommage à grand Kallé.* 1985. Limete-Kinshasa.

Horton, Christian Dowu. 1979. *Indigenous Music of Sierra Leone: An Analysis of Resources and Educational Implications.* Ph.D. dissertation, University of California, Los Angeles.

Imfeld, Al, ed. 1980. *Verlernen, was mich stumm macht: Lesebuch zur afrikanischen Kultur.* Zurich.

Isaacs, Adam. 1984. Interview with Manu Dibango in *Melody Maker* (September 9, 1989).

Ita, Chief Bassey. 1984. *Jazz in Nigeria: An Outline Cultural History.* Lagos.

Jahn, Janhienz. 1972. *Who's Who in African Literature.* Tubingen.

Johnson, Rotimi. 1989. "The Language and Content of Nigerian Popular Music." In *Perspectives on African Music,* edited by Wolfgang Bender, 91–102. Bayreuth African Studies Series No. 9.

Johnston, Thomas Freerick. 1972. *The Music of the Shangana-Tsonga*. Los Angeles. Univ. of the Witwatersrand.

Junior, Justin Morel. 1979. *Musique et tradition orale en Guinée*. Memoire de diplome de fin d'etudes superieurs. Conakry.

Kaba, Lansiné. 1976. "The Cultural Revolution, Artistic Creativity, and Freedom of Expression in Guinea." *Journal of Modern African Studies* 14, 2 (1976): 201–18.

Kala-Lobe, Henri. 1982. "Music in Cameroon." *West Africa* 3045 (December 8, 1982): 2881–3.

Kauffman, Robert. 1975. "Shona Urban Music: A Process Which Maintains Traditional Values." *Urban Man in Southern Africa*, edited by C. Kileff and W. C. Pendleton, 127–44. Gwelo.

Kazadi, Pierre. 1971. "Congo Music: Africa's Favorite Beat." *Africa Report* (April 1971): 25–27.

———. 1973. "Trends of Nineteenth and Twentieth Century Music in the Congo-Zaire." In *Musikkulturen Asiens, Afrikas und Ozeaniens im 19. Jahrhundert*, edited by R. Günther, 267–283. Regensburg.

Kebede, Ashenafi. 1982. *Roots of Black Music: The Vocal, Instrumental, and Dance Heritage of Africa and Black America*. Englewood Cliffs.

Keil, Charles. 1979. *Tiv Song: The Sociology of Art in a Classless Society*. Chicago.

Kerker, Armin. 1980. "Francis Bebey in einem Gespräch mit Arnim Kerker." *Verlernen, was mich stumm macht: Lesebuch zur afrikanischen Kultur*, edited by Al Imfeld, 211–18. Zurich.

Kilson, Marion. 1971. *Kpele Lala: Ga Religious Songs and Symbols*. Cambridge, Mass.

King, Bruce. 1966. "Introducing the High-Life." *Jazz Monthly* (July 1966): 2–8.

Kirby, Percival R. 1959. "The Use of European Musical Techniques by the non-European Peoples of Southern Africa." *Journal of the International Folk Music Council* 11 (1959): 37–40.

Knight, Roderic. n.d. Liner notes to record *Kora Music from the Gambia*. Folkway Records FW 8510.

———. 1972. Liner notes to record *Kora Manding: Mandinka Music of the Gambia*. Ethnodisc Recording ER 12102.

———. 1973. "Mandinka Jaliya: Professional Music of the Gambia." Ph.D. dissertation, Univ. of California.

Konaté, Yacouba. 1987. *Alpha Blondy: Reggae et société en Afrique Noire*. Paris and Abidjan.

Kubik, Gerhard. 1974. *The Kachamba Brothers' Band: A Study of Neo-Traditional Music in Malawi*. Zambian Papers 9. Lusaka.

———. 1981. "Neo-Traditional Popular Music in East Africa Since 1945." *Popular Music* 1 (1981): 83–104. Cambridge.

210                          BIBLIOGRAPHY

————. 1982. *Ostafrika. Musikgeschichte in Bildern,* Vol. 1, *Musik-ethnologie,* Part 10. Leipzig.

————. 1983a. "Musikgestaltung in Afrika." In *Musik in Afrika,* edited by A. Simon, 27–40. Berlin: Museum für Völkerkunde.

————. 1983b. "Beziehungen zwischen Musik und Sprache in Afrika." In *Musik in Afrika,* edited by A. Simon, 49–57. Berlin: Museum für Völkerkunde.

————. 1983c. "Mehrstimmigkeit in Zentral- und Ostafrika." In *Musik in Afrika,* edited by A. Simon, 84–102. Berlin: Museum für Völkerkunde.

————. 1983d. "Die Amadinda-Musik von Buganda." In *Musik in Afrika,* edited by A. Simon, 139–65. Berlin: Museum für Völkerkunde.

————. 1983e. "Transkription afrikanischer Musik vom Stummfilm." In *Musik in Afrika,* edited by A. Simon, 202–16. Berlin: Museum für Völkerkunde.

————. 1983f. "Verstehen in afrikanischen Musikkulturen." In *Musik in Afrika,* edited by A. Simon, 313–26. Berlin: Museum für Völkerkunde.

————. 1983g. "Kognitive Grundlagen afrikanischer Musik." In *Musik in Afrika,* edited by A. Simon, 327–400. Berlin: Museum für Völkerkunde.

————, assisted by Moya Aliya Malamusi, Lidiya Malamusi and Donald Kachamba. 1987. *Malawian Music: A Framework for Analysis.* Zomba.

————. 1988. "Nsenga/Shona Harmonic Pattern and the San heritage in southern Africa. *Ethnomusicology* 32, No. 2.

————. 1988. *Zum Verstehen afrikanischer Musik.* Leipzig.

————. 1989. *Westafrika. Musikgeschichte in Bildern,* Vol. 1, *Musikethnologie,* Part 11. Leipzig.

Laade, Wolfgang. 1971. *Neue Musik in Afrika, Asien, und Ozeanien.* Heidelberg.

Lambert, H. E. 1962/63. "The Beni Dance Songs." *Swahili* 33 (1962/63): 18–21. Dar es Salaam.

Law, Ken. n.d. Film: *Pennywhistle Boys: Lala Sana.*

Laye, Camara. 1966. *L'Enfant Noir,* edited by Joyce Hutchinson. Cambridge.

Lee, Hélène. 1988. *Rockers d'Afrique: Stars et légendes du rock mandingue.* Paris.

Lonoh, Michel. 1984. *Essai de commentaire de la musique conglaise moderne.* n.p.

Low, John. 1982. "Shaba Diary: Trip to Rediscover the Katanga Guitar Styles and Songs of the 1950s and 1960s." *Acta Ethnologica et linguistica* 54 (1982). Vienna.

————. 1982b. "A History of Kenyan Guitar Music 1945–1980." *African Music, Journal of the International Library of African Music* 6, No. 2, 17–36.

Lynn, Leonard. 1967. *The Growth of Entertainment of Non-African Origin in Lagos from 1866–1920*. M.A. Thesis. Ibadan.

Makeba, Miriam, with James Hall. 1987. *Makeba: My Story*. London.

Malamusi, Moya Aliya. 1984. "Music Scene in Zambia." *Jazzforschung* 16 (1984): 189–98.

Mapoma, Mwesa Isaiah. 1980. *The Determinants of Style in the Music of Ingomba*. Ph.D. Dissertation, University of California.

Marre, Jeremy. 1985. *Beats of the Heart: Popular Music of the World*. New York.

Martin, Stephen H. 1980. *Music in Urban East Africa: A Study of the Development of Urban Jazz in Dar es Salaam*. Ph.D. Dissertation, University of Washington.

————. 1982. "Music in Urban East Africa: Five Genres in Dar es Salaam." *Journal of African Studies* 9 (Fall 1982): 155–63.

Martins, Bayo. 1982. *The Message of African Drumming*. Heidelberg.

Matondo ne Mansangaza, Kanza. 1972. *Musique Zairoise Moderne*. Kinshasa.

May, Chris, and Chris Stapelton. 1988. *African All Stars*. London.

Mensah, Atta Annan. 1971/72. "Jazz: The Round Trip." *Jazzforschung* 3/4. (1971/72).

Mitchell, J. Clyde. 1956. *The Kalela Dance*. The Rhodes Livingstone Papers 27. Manchester.

Mkufya, W. E. 1982. *The Dilemma*. Dar es Salaam.

Monga, Célestine. 1983. Interview with Tabu Ley. *Jeune Afrique* 1157 (March 9, 1983).

Moore, Carlos. 1982. *Fela Fela This Bitch of a Life*. London.

Mytton, Graham. 1983. *Mass Communication in Africa*. London.

Nettl, Bruno, ed. 1978. *Eight Urban Musical Cultures: Tradition and Change*. Urbana.

"Nigeria's Own Highlife Stars." *West African Review* 29, No. 373 (1958): 808–10.

Nketia, Joseph H. Kwabena. 1979. *Die Musik Afrikas*. Wilhelmshaven.

Ofomata, G. E. K., ed. Forthcoming. *Studies in Igboland*.

Okafor, Richard Chijoke. 1980. *Igbo Minstrels*. Ph.D. dissertation, The Queens University, Belfast.

Okagbare, B. C. 1969. *Songs of I. K. Dairo, M. B. E. and His Blue Spots*, Apapa.

Oyelami, Muraina, and Wolfgang Bender. Forthcoming. *Juju-Music: Lyrics of Joruba Popular Music from Nigeria*. Songtexts of African

Popular Music. no. 1, *Nigeria/Yoriba*, edited by Wolfgang Bender, Iwalewa Haus. University of Bayreuth.

Pongweni, Alec J. C. 1982. *Songs that Won the Liberation War.* Harare.

Powne, Michael. 1968. *Ethiopian Music: An Introduction.* London.

Ranger, T. O. 1975. *Dance and Society in Eastern Africa 1890–1970: The Beni Ngoma.* Berkeley.

Rejholec, Jutta. 1984. *Zur Umstrukturierung kolonialer Kulturinstitutionen: Probleme und Perspektiven der Museen in Senegal.* Series F, Bremer Afrika Archiv, Vol. 18. Bremen.

Ricard, Alain. 1977. "The Concept Party as a Genre: The Happy Stars of Lome." In *Forms of Folklore in Africa*, edited by B. Lindfors, 222–36. Austin.

———. 1978. Film: *Principes d'Asihu (Concert Togolais).* 16mm, color. Togo.

Roberts, John Storm. 1965. "Kenyas Schlager-Texte." *Afrika heute* 14/15 (August 1965): 201–5.

———. 1973. *Black Music of Two Worlds.* London.

———. n.d. Cover notes to *The Nairobi Sound*, OMA 101.

———. n.d. Cover notes to *The Tanzania Sound*, OMA 106.

Rycroft, David 1961. "The Guitar Improvisations of Mwenda Jean Bosco." *African Music Society Journal* 2, no. 4 (1961): 81–98 (Part 1) and 86–102 (Part 2).

Schachter, Ruth. 1958. "French Guinea's R. D. A.: Folksongs." *West African Review* 29 (August 1958): 673–81.

Senghor, Leopold Sedar. 1963. *Botschaft und Anruf: Sämtliche Gedichte.* Munich.

Simon, Arthur, ed. 1983. *Musik in Afrika: 20 Beiträge zur Kenntnis traditioneller afrikanischer Musikkulturen.* Veröffentlichungen des Museums für Völkerkunde Berlin. Neue Folge 40. Abteilung Musikethnologie IV. Berlin.

Sow, Sadio Lamine. 1981. "Le Conteur des Ondes." *Jeune Afrique* 1078 (2 Septembre 1981): 64f.

Sprigge, Robert. 1961. "The Ghanaian Highlife: Notation and Sources." *Music in Ghana* 2 (1961): 40–94.

Taylor, Richard. 1977. Film: *Afro Rock: Sweet Sound of Honey.* BBC.

Tenaille, Frank. 1987. *Toure Kunda.* Paris.

Tracey, Hugh. 1952. *African Dances of the Witwatersrand Gold Mines.* Johannesburg.

UNESCO. 1979. *Cultural Policy in the Revolutionary People's Republic of Guinea.* Paris.

Vail, Leroy, and Landeg White. 1978. "Plantation Protest: The History of Moçambican Song." *Journal of Southern African Studies*, 5, No. 1 (Oct. 1978): 1–25.

——. 1980. *Capitalism and Colonialism in Mocambique.* London.

Voss, Harald. 1962. *Rundfunk und Fernsehen in Afrika.* Bonn.

Wallis, Roger, and Krister Malm. 1984. *Big Sounds from Small People: The Music Industry in Small Countries.* London.

Waterman, Chris. 1985. *Juju Roots: 1930s-1950s;* Cover notes to Rounder Records 5017.

——. 1986. Juju: The Historical Development, Socioeconomic Organization, and Communicative Functions of a West African Popular Music, Ph.D. dissertation, University of Illinois.

Wegner, Ulrich. 1984. *Afrikanische Saiteninstrumente.* Veröffentlichungen des Museums für Völkerkunde Berlin. Neue Folge 41. Abteilung Musikethnologie V. Berlin.

Weimer, Bernd. 1980. "Black Consciousness und die Kultur der Befreiung: Bernd Weimer im Gespräch mit Fefifi Tladi." *IKA* 15 (August 1980): 17–24.

Zemp, Hugo. 1964. "Musicien autochtones et griots malinke chez les Dan de Cote d'Ivoire." *Cahiers d'études africianes* 15, vol. 4 (1964): 370–82.

Zindi, Fred. 1985. *Roots Rocking in Zimbabwe.* Gweru.

## Dictionaries

*The Greenwood Encyclopedia of Black Music: Biographical Dictionary of Afro-American and African Musicians.* 1982. London.

## Bibliographies

Gaskin, L. J. P. 1965. *Selected Bibliography of Music in Africa.* (African Bibliographical Series B). London.

Merriam, Alan P. 1951. "An Annotated Bibliography of African and African-Derived Music Since 1936" *Africa* 21, 4 (October 1951): 319–29.

Thieme, Darius L. 1964. *African Music: A Briefly Annotated Bibliography.* Washington.

Varley, Douglas H. 1970. *African Native Music: An Annotated Bibliography.* (Reprint of 1936 edition). London.

## Periodicals

a) Scholarly Journals: *African Music; Ethnomusicology; The Black Perspective in Music; Journal of Black Studies; African Arts; Yearbook of Traditional Music; Popular Music; Popular Music and Society; Jazzforschung/Jazz Research; Musical Traditions.* b) Popular Magazines: *Africa Music; Bingo; Blues and Soul.*

# DISCOGRAPHY

■

Due to the immeasurable amount of African music available, any discography can offer only a fraction. In the following, only a few representative records of well-known musicians are listed here in respect to regions and styles. A complete listing certainly would go beyond the scope of this book. Interested readers are referred to Ronnie Graham's extensive discography (Ronnie Graham: The DaCapo Guide to Contemporary African Music. New York: DaCapo Press, 1988). Musicians like Sunny Adé or Fela, who have recorded twenty, thirty, or more records, are listed only with selected titles.

Series of traditional music have not all been listed completely. Complete listings may be requested from the respective recording companies.

A star (*) indicates that the record is probably available in stores. Records I wish to recommend are identified by a dagger (†).

## Africa, General

### MODERN

*Africa Dances,* Authentic Records 601, (A compilation of singles from Zaire, Congo, Ghana, Nigeria, Sierra Leone, South Africa, Kenia, Tanzania, Mozambique, Uganda, and Ethiopia).*

### TRADITIONAL

*African Music,* recorded by Laura C. Boulton on the Straus West Africa Expedition of Field Museum of Natural History (Malinke, Bambara, Touareg, Bakwiri, Kru, Bini—Mali Cameroun, Nigeria), Folkway, Records, FW 8852, 1957.*

*Tribal Folk and Cafe Music of West Africa,* recorded by Arthur S. & Lois Alberts, 1950.

## To Chapter One

*French Africa,* The Columbia World Library of Folk and Primitive Music, collected and edited by Alan Lomax, edited by André Schaeffner and Gilbert Rouget, Columbia Masterworks 91A 02015.

*The Griots—Ministers of the Spoken Word,* recorded in West Africa by Samuel Charters, Ethnic Folkways Records FE 4178, 1975.*

Colonial music: *Chants et Musiques de Traditions des Troupes Coloniales (1900–1958),* Disques Serp MC 7065.

### Guinea

#### MODERN

*Syliphone Discothèque 71,* Syliphone SLP 35, 1972, (collection of Kélétigui et ses Tambourinis, Bembeya Jazz National, Myriam's Quintette, Virtuose Diabaté, Balla et ses Balladins, and Bafing Jazz Mamou).

*Discothèque 73,* Syliphone SLP 45, 1975, (collection of Myriam Makeba, Bembeya Jazz National, Super Boiro Band, Horoya Band National, Kélétigui et ses Tambourinis).

*Orchestre de la Paillote,* sous la direction de Traore Kélétigui, Syliphone SLP 1.

*Jardin de Orchestre du Guinée,* sous la direction de Onivogui Balla, Syliphone SLP 2.

*Horoya Band National,* Syliphone SLP 41.*

*Super Boiro Band,* Syliphone SLP 46, 1975.*

Camayenne Sofa: *La Percée,* Syliphone SLP 52.*

Balla et ses Balladins: *Objectif Perfection,* Syliphone SLP 75, 1980.*

Bembeya Jazz National: *Regard sur le Passé,* Syliphone SLP 10 or SLP 64.*

Bembeya Jazz National: *Special Receuil-Souvenir de Bembeya Jazz National (Mémoire de Aboubacar Demba Camara),* Syliphone SLP 44.

Bembeya Jazz National: *10 Ans de Succès,* Syliphone SLP 24.

Les Amazones de Guinée: *Au Cœur de Paris,* Syliphone SLP 76.*

Sona Diabate des Amazones: *Sons de la Savane,* Syliphone SLP 77.*

M'Mah Sylla: *Le Rossignol de Guinée,* Syliphone SLP 78.*

*Kouyaté Sory Kandia,* Syliphone SLP 12, 1971.*

Kouyaté Sory Kandia: *L'Épopée du Mandigue,* Vol. 1–3, Syliphone SLP 36, 37, 38.*

## NEOTRADITIONAL

*Les Ballets Africains,* Ensemble national de la République de Guinée, Bel
Air 411 043.
Keita Fodéba, Mouangué, Kante Facelli: *The Voices and Drums of Africa,*
Monitor MFS 373.
*Ballets Africains* de la République de Guinée, Syliphone SLP 14.
*Folklore et Ensembles Instrumentaux,* Syliphone SLP 43.*

## TRADITIONAL

*Musique Malinké, Guinée,* Enregistrements de G. Rouget, Collection
Musée de l'Homme Disques Vogues LDM 30 3113.
Guinea Conakry: *Här Spelar vi Som vi Vill,* Musiknätet Waxholm MNW
6F, 1976.
Musicians in Exile: Fodé Youla and Africa Djolé, *Basikolo—Percussion
Music from Africa,* FMP-Records SAJ 48, 1984, *.

## Guinea-Bissau—Cabo Verde

### MODERN

*Sa'ba' Miniamba',* La Do Si Discos 779013.
N'Kassa Cobra: *Unidade-Luta-Progresso,* La Do Si Discos 780118.

### POLITICAL

*Música Cobaverdiana—Protesto e Luta,* Verlag J. Sendler V.J.S.1.†

## Senegal

### MODERN

Le Sahel: *Bamba,* Musiclub MUS-LPS-001.
*Star Band de Dakar:* (N'Deye N'Dongo), IK 3029.
Étoile de Dakar: *Xalis,* M. Diaw DA 001.
Étoile de Dakar: *Absa Gueye,* African Music Pam 02, 1984.*
Youssou N'Dour et le Super Étoile de Dakar: *Mouride,* E.D.008.*
Youssou N'Dour et le Super Étoile de Dakar: *Immigrés/Bitim Rew,* Cel-
luloid CEL 6709.*
Star Number One: *Maam Bamba,* Disques Gruit GRLP 7601.
L'Orchestre N'Guewel de Dakar: *Xaadim,* Discafrique DARL 008.
Orchestre de Ouza et ses Ouzettes de Dakar: *Lat Dior,* Jambaar Records,
JM 5003.
Xalam, Ade: *Festival Horizonte Berlin 1979,* XPS 001.*
*Touré Kunda:* (Turu), Celluloid 6599, 1981.*
Super Jamano de Dakar: *Géédy Dayaan,* Disques Griot GR 7604.
*Cosaan Orchestra de Dakar:* (Cosaan), Sonafric SAF 50038, 1976.

## NEOTRADITIŌNAL

Lamine Konté: *La Kora du Sénégal*, Arion ARN 33179.*

Lamine Konté: *Sénégal la Kora*, Vol. 2, Arion 33313.*

Lamine Konté: *Chant du Nègre . . . Chant du Monde*, Arion ARN 33395, 1977.*

## TRADITIONAL

Lalo Kéba Drame: *Hommage A*, Sonafric SAF 3030.

*Sekou Batourou Kouyaté et sa Cora*, Disques Kouma, KLP 1041, 1976.

## CHRISTIAN

La Chorale de Diembering: *Chants & Rhythmes de Casamance*, Arion ARN 33695, 1982.*

*Messe et Chants au Monastère de Keur Moussa*, Sénégal, Arion ARN 33565, 1980.*

## Gambia

### MODERN

Guelewar: *Sama Yaye Demna N'Darr*, Valerie VAL 001.

Ifang Bondy: *Saraba*, Disques Griot GR 7603.

Bubacar Jammeh: *Kiang Jenyerr Kulumba*, Vol. 1, Jammeh Records J.R. 106, 1982.*

Saraba: *Papa Music!*, Inner Music 01.*

### TRADITIONAL

*Kora Manding—Mandinka Music of the Gambia*, Recorded by Roderic Knight, Ethnodisc ER 12102, 1972.

Jali Nyama Suso: *Mandinka Kora—Gambie*, Recorded by Roderic Knight, OCORA OCR 70, 1972.

Jali Nyama Suso, *Songs from the Gambia*, Recorded by Samuel Charters, Sonet SNTF 729, 1977.

Alhaji Banseng Konte, Dembo Konte, Ma Lamini Jobate: *Gambian Griot Kora Duets*, Folkways FW 8514, 1979.*

Amadu Banseng Jobareth: *Master of the Kora*, Eavadisc EDM 101, 1978.

Foday Musa Suso: *Kora Music from the Gambia*, Folkways Records FW 8510.

Konte Family: *Kora Music and Songs From the Gambia*, Virgin Records VX 1006, 1982.

# Mali

*Mali: Canti epici, storici, politici e di propaganda del governo socialista di Mobido Keita (1960–1968),* registrazioni inedite di Radio Mali, Vols. 1 and 2, Albatros VPA 8326, 8327.

## MODERN

*Orchestre Régional de Ségou: Les Meilleurs Souvenirs de la 1ère Biennale artistique et culturelle de la Jeunesse (1970),* Mali Music, Production du Ministère de l'Information, Bärenreiter-Musicaphon BM 30 L 2601.

*Orchestre Régional de Mopti,* as above, Bärenreiter-Musicaphon BM 30 L 2602.

*Orchestre Régional de Sikasso,* as above, Bärenreiter-Musicaphon BM 30 L 2603.

*Orchestre Régional de Kayes,* as above, Bärenreiter-Musicaphon BM 30 L 2604.

*L'Orchestre National "A" de la République de Mali,* as above, Bärenreiter-Musicaphon BM 30 L 2605.

*Orchestre Rail-Band de Bamako,* as above, Bärenreiter-Musicaphon BM 30 L 2606.

*Concert "Rail Band" du Mali,* Disques Kouma KLP 1042.

*Mélodias "Rail Band" du Mali,* Disques Kouma KLP 1043.

*Les Ambassadeurs du Motel,* Sonafric SAF 50.014.

Salif Kéïta, *Ambassadeur International Mandjou,* Celluloid CEL 6721.

Les Ambassadeurs Internationaux: *(Djougouya),* Celluloid CEL 6635.

*Maravillas de Mali,* Bellot Records MAG 124.

*Super Biton Balandzan,* Tangent TAN LP 7008.

## NEOTRADITIONAL

*Les Meilleurs Souvenirs de la 1ère Biennale artistique et culturelle de la Jeunesse (1970),* Mali Music, Production du Ministère de l'Information, Bärenreiter-Musicaphon BM 30 L 2651.

Mokontafé Sako: *Farafina Moussow,* Sonafric SAF 40 012, 1976.

Mokontafé Sako: *Les Aigles du Mali,* Sonafric SAF 50 033, 1976.

Fanta Damba: *(Loterie Nationale),* Songhoï Records SON 8201, 1975.

Fanta Damba: "La Tradition Epique:" *Musique du Mali.* Mali Music, Production du Ministère de l'Information, Première Anthologie de la Musique Malienne, Bärenreiter-Musicaphon 6 BM 30 L 2551.

Fanta Sacko: ("Jelike Jan"), as above, *Musique du Mali,* Bärenreiter-Musicaphon 1 BM 30 L 2551.

### TRADITIONAL

Bazoumana Sissoko: "Le Vieux Lion I," as above, *Musique du Mali*, Bärenreiter-Musicaphon 2 BM 30 L 2551.

Bazoumana Sissoko: "Le Vieux Lion I," as above, *Musique du Mali*, Bärenreiter-Musicaphon 3 BM 30 L 2551.

*Le Mali des Steppes et des Savennes: Les Mandingues.* Mali Music, Production du Ministère de l'Information, Première Anthologie de la Musique Malienne, Bärenreiter-Musicaphon 1 BM 30 L 2501.

*Le Mali du Fleuve: Les Peuls*, as above, Bärenreiter-Musicaphon 2 BM 30 L 2502.

Le Mali des Sables: Les Songoy, as above, Bärenreiter-Musicaphon 3 BM 30 L 2503.

*L'Ensemble Instrumental* (Médialle d'or au festival culturel panafricaine d'Algier), as above, Bärenreiter-Musicaphon 4 BM 30 L 2504.

*Cordes Ancienne*, as above, Bärenreiter-Musicaphon 5 BM 30 L 2505.

*Les Dogon: Le chants de la vie—le rituel funéraire*, Disques OCORA OCR 33.

### CHRISTIAN

*Messe des Déshérités*, enregistrée à Bamako (Mali), Barclay 920177.

## To Chapter Two

### Zaire

#### MODERN

Kongo Retro Band: *Anthologie de la Musique Kongo* (Angola—Zaire—Congo), Vol. 1, Universal Music Records UNIMUSIC LPS 13.270, †.

Le Kongo Retro Band Rapelle: *Anthologie de la Musique Kongo* (Angola—Zaire—Congo), Vol. 1, Universal Music Records UNIMUSIC LPS 13.271, †.

Joseph Kabassele et l'African Jazz: *Hommage au Grande Kalle*, Vols. 1 & 2, African 360 142, 360 143, †.

Docteur Nico et l'ochestre Africa Fiesta: *Toute l'Afrique Danse*, Sonafric SAF 50.003, 1975.

Tabu Ley Rochereau et l'orchestre Afrisa: *Extrait de l'enregistrement direct au Festival Mondial des Arts Négro-Africains de 1977 au square Tafawa Balewa et au National Theatre de Lagos*, African 360.097/098, 1977.

Tabu Ley et Mbilia Bel avec l'Afrisa International: *Loyenghe*, Genidia GEN 107/108, 1983.

*Abeti (Bibile)*, African Music Explosion Records AME 9101, 1975.

Tout Choc Zaïko Lang-Langa 1974–1978: *Bakundé Ilo Production in Oldies and Goodies*, Manglo Corporation MGL 003/85.

*Franco 20ème Anniversaire, 6 juin 1956–6 juin 1976,* African
360.082/83, 1976.
Franco et Sam Mangwana: (*Coopération*), Edipop POP 017, 1982.†
Sam Mangwana: *Tiers Monde Coopération–Nouvelles Formule,* Indus-
trie Africaine du Disque IAD 003, 1983.†
Sam Mangwana: *Canta Moçambique—Vamos Para o Campo!,* S.A.M.
Productions SAM 004.†
Sam Mangwana, *Maria Tebo,* Discafrique DARL 012.
*Le Poète Simarro Massiya Maya,* I.A.D. PF77012.
Souzy Kasseya: (*Mr. Simon*), Earthworks ELP 2008, 1985.


TRADITIONAL
"Congo Republic (Leopoldville) and Ruanda," recorded by Hugh Tracey,
*The Music of Africa Series,* No. 22, GALP 1017.
"Music of Northern Zaire (Sudanic)," recorded by Hugh Tracey, *The Mu-
sic of Africa Series,* No. 22, GALP 1251.
*Africa: The Sounds and Music of Congo,* Monitor Records MFS 735.
*Musique de l'Ancien Royaume Kuba,* Disques Ocora OCR 61.


NEOTRADITIONAL
*Sanza and Guitar-Music of the Bena Luluwa of Angola and Zaire,*
recorded by Barbara Schmidt-Wrenger, Lyrichord LLST 7313.*


CHRISTIAN
*Missa Luba,* Les Troubadours du Roi Baudouin, Philips 850.071.


## Burundi

TRADITIONAL
*Music from Burundi,* Albatros VPA 8137, 1972.*


## Rwanda

TRADITIONAL
"Music from Rwanda," Unesco Collection, *An Anthology of African
Music,* Bärenreiter Musicaphon BM 30 L 2302.*


## Ivory Coast

MODERN
Amadou Blake: *Taximen,* Sacodis LS7-78, 1978.*†
Alpha Blondy and the Natty Rebels: *Jah Glory,* Moya Productions Moy
33001.*

Coffin's Reggae and Rhythm Festival: *Jim Jim,* International Crac CR 3001.

Ernesto Djedje: *Golozo,* S.I.I.S. (Société Ivorienne pour l'Industrie du Son) 004.

Ernesto Djedje: *Souvenir,* SED 3301, 45 rpm, 12''.

Amedee Pierre: *Hier & Aujourd'hui,* S.I.I.S. 0021.*

Aicha Kone: (*Aminata*), WAM 3001.*

### TRADITIONAL

*Musique Gouro de Côte d'Ivoire,* Disques Ocora OCR 48.

*Masques Dan Côte d'Ivoire,* Disques Ocora OCR 52.

"Ivory Coast," *Musical Atlas,* Unesco Collection, EMI Odeon C 064-17842, 1972.*

*Côte d'Ivoire, Chants et Danses de Boundiali,* Agence de Coopération Culturelle et Technique ACCT 18211.*

"The Music of the Senufo," Unesco Collection, *An Anthology of African Music,* Bärenreiter Musicaphon BM 30 L 2308.*

## Togo

### MODERN

Yta Jourias: *Pouvoir Noir,* Sonafric SAF 50006, 1975.

Mamo Lagbema, *Laisses Vouler,* Inter-Disque FATAO 0113.

Dama Damawuzan: *Tirez-Tirez,* 45 rpm, 12'', Production A.P.101.†

### TRADITIONAL

*Togo-Music from West Africa,* Rounder Records 5004, 1978, *.

*Musique Kabiye, Togo,* Disques Ocora OCR 76.

## Benin

### MODERN

Gnonnas Pedro: *La Musica en Vérité,* Ledoux Records LED 2B ASL 7009, 1980, *, †.

T. P. Orchestre Poly Rhythmo de Cotonou, Benin: (*Davi Dijinto*), Albarika Stores ALS 048.

### TRADITIONAL, NEOTRADITIONAL

*Musiques Dahoméennes,* Disques Ocora OCR 17.†

"Dahomey," *Musical Atlas,* Unesco Collection, EMI Odeon C 064-18217, 1976.

## Burkina Faso (former Upper Volta)

### MODERN

Kone Idrissa: *Volta Jazz,* Sonafric SAF 50058, 1977.

*Echo del Africa National: Récit Historique de Bobo Dioulasso,* Sonafric SAF 50035, 1976.†

*Les Imbattables Léopards O-Idy-Idrissa (Bissongo),* Sonafric SAF 61.013, 1979.

Hamidou Ouedraogo: (*Pogo Zaiga Yandre*), Songhoï Records SON 8204, 1976.

### TRADITIONAL

"Savanna Rhythms," *Music from Upper Volta,* Explorer Series, Nonesuch H-72087, 1981.*

"Rhythms of the Grasslands," *Music of Upper Volta,* Vol. II, Explorer Series, Nonesuch H-72090, 1983.*

*Musique de Pays Lobi,* Disques Ocora OCR 51.

*Musique Bisa de Haute Volta,* Disques Ocora OCR 58.

## Niger

### TRADITIONAL

*Les Nomades du Niger,* Enregistres par Moussa Hamidou, BAM ID 5886.

*Niger, La Musique de Griots,* Disques Ocora, OCR 20.

## Chad

### MODERN

Maître Gazonga: *Les Jaloux Saboteurs,* Tangent TAN LP 7003.*

### TRADITIONAL

"Chad (Kanem)," Unesco Collection, *An Anthology of African Music,* Bärenreiter Musicaphon BM 30 L 2309.

## Cameroun

### MODERN

Francis Bebey: *African Moonlight. African Music with the Sanza,* Trikont, Unsere Stimme LC 4270, 1984.*

Manu Dibango: *Makossa Man,* Atlantic SD 7276, 1974.

Manu Dibango: *Ceddo,* Bande Originale du Film, Fiesta 362 002, 1977.*

Manu Dibango: *L'Herbe Sauvage,* Bande Originale du Film, Fiesta 362 005, 1977.*

Manu Dibango: *Le Prix de la Liberté,* Bande Originale du Film, Fiesta 362 015, 1978.*

## TRADITIONAL

"Cameroon," *Musical Atlas,* Unesco Collection, EMI Odeon C 064-18265, 1977, (Baka Pygmy Music).*

*Musique Traditionelle du Cameroun, Chantes de Bamum,* Sonafric SAF 50057, 1977.*

*Music of the Cameroon: The Fulani of the North,* Lyrichord LLST 7334.*

*Musique Traditionelle D'Afrique: Flûte et Rhythmes du Cameroun,* SFP 52.011.*

## CHRISTIAN

*The Mass at Yaoundè,* Arion FARN 91025, 1975.

Athanase Ateba et la Chorale Camerouneaise Oyenga Beti: *Odin Nti Zamba Woe,* Sonafric SAF 50018, 1976.

# Gabon

## MODERN

Orchestre de la Gendamerie Nationale Gabonaise: *International Akweza,* LSB 701175.

A. Sambat: *Le Transgabonais—Un Rêve Devenu Réalité,* SAMBG 682.

*Tina,* EMI Pathé C 062-15799.

*Bantu: Musique Traditionelle, Musique Moderne,* CICIBA (Centre International des Civilisations Bantu) 8401-8402.*†

## TRADITIONAL

*Musique du Gabon,* Disques Ocora OCR 41.

*Gabon: Musique des Mitsogho et des Batéké,* Collections Musée de l'Homme, Disques Ocora OCR 84.

*Gabon: Chantres du quotidien/Chantres de l'épopée,* Ocora 558 515.

*Gabon—Musica da un Microcosmo Equatoriale,* Albatros VPA 8232, 1975.*

# Central African Republic

## TRADITIONAL

"Central African Republic," Unesco Collection, *An Anthology of African Music,* Bärenreiter Musicaphon BM 30 L 2310.*

"Ba-Benzélé Pygmies," Unesco Collection, *An Anthology of African Music,* Bärenreiter Musicaphon BM 30 L 2303.*

*Musique Centrafricaine,* Disques Ocora OCR 43.

*Musique Banda: République Centrafricaine,* Collection Musée de l'Homme, Disques Vogue LD 765, 1971.

## People's Republic of Congo

### MODERN

Franklin Boukaka ses Sanzas et son Orchestre Congolais: *Survivance,* Gilles Sala GS 8403 (1967), 1987.*†

Orchestre Bantous de la Capitale, *Special 20e Anniversaire: Rhythme Loketo Chaud-Loketo M'Ba,* Musi-Club BAE 4005.

Loko Masengo: *Non Stop Tchiabuala,* Safari Sound SAS 041.

Master Mwana-Congo: *Kounkou Ignace,* Disques Sonics SONICS 79 403.

Pamelo Mounk'a: (*L'Argent Apelle l'Argent*), Disques Sonics SONICS 79 406.

Grand Marcus: *Rhythmes et Voix du Congo,* Emmanuel Bouetoumoussa EB 8202.

Le Prince Youlou Mabiala et l'orchestre Kamimaze Loningisa: *Couper-Soucis,* Publi-Son PS 002, 1985.

José Missamou canta: *El Salsero de Brazzaville—El Centenario de Brazzaville, 1880–1980,* Tchi-Tchi TC 393.

### TRADITIONAL

*Musique Congo,* Disques Ocora OCR 35.

*Polyphonies Mongo,* Disques Ocora OCR 53.

## To Chapter Three

### Sierra Leone

### MODERN

Afro National: *Tropical Funkmusic,* Mokassa International Records M 2328, 1978.†

Super Combo Kings of Sierra Leone: *Super Combo's Greatest Hits,* Sierra SRA 1001.

Big Faya and the Sierra Leone Military Band, OAU 1980 Siera Leone, 1980.

### TRADITIONAL

Sierra Leone—Musiques traditionelles, Ocora OCR 558 549, 1979.*

## Ghana

### MODERN

Professional Uhuru Dance Band: *Uhuru Special Hi-Life Numbers*, DECCA WAPS 31, 1971.

Ramblers International: (*Akwanuma Hiani*), DECCA WAPS 334, 1976.

African Brothers Band (International): *High-Life Time*, Afribros PAB 003, 1974.

Wulomei in: *Drum Conference*, Polydor 2940 001, 1975.

Eric Agyeman: *Highlife Safari*, Apogée Productions BEBLOP 013, 1979.*†

Atakora Manu: Disko Hi-Life, Makossa International Records M7074, 1981.*†

C. K. Man & His Carousel 7, *Funky Highlife*, Essebions EBLS 6131, 1975.

Super Sweet Talks: *Adjoa*, Sacodis LS 53.*†

Mc God & the People's Band: *Taste Me . . .*, African Music PAM 01.*

African Brothers Band: *Me Poma*, Stern's 1004, 1984.*

*The Guitar and the Gun: A Collection of Ghanian Highlife Dance Music*, Africagram Records, A DRY 1, 1983.*†

*Soul to Soul: Music from the Original Soundtrack*, Atlantic ATL 40 290, 1971.

### NEOTRADITIONAL

Mustapha Tettey Addy: *Masterdrummer from Ghana*, Vol. 2, Tangent Records TGS 139, 1980.*

Asiakwa Brass Band: *Agayata Wuo*, Brobisco KBL 136.†

### TRADITIONAL

*Drums of West Africa: Ritual Music of Ghana*, Lyrichord LLST 7307.*

*Africa: Ancient Ceremonies. Dance Music & Songs of Ghana*, Explorer Series, Nonesuch H-72082, 1979.

### CHRISTIAN

Western Melodic Singers: *Ewuradze Maba*, Essiebons EBLS 6148, 1976.

## Liberia

### MODERN

Kapingbdi: *Don't Escape*, Trikont unsere Stimme, US 0081, 1981.*

Miatta Fahnbulleh: *Kokolioko / Amo Sakee Sa*, 45 rpm 12'', Rokel SD-RK 02, 1978.†

TRADITIONAL/NEOTRADITIONAL

*Folkways of Liberia,* Folkways Records FE 4465.*

"The Music of the Dan," Unesco Collection, *An Anthology of African Music,* Bärenreiter Musicaphon BM 30 L 3201.*


## Nigeria

MODERN

*Hi-Lifes You Have Loved,* Decca WAPS 45, 1972.†

Stars of West Africa: *High Life Hits,* Vol. 2, Decca WAPS 23, 1963.†

West African Rhythm Bros., Nigerian Union Rhythm Group, Ayinde Bakare & His Meranda Band, Rans Boi Ghana Highlife Band, *Highlife Volume 2,* Melodisc MLP 12-134.†

I. K. Dairo (MBE) and His Bluspot Band: *I. K. Dairo in the Sixties,* Afrodisia DWAPS 2096, 1980.*†

Dr. Victor Olaiya: *In the Sixties,* Polygram POLP 066.*†

Rex Lawson's: *Victories,* Philips PRL 13408.

Zeal Onyia: *Returns,* Tabansi Records TRL 110.*†

Ebenezer Obey and His International Brothers: *In London,* Decca WAPS 28, 1969.†

Chief Commander Ebenezer Obey and His Inter-Reformers Band: *Eyi Yato,* OTI LP 508, 1981.†

Sunny Ade & His African Beats, Vol. 4: *Late General Ramat Muritala Mohammed,* SALPS 4, Decca 278.172, 1976.†

King Sunny Ade & His African Beats: *The Royal Sound,* Sunny Alade Records SALPS 16, 1979.

King Sunny Ade & His African Beats: *Aura,* Island/Ariola 206 418-320, 1983/84.*

Sir Shina Adewale & His International Superstars: *Superstar Verse 3,* Wel-Kadep Records WKLPS 3, 1978.

Admiral Dele Abiodun and His Top Hitters Band: *The Beginning of the New Era,* Adawa Super Records ASLP01, 1981.

Segun Adewale: *Play for Me,* Stern's African Record Centre, STERNS 1003, 1983.*

Segun Adewale: *Ojo Je,* Stern's African Record Centre, STERNS 1009, 1985.*

Chief Stephen Osita Osadebe: *Onu Kwulunjo, Okwue Nma,* Polygram POLP 056, 1981.

Doctor Sir Warrior and His Original Oriental Brothers International Band: *Chi Awu Otu,* Decca Afrodisia DWAPS 2164, 1982.

Oriental Brothers International Band: *Obi Nwanne,* Decca Afrodisia DWAPS 2090, 1980.

Oliver de Coque and His Expo '76: *Easter Special,* Olumo Records ORPS 128, 1981.

Ikenga Super Stars of Africa: *(Nwa Enwe Nne),* African DWA 2150, 1981.

Prince Nico Mbarga & Rocafil Jazz: *(Sweet Mother),* Decca 278,159 (ASALPS 6), 1976.*

Fela Ransome Kuti & the Africa '70: *Question Jam Answer,* Vol. 2, Editions Mokassa EMI 23.09.1975.

Fela Anikulapo-Kuti & the Africa 70: *International Thief Thief,* Kalakuta Records 203554, 1979.

Fela Anikulapo-Kuti & the Africa 70: *Zombie,* Creole CRLP 511, 1977.†

The Lijadu Sisters: *Mother Africa,* Decca Afrodisia DWAPS 2021, 1977.

*The Best of Victor Umwaifo,* Mokassa M 2358, 1981.

Sonny Okusun: *(Fire in Soweto),* EMI Pathe Marconi 2 C 064 82447, 1978.*†

Alhaji (Chief) Sikiru Ayinde Barrister and His Supreme Fuji Commanders: *Nigeria,* Siky Oluyole Records SKOLP 022, 1983.*

Alhaji (Chief) Kollington Ayinla and His African Fuji '78 Organisation: *Mo Tun De Pelu Ara,* Kollington Records KRLPS 1.*

### NEOTRADITIONAL

Ododo Atilowu Group: *Ododo Atoligwu-Igbo Ukwu,* Tabansi Records TRL 151.

Chief Ezigbo Obiligbo: *Melody Sound Studio,* Melody MSLP 1.

Christy Essien Igbokwe: Give Me a Chance, Decca Afrodisia DWAPS 2107, 1980.

### TRADITIONAL

*Black Music: Beispiele afrikanisher Musik I und II,* Gert Chesi, Black Magic M 6130.

*Nigeria: Musique du Plateau,* Disques Ocora OCR 82.

"Nigeria—Hausa Music I," Unesco Collection, *An Anthology of African Music,* Bärenreiter Musicaphon BM 30 L 2306.

"Nigeria—Hausa Music II," Unesco Collection, *An Anthology of African Music,* Bärenreiter Musicaphon BM 30 L 2307.

"Nigeria III Igbo Music," Unesco Collection, *An Anthology of African Music,* Bärenreiter Musicaphon BM 30 L 2311.

### CHRISTIAN

Good Women Choir C.A.C. Ibadan & District (led by Mrs. D. A. Fasoyin): *Mo Nwoju Olorun,* Ibikun Orisun Ire Records MOLPS 58, 1978.

The Gospel Choral Group (led by Prince S. O. Akinpelu): *Eni Kan Nbe Feran Wa*, Decca WAPS 377, 1977.

# To Chapter Four

### TRADITIONAL

*British East Africa*, The Columbia World Library of Folk and Primitive Music, Collected and Edited by Alan Lomax, Edited By Hugh Tracey, African Music Society, Columbia Masterworks 91A 02017.

## Kenya

### MODERN

*Songs the Swahili Song: Classics from the Kenya Coast*, Contemporary African Music Series, Original Music OMA 103.\*†

*The Nairobi Sound: Acoustic and Electric Guitar Music of Kenya*, Contemporary African Music Series, Original Music OMA 101.\*†

Daudi Kabaka: *The Cavaliers Band*, Sonafric SAF 61005, 1978.

(Victoria Jazz Band, DO 7 Band, International de Nelly): *Kenya Partout*, Vol. 2, Playa Sound SP 2085, 1976.

Daniel Kamau: *Kenyafrica 1*, Playa Sound PS 33001, 1976 (also on RCA DK 01, 1976).

Les Wanyika: *Proudly Presents New Dance Lesles*, Polydor POLP 513.

Orchestre Les Mangelepa Featuring Embakasi: *1st Anniversary Album*, ASLP 913.

Orchestra Super Mazembe: *Kaivasaka*, Virgin V 2263, 1983.

Slim Ali and The Hodi Boys: *Sweet Mother*, Reprise Records SKRLP 02/RRC 2235.

Kalambya Sisters: (*Katelina*), Zensor ZS 1983, 45 rpm 12″.\*†

### TRADITIONAL

*Original afrikanische Ritualmusik: Magischer Kreis II*, Xymax Musikproduktions GmbH, 29202-1 LP, 1984.

*Musikalische Mythologie in Ost-Africa: Magischer Kreis III*, Xymax Musikproduktions GmbH, 29203.

## Uganda

### TRADITIONAL

*The Music of Africa Series*, No. 24, "Uganda," recorded by Hugh Tracey, Gallotone GALP 1319.

CHRISTIAN

*Erweckung in Ostafrika.* Eine Dokumentation mit Bischof Festo Kivengere und Chöre aus Uganda. Missionstrupp Frohe Botschaft, MFB 704.

## Tanzania

MODERN

*The United Republic of Tanzania with the Tanzania Police Band,* AIT 502, 1973.
(Juwata Jazz Band; L'Orchestre Dar International; Mwenga Jazz Band): *Hits of Tanzania,* Vol. 1, AIT Moto Moto HTLP 03.
Orchestra Makassy: *Agwaya,* Virgin Records 204 948-320, 1982.*

TRADITIONAL

*Musik Fran Tanzania,* Caprice CAP 1089, 1974.*
*The Music of Africa Series,* No. 25, "Tanganyika," recorded by Hugh Tracey, Gallotone GALP 13120.

CHRISTIAN

Der Konde-Chor aus Tansania: *Nimm meine Hände,* Verlag der Evang.-Luth. Mission, Erlangen MNA 4.*
Makumira Chor: Sita Ya Mungu—Neue Lieder aus Tansania, Verlag der Vereinigten Evangelischen Mission, Wuppertal, Verlag der Evang.-Luth. Mission, Erlangen VEM 7.*

## Ethiopia

*Ethiopian Urban Tribal Music—Mindanoo Misitiru,* Vol. 1, Lyrichord LLST 7243; *Gold from Wax,* Vol. 2, Lyrichord LLST 7244.

TRADITIONAL

*Ethiopia,* Vol. 1, "Music of the Central Highlands," recorded by Jean Jenkins, Tangent TGM 101; Vol. 2, "Music of the Desert Nomads," recorded by Jean Jenkins, Tangent TGM 102; Vol. 3, "Music of Eritrea," recorded by Jean Jenkins, Tangent TGM 103.
*Musik der Hamar—Südäthiopien,* Aufnahmen und Kommentar Artur Simon, Museum Collection Berlin (West) MC 6.

## Sudan

*Musik der Nubier—Nordsudan,* Aufnahmen und Kommentar Artur Simon, Museum Collection Berlin (West) MC 9.

*Dikr und Madih—Sudan,* Aufnahmen und Kommentar Artur Simon, Museum Collection Berlin (West) MC 10.

*Soudan Pays des Nouba,* Documents Sonores Authentiques de Pierre et Elaine Dubois, Disques VDE-Gallo, VDE 30-294.

# To Chapter Five

## Zambia

### MODERN

*The Best of Paul Ngozi,* 10 smash hits 1976–1979, Sound Project P.N.L. 003.

Rikki Ililonga: *Same Name Music,* Sepiso RILP 005.

*The Blackfoot: The Foot Steps,* Zambia Music Parlour ZMPL 28, 1978.

*The Best of The Five Revolutions* (featuring the hit single *Muamfwilwa*), Zambia Music Parlour ZMPL 43.

Nashil Pichen Kazembe with Orchestre Super Mazembe: *African Super Stars,* Vol. 2, AIT LP/NPK 2.

Smokey Haangala: *Aunka Ma Kwacha,* Teal Records, RAK 1.

Smokey Haangala: *Waunka Mooye,* Teal Records, LRLP 2, 1980.

### NEOTRADITIONAL

Serenje Kalindula Band: *Amanyamune,* Zambia Music Parlour, ZMPL 31, 1979.

Spokes Chola and Mansa Radio Band: *Kalindula,* Zambia Music Parlour ZMPL 23.

### TRADITIONAL

*Inyimbo: Songs of the Bemba People of Zambia,* recorded by Isaiah Mwesa Mapoma, Ethnodisc Recordings ER 12103.

*La Voix de Masques de Zambie: Rituels d'Initiation Makishi et Nyau,* Troupe National de Danse de Zambie, Arion ARN 33605, 1982.*

### CHRISTIAN

Mercyful Paradise Church Choir, United Church of Zambia: (*Mumulu Mukakumbi*), Zambia Music Parlour ZMPL 34.

Chitsitsimutso Choir: (*Kuli Malo Abwino*), Multimedia Zambia.

## Zimbabwe

### MODERN

*Chimurenga-Lieder: Musik des revolutionären Volkskrieges des Volkes von Zimbabwe,* Sendler VJS 5.

Elijah Mdzikatire and the Ocean City Band: *Gukura Hundi,* Teal Record Company, Zimbabwe ZML 1000, 1980.

Oliver and the Black Spirits: *Africa,* Gallo, Kudzanayi BL 241, 1980.

*The Best of Devera Ngwena Jazz Band,* Teal Records, Zimbabwe ZML 1010.*

Thomas Mapfumo & the Acid Band: *Hokoyo,* Afro Soul ASLP 5000.

Thomas Mapfumo & the Blacks Unlimited: *Mabasa,* Earthworks/Rough Trade ERT 1007, 1984.*

*Viva Zimbabwe: Dance Music from Zimbabwe,* Earthworks ELP 2001, 1983.*

The Pied Pipers: *People of the World Unite,* WEA, Gramma WIZ 5000.*

## TRADITIONAL

Ephat Mujuru Ensemble: *The Mbira Music of Zimbabwe: The Spirit of the People,* Teal Record Company, Zimbabwe ZML 1003.*

Dumisane Abrahan Maraire: *The African Mbira: Music of the Shona People of Rhodesia,* Nonesuch Explorer Series H-72054.*

*Africa Shona Mbira Music,* recorded by Paul Berliner, Nonesuch Explorer Series H-72077, 1977.*

## Malawi

### MODERN

"The Kachamba Brothers' Band: (Wodala Sofia)," *Acta Ethnologica et Linguistica,* Series Phonographica No. 1, 1972.*

Donald Kachamba's Band: *Simanje-Manje and Kwela from Malawi,* AIT GKA 1, 1978.*

Donald Kachamba's Kwela Band: (*Lusaka Song*), 0120240, 1978.*

## Mozambique

### MODERN

(Grupo Bantu; Magide Mussá; José Mafer; Os Planetas; Camal Jivá): *Varios,* Vol. 1, INLD, Ngoma 0049, 1980.

Awendila, Wili & Anibal Wasanti, *Bayly* (Somodiscos), LMB 003, 1978.

### POLITICAL

*Coral das FPLM,* INLD, Ngoma 0040, 1980.

## Angola

### MODERN

(Minguito; Prado Paim; Teta Lando; Nito Nunes, Dia Kimuezo Super

Coba; Conjuno Merengue): *Ritmo os Melhores de Angola 1*, CDA 6005.
David Ze Mutudi: *Ua Ufolo-Viuva Da Liberdade*, CDA NALP 6002.
Teta Lando: *Indepedencia*, CDA NALP 6000.
Bonga: *Angola 72*, Hallmark Records LP 137.
Bonga: *Raizes: Cançoes e Poemas de Angola, Brasil, Cabo Verde*, Morabeza Records 6810619.

## TRADITIONAL
*Music and Musicians of the Angolan Border—The Tshokwe*, Lyrichord LLST 7311.
*Mukanda Na Makisi/Angola*, Recordings and Commentary Gerhard Kubik, Museum Collection Berlin (West) MC 11.

## POLITICAL
*Canti Rivoluzionari Dell' Angola: Il Popolo al Potere*, Folk Internationale, CETRA LPP 293.

## Madagascar

### MODERN
Henri Ratsimbasafy: *Madagaskar—Le Lamba Blanc*, Playa Sound LPP 196, 1979.
Rossy: *Nehmt die Kabossy, spielt die Valiha*, Atelier im Bauernhaus, PL 528, 1983.*

### TRADITIONAL
*Valiha Madagaskar*, Disques Ocora, OCR 18.
*Musique Malagache*, Disque Ocora, OCR 24.

### CHRISTIAN
Ankalazo Ny Tompo: *Religiöse Lieder aus Madagaskar, Sounds & Songs*, Missio Aktuell Verlag MAV 3041, 1980.*

# To Chapter Six

## South Africa

### MODERN
(Little Lemmy, Lemmy Special, among others): *Something New From Africa*, Decca LK 4292, 1959.
(Miriam Makeba, Lemmy Special, Malombo Jazz, among others): *Music Sounds of Africa*, Gallo GL 1578, 1969.

King Kong: *All African Jazz Opera,* Gallo KL 778, 1966.*

The Dark Sisters: *Star Time,* Vol. 4, EMI HMV 33JP 1003, 1968.

*The Best of Mahotella Queens,* Gallo Gumba Gumba BL 123, 1977.*

The Soweto Boys: *(Ka Ka),* WEA Soweto 96 008, 1977.

The Soul Brothers: *Mshoza Wami,* April Music Masterpiece LMS 526.

Babsy Mlangeni: *Nantsi le Indoda,* CCP Record Co. Black Music BMC (E) 545, 1979.

Harari: *Rufaro-Happiness,* Gallo The Sun GL 1874, 1976.

Steve Kekana: *Umenziwa Akakhohlwa,* EMI Brigadiers JPL (E) 4005, 1980.*

Kati Elimnyama: *Ngisize Baba Wami,* WEA Chocolate City CNH 2007, 1983.*

Mzikayifani Buthelezi: *Kulukhuni Ukuba Indoda,* Boots BOL (R) 123, 1083.*

Thomas Chauke Na Shinyori Sisters: *Shimatsatsa No. 2—Don't Be Surprised,* WES Beat City QBH 1030, 1983.*

Uthwalofu Namankentshane: *Inselelo,* WEA City Lights, CGH 5009, 1983.*

Brenda & the Big Dudes: *Let's Stick Together,* EMI Family FLY 8, 1984.*

Sakhile: *New Life,* Teldec Jive Africa 6.25998, 1984.*

Juluka: *The International Tracks,* Music Inc. MINC(O) 1098, 1984.*

(Philip Tabane): *Malombo,* Kaya Records Co., Kaya (E) 300, 1984.*

*Music of Black South Africa,* Sound Track Music of the Film "Rhythm of Resistance," Virgin Records, V2113, 1978.

The Cockerel Boys—Abafana Baseqhudeni: *From Africa—From Soweto: Mubube Jive & Soul,* L-R Records LR 44.009, 1982.

*Soweto Compilation,* Zensor 05, 1982.*†

EXILE

Miriam Makeba: *Makeba!,* WEA Reprise RRC 2213, 1968.†

Miriam Makeba: *African Convention,* Pläne 88 199, 1980.*

Miriam Makeba: *A Promise,* Pläne 88 203, 1980.*

Miriam Makeba: *Country Girl,* Pläne 88 245, 1981.*

Jabula: *African Soul,* Pläne 88 154, 1978.*

Dudu Pukwana: *Zila,* Jika Records ZL 1, 1981.

"Dollar Brand" Abdullah Ibrahim: *African Marketplace,* WEA Elektra ELK 52217, 1980.*†

"Dollar Brand" Abdullah Ibrahim: *Matsidiso,* Pläne 88 231, 1981.*

"Dollar Brand" Abdullah Ibrahim: *South African Sun Shine,* Pläne 88 293, 1982.*

Letta Mbulu: *There's Music in the Air,* A&M Records AMLH 64609, 1976.*

Hugh Masekela: *Techno Bush*, Teldec Jive Africa 6.25983, 1984.*
Hugh Masekela: *Waiting for the Rain*, Teldec Jive Africa 6.26155, 1985.*

## TRADITIONAL

*Music of Africa—African Dances of the Witwatersrand Gold Mines*, Series No. 12/13, recorded by Hugh Tracey, Gallo DLPL 319/20, 1973.*

*Music of Africa—The Zulu Songs of Princess Constance Magogo*, Series No. 37, Gallo SGALP 1678, 1973.*

*Music of Africa—From the Roadside*, Series No. 18, recorded by Hugh Tracey Gallo GALP 1110.*

## CHRISTIAN

*Ntate, Roma Nna!, Lieder aus dem südlichen Afrika*, Verlag des Evang. Luth. Missionswerkes in Niedersachsen 66.21 251-01-2.*

## POLITICAL

*Uhuru Wa Afrika—Freiheit Für Afrika*, African National Congress (ANC), MAS 009.

# Namibia

## POLITICAL

*The SWAPO Singers: One Namibia One Nation*, Swapo Department of Information and Publicity in London, 6812 258.